Thank You!: John Antosiewicz, Marty "The Astounding B Monster" Baumann, Matthew Bradley, Bob Burns, Xandra Conkling, Frank Dietz, Eric Edson, Jon Fedele, Stan Follis, Kerry Gammill, Richard Heft, Ron Honthaner, Doug Kennedy; the late Alyce, Donna and Marilyn King; Arthur and Stephen Kirkman, Robert J. Kiss, Dave McDonnell, Doug Menville, Greg Nicotero, Nan Peterson, Gary D. Rhodes, Mary Runser, Dan Scapperotti, David Schecter, Sue Svehla, Evil Wilhelm, Wade Williams — and the late Tom Boutross, Robert Clarke and Robin C. Kirkman.

Cover Artwork: Inspired by the classic movie posters and paperback covers of the 1950s-60s, illustrator Marty Baumann *(martybaumann.com)* rendered this striking retro-contemporary painting. Marty's credits include work for Pixar Animation Studios, Walt Disney Pictures, Hasbro and Universal Studios.

Back Cover Artwork: In 1958, Sun Demon sound man Doug Menville drew a sketch (view it in the Supplemental Photo Gallery) that he hoped would be used as a starting point by the movie's eventual poster artist. It wasn't — but in 2011, it was refined and colorized by illustrator Kerry Gammill *(KerryGammill.com)* for this book's back cover. Kerry's art credits include the comic books *Superman, X-Men, Fantastic Four* and *Bela Lugosi's Tales from the Grave.* He has also worked as a conceptual artist for movies and TV (*Phantoms, Virus, Species II, The Outer Limits,* more).

Scripts from The Crypt: The Hideous Sun Demon
© 2011 Tom Weaver. All Rights Reserved.

No part of this book may be reproduced in any form or by any means, electronic, mechanical, digital, photocopying or recording, except for the inclusion in a review, without permission in writing from the publisher.

The Hideous Sun Demon is a copyrighted work owned and controlled universally and in perpetuity by Wade Williams. All rights reserved. All stills, script and posters use licensed by Wade Williams.

Published in the USA by:
BearManor Media
PO Box 1129
Duncan, Oklahoma 73534-1129
www.bearmanormedia.com

ISBN 978-1-59393-700-3

Printed in the United States of America.
Book design by Brian Pearce | Red Jacket Press.

TABLE OF CONTENTS

Introduction 7

The Sun Demon Speaks! 10

Notes on The Scripts 23

The Scripts: *Sauros* 27

The Scripts: *The Hideous Sun Demon* 133

The Scripts: *Sorceress* 275

The Sun Demon: Its Drive-In World Premiere 301

Hideous Sun Demon: The Special Edition 313

About Robert Clarke 319

Fun Facts 323

Showmanship Manual 339

Afterword 349

Supplemental Photo Gallery 353

Dedicated to
Robert Clarke (1920–2005)
and Robin C. Kirkman (1930–2010)

INTRODUCTION

Sun Demon Associate Producer **Robin C. Kirkman** Recalls the Movie and Robert Clarke

I've met some pretty famous people (architect Frank Lloyd Wright, pianist Vladimir Horowitz). I've run my own business, a bookstore housed in a cozy nook in Southern California. I've done a little preaching in church. Incredible experiences all, but far overshadowed by the grandest of my life: my participation in a little horror film in the late '50s called *The Hideous Sun Demon*.

Subsequently, when I was in the employ of Multnomah County in Oregon, I had the poster for the film on display in my cubicle. On one occasion, I brought my 16mm print in for a showing. It was a hit, and presentations later became an annual event (though with a VHS copy, as the print broke during a rewind), with newer employees now discovering that they had a "Hollywood man" in their midst. I always gave a brief introduction, and everyone cheered at the opening credits when **Associate Producer: Robin C. Kirkman** filled the screen.

Of course, replays were a must for the scene that showcased my one turn as an actor, playing the ill-fated cop that Dr. Gil McKenna (Robert Clarke), in his haste to evade capture, runs down with his car. My co-workers loved the story of how I went through take after take, trying to get that shot right, too scared to get close enough to the car to sell the illusion that I was being hit. Plus, I had changed somewhat since 1957 — I now had a little less hair on top, and wasn't immediately recognizable.

Often, during lunch breaks, I walked the area around work with a friend and co-worker, Terry. One summer afternoon, we stopped by a nearby video rental

Student turns stuntman: In addition to his other *Demon*ic duties, Robin C. Kirkman plays the cop who doesn't quite dodge Gil's getaway car.

store. I had heard that they stocked *The Hideous Sun Demon*, and we asked about it. We were directed to the Cult Horror section, and sure enough, there it was! We started to leave. I hadn't planned on saying anything to those in the store about my connection to the film, but Terry had different ideas. He told them, in delightfully dramatic fashion, who I was. One would have thought Bob Clarke himself had walked into the place. I became a celebrity on the spot. I couldn't believe it!

In later years, Bob wouldn't let a phone call go by without thanking me for my work on the film, stressing that it wouldn't have been completed without me. I always assured him that it was his vision, his energy and his enthusiasm that brought forth *The Hideous Sun Demon*. It was his dream, his baby, all the way.

At the time it was made, I was a young (late 20s) "kid" looking for adventure. A group of us cinema students from USC gathered around Bob and formed a production unit. I had some money, and I offered to invest in the film. Perhaps some might question my wisdom; after all, this was Hollywood. Can you trust "Hollywood people"? Regarding *this* Hollywood person (Bob), I will emphatically state, "*Yes!*" We all worked hard, and it was a *blast*!

I look back at those years…1955, when my parents died and I got part of my inheritance; 1960, when my trust became available to me; and 1970, when it was all gone. All that foolishness, living high on the hog. I regret all of it, with one great exception: I would never trade my involvement with, and investment in, *Hideous Sun Demon* for anything. Nothing in my life compares to that, and I wouldn't change it for the world.

I was deeply saddened to hear, in 2005, of Bob's passing.

Thank you, Mr. Robert Clarke, for a most unforgettable experience. You and our "little movie" left the biggest impact of anyone or anything on my life, and I am, as I have always been, and will forever be, profoundly grateful.

Robin C. Kirkman
August 17, 2010

Kirkman, 80, died at Kaiser Permanente Sunnyside, a medical center in Clackamas, Oregon, several weeks after penning this introduction.

THE SUN DEMON SPEAKS!

by Robert Clarke
as told to Tom Weaver

The following is an excerpt from the autobiography Robert Clarke: To "B" or Not to "B" *(Luminary Press, 1996) by Clarke and Tom Weaver. We pick up Clarke's story in 1957, at the point where he wraps up filming the sci-fi cheapie* The Astounding She-Monster.

For *The Astounding She-Monster*, producer-director Ronnie Ashcroft paid me $500 for the week's work, which was about right for a picture of this sort, and Ronnie also promised me a four percent share of the money *he* made as producer. I thought that was a nice gesture and I thanked Ronnie, but I was certain that I'd never see a nickel over and above the 500 a week. It wasn't that I didn't trust Ronnie, it was the fact that I knew how crooked many distributors were back then; I was sure that Ronnie's producer's share would come to nothing and that I'd be getting four percent of nothing. But my four percent *did* come, in the form of a check here, a check there, and soon it exceeded the 500 I'd made as my straight salary. Thanks to Ronnie's generosity — and integrity, and honesty — over a period of time I received a total of an additional $3000.

Making that pile of money got me thinking. Since I knew how much I made off my four percent, it didn't take much multiplication to get a rough idea what Ronnie must have earned. If Ronnie could make that amount of money off of a quick, cheap film like *The Astounding She-Monster*, it sort of stood to reason that a science fiction film with a bit more quality and substance to it ought to make as much. Or more.

The most important consideration was that *my* science fiction film would be commercially successful. At that time, "commercially successful" usually either meant a Western or a monster picture. I opted for the latter — an honest-to-God monster sci-fi. My idea was to do a picture that would be a variation on the old Robert Louis Stevenson story *Dr. Jekyll and Mr. Hyde*. To be truthful, I never read Stevenson's story but, when I was 12 years old, I sneaked off from grade school with a friend and we went to see *Dr. Jekyll and Mr. Hyde* [1931] with Fredric March and Miriam Hopkins. I didn't tell my Mom because I was afraid she wouldn't let me go. (Of course, she was scared and furious when I got home — furious that I went to the movies, but scared until I got back.) I never forgot that day, or how

 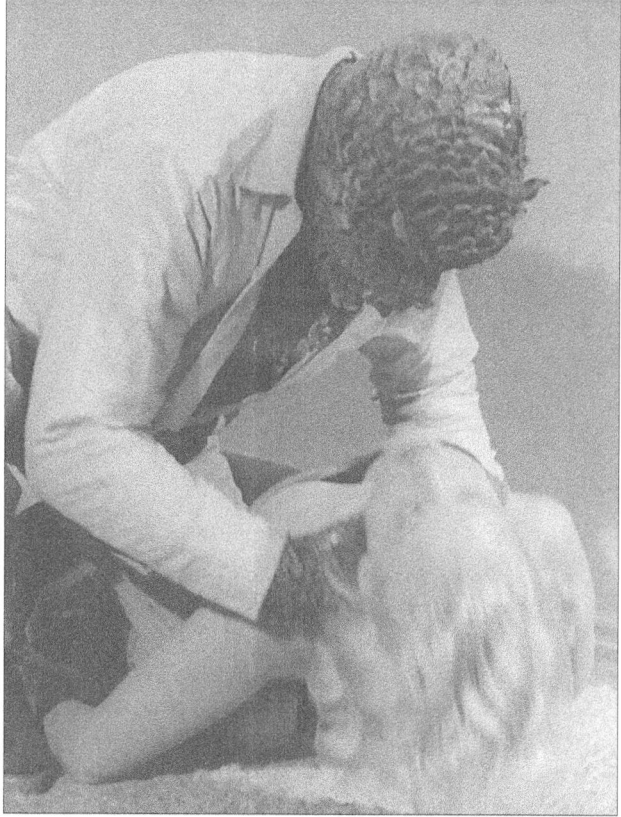

Buddy, can you paradigm?: Robert Clarke modeled the *Sun Demon* story after one of his movie favorites, the 1931 Fredric March *Dr. Jekyll and Mr. Hyde*. Left: March and Miriam Hopkins in *Jekyll*; Right: Clarke and Nan Peterson in *Sun Demon*.

very impressed I was with that movie. So I started out with this plan: to produce, direct and star in a science fiction monster picture in which I would be playing the Jekyll and Hyde characters.

It was at that point that I got Phil Hiner involved. I had met Phil in Chicago, when I was an inspector for the Civil Service Signal Corps there in 1941 and '42. Phil was a part-time writer then; he later moved out here to the West Coast and worked for an aircraft manufacturer, writing how-to books. Phil's real interest, however, was in writing fiction, so we collaborated on the script, flip-flopping Robert Louis Stevenson's basic plot. Instead of having a physician drink a potion that changes him into a monster, our plot had as its main character a scientist who is accidentally exposed to fissionable materials. This upsets his chromosome balance so that he reverts, in the sun's rays, into a reptilian sort of monster. Remembering the old Fredric March film, I gave the character two girlfriends, one serious and loyal, the other a bad girl from the wrong side of the tracks. Twisting that story around, I hoped that we could come up with a good, solid plot. (And I think, thanks to Robert Louis Stevenson and the Fredric March movie, that we did.) Phil turned our treatment into a screenplay that had the title *Sauros* (the Latin word for reptile).

To make the movie's "science" sound semi-plausible, I went to the University of Southern California library's biology section to do some research. I had heard that the human fetus evolves from a one-cell organism to a fish to a reptile before it takes on the characteristics of a mammal. It was simple enough to develop a screenplay where some poor soul finds himself going through that process, *backwards*. The very book in which I did my research is seen in the movie, in an insert shot.

I also took a USC screenwriting class under Malvin Wald, trying to get a little feeling for the elements necessary for a picture. While there, I met a number of young fellows who were enrolled in the Cinema Department: Tom Boutross, Robin Kirkman, Vilis Lapenieks and others. All these students were in their

Clarke told interviewer Marty Baumann, "When Alyce and I were first married, I took our last $5000 and started making this movie. Does that sound like Ed Wood?" Pictured: Clarke, Nan Peterson, d.p. John Morrill.

early- to mid-20s, and several of them lived together shared a large two-story house they called Cinemanor. When they all showed a lot of enthusiasm about becoming part of my project, we arranged to have a couple of meetings, the first one at their place and the second in a classroom at USC. They all had the willingness, spirit and desire; I was very lucky to get them. Robin even offered to invest in the movie, which was a big step toward getting into production.

Robin turned out to be a very loyal friend through the entire *Sun Demon* experience. Tom Boutross became my co-director and he also edited the film. Vilis Lapenieks photographed, alternating with another couple of fellows, John Morrill and Stan Follis. (We shot on weekends, and sometimes one or more of these guys had other plans. So we always went with whoever was available.) Screen credit for the script went to another USC student, E.S. Seeley Jr., who was a friend of Robin Kirkman's. Seeley was an esoteric type of fellow, professorial in demeanor, and later on he tried to take more credit for the writing than he deserved.

Seeley kept bugging us for more money, more money; then, to our relief, he went abroad on some kind of trip, giving us a respite. But he then began writing nasty letters to Robin, threatening us with litigation unless we coughed up additional funds. He was very erratic and quite difficult — a real character. (And, no, he received no additional moneys.)

After Seeley turned in *his* draft, I still felt that there were rough edges. My very dear friend Beatrice Halstead worked as a secretary for George Murphy, the actor-tap dancer; she was also my business manager. Mrs. Halstead hooked me up with a writer named Doane Hoag, who worked in industrials quite a bit, and Doane did a good job of polishing up the dialogue. When we were trying to come up with a name for our new company, Mrs. Halstead thought of my wife Alyce, one of the King Sisters, and suggested, "Why don't you use Alyce's stage name, 'King'? 'Clarke-King Enterprises'?" That's where the name of the company came from.

Since *Sun Demon* would be non-union, I was a bit restricted in who I could cast, but I thought it would

Eager to do more in Hollywood than act, 37-year-old Robert Clarke hoped that *Sun Demon* would open the door to a film producing career. *Left to right:* Fred La Porta, Clarke, Patricia Manning, Patrick Whyte.

be nice to have another semi-recognizable name in the picture. I tried to hire Andrea King. Andrea had been a Warner Bros. contract player in the 1940s, she had acted in Ronnie Ashcroft's *Outlaw Queen* (1957) with me, and I thought she'd be apt to agree. But Andrea said, "I can't do anything without my agent," and she sort of high-hatted me. (Well…who could blame her?) So I got passed over by Andrea King, and then by an

Unrequited love: Patricia Manning as Gil's loyal colleague Ann Lansing.

old friend of mine from Oklahoma, Amzie Strickland. Amzie and I went to high school together (different schools, same time), and she later made it big in radio acting in New York in the '40s. I approached Amzie about *Sun Demon*, and she gave the same answer that Andrea did: "I'm sorry, but I can't do anything without talking to my agent Meyer Mishkin." It quickly became pretty obvious, since we were paying 25 bucks a day, that we were going to have to go with unknowns.

We proceeded to get our cast through members of the crew who knew of aspiring actors and actresses around USC. We told them that this was a non-union picture and we had them come out and read. For the good and bad girls, we got Patricia Manning and Nan Peterson. They were both very sincere in their efforts. Patricia was quite good in the more dramatic role, and Nan had the sex appeal and the obvious physical equipment and looks to be the bad gal (and to appeal to the guys). Playing George the gangster, Peter Similuk had a menacing look and spoke his lines pretty well. One fellow that didn't come off too well was Robert Garry, who played my hospital doctor. But I ought not to be too critical, since many of these people weren't professional actors. For instance, the man who played the German doctor was named Fred Pincus, and he made glassware for hardware stores. He had a very obvious accent, and so I asked him, "Do you want to be in this movie?" I figured that if he could just remember and say the words, his accent would make it appear like he was acting. That was the first time he ever acted — and the last. (He wanted to be billed as Fred La Porta, and so that's what we did. I didn't know then why he wanted his name changed, and I don't know now.) Patrick Whyte, who had a fairly sizable part as Dr. Buckell, had played a number of small roles in movies and on TV, and he thought of himself as an actor's actor. He helped considerably: He had enthusiasm, he made some good suggestions and he gave it his best all the time.

For some of the supporting parts, I turned to my in-laws, the King family. Suzy, the little girl in the movie, was played by Xandra Conkling, my niece. Her mother, in the film *and* in real life, was Donna King, my wife's sister; she was one of the original King Sisters during the Big Band era. My mother-in-law Pearl Driggs was the elderly lady sitting out on the hospital roof when I first transform into the Sun Demon. (The King Sisters' real name was Driggs, which they changed for obvious reasons — Driggs sounded too much like *dregs*. So they took their father's middle name, King, and used that instead.) We used my nephew David Sloan as the young newsboy on the street, selling papers about the manhunt for the Sun Demon. Del Courtney, who played the disc jockey, was the fiancé of my sister-in-law Yvonne King; he was an orchestra leader and a deejay in San Francisco. Yet another King Sister, Marilyn, wrote and sang the song "Strange Pursuit" which is heard in the film (mouthed by Nan Peterson). In 1982, when Paramount put together a campy compilation of monster movie clips called *It Came from Hollywood*, they used the scene of Nan singing that song and paid Marilyn $500 for the use of it. I'm also in that scene and so Paramount paid me a few dollars. I can't recall now how much, because it was so minimal, but it wasn't as much as Marilyn got, I remember *that*.

The King family, by the way — the sisters, the kids, Del Courtney, all of them — were wonderful. Everybody pitched in to help, and everybody received a *very* minimal amount of money. Donna's son Chris told me that he was recently in San Jose and he mentioned to some guy there that his uncle was the Sun Demon. Well, the guy practically had a *stroke*. "Really? Your uncle was the Sun Demon?! You're kidding. Not *really*....*Really*?" The guy did everything but back flips. (And I wonder if the guy would have been nearly as impressed if, instead of *Hideous Sun Demon*, Chris had dropped the name of the King Family!)

I can't recall precisely when we began production on *Sun Demon*, but it was very close to the time when Alyce gave birth to our son Cam. That puts our starting date at the very end of 1957 or the first part of 1958. We shot only on weekends: We'd have a spot picked for our shooting on a given weekend, we'd rent our lighting, camera and sound equipment on a Friday afternoon and we would therefore get two days of shooting out of a one-day rental. We shot it on 12 weekends over the course of 13 weeks. (My dad died on Friday, February 28, 1958, and that weekend we of course did not work.) Believe it or not, we started with $10,000 cash: Robin Kirkman and I each put in $5,000. That must seem ridiculous today but back *then*, making the sort of picture we were making, we felt that we had a shot at making a good, modest science fiction movie.

One of the reasons we were able to make *The Hideous Sun Demon* as economically as we did was the fact that we shot on practical locations. (This was something that Roger Corman was known for, and we just followed his lead.) For instance, when we needed a scene in a bar, we just walked into a bar in Santa Monica and asked the owner how much he would charge us to come in there and shoot. The exterior of Dr. McKenna's house was actually a Catholic school; it was an old mansion formerly owned by silent movie star Antonio Moreno. The interiors, however, were shot at a different location, a big old four-story rooming house on Lafayette Park Avenue. It also had been a mansion in the early days of Los Angeles history, and

Clarke and (in wheelchair) his mother-in-law Pearl Driggs in the hospital rooftop scene. In background are d.p. Vilis Lapenieks and (behind the board) USC Cinema student Erik Darstaad, an uncredited cameraman on the movie.

I'd been in it a few years before, when part of an episode of *I Led Three Lives* was shot there. When I decided to try to use it in *Sun Demon*, I contacted the lady who ran the place and told her I was interested in renting it for a movie.

"Will you pay me as much as *they* did?" she asked, referring back to the *I Led Three Lives* people.

"Perhaps," I warily replied. "How much was that?"

Kirkman, co-director Tom Boutross and Clarke between takes during the dramatic "Cheese it! The cops!" scene.

"Well, *they* paid me $25 a day."

Needless to say, that was practically a steal — so much of a bargain, in fact, we actually wrote some extra scenes to be shot in the house, because the price was so right.

The scene where I transform on the hospital roof was shot atop a hospital on South Hope Street in downtown L.A. It's now called the California Medical Center. We also used its ambulance driveway and a room inside (for the scene where I smashed the mirror). Also downtown was the power plant where we shot scenes of Atomic Research, Inc.

Using real locations gave our low-budget picture production values. In other words, the ocean is the ocean, whether it's a small-budget picture or an MGM blockbuster. Shots of me walking along the cliffs were photographed at Bass Rock, and the beach scene with Nan Peterson was shot near Trancas, which is now a very fashionable area. We had sound equipment there for that scene but the roar of the ocean drowned out our voices. In post-production, Nan and I had to loop every line.

The oil fields were in the Long Beach area of what had been Signal Hill in the early 1900s. Many of those old wooden derricks still stand and still pump oil. The gas storage tank was located near the Union Station train depot, and it was made available to us through the Southern California Gas Company. It was about 300 feet high, and when I took the dummy of the Sun Demon up to the top to throw it off, my voice (as big and loud as it was) could not be heard by the camera crew down below. We had a very difficult time communicating.

One of the people partly responsible for the popularity of the movie was the fellow who fashioned the Sun Demon mask and costume, Richard Cassarino. Before I found Dick, I first looked up Jack Kevan, the very creative makeup man who made the Gill Man costume for *Creature from the Black Lagoon* (1954). I visited Jack in his Beverly Hills home and told him what I wanted. Jack, however, was used to working for the big studios, and he told me that he'd have to charge me about $5000. He wasn't overpricing it, but he also wasn't within *my* price range (or even close). That's when I came upon Dick Cassarino, who was a film buff and a sometimes-actor. He made a life mask of me and then he fashioned the Sun Demon mask on that. For the scenes in which the Sun Demon was shirtless, I wore the top half of a neoprene skin-diving wetsuit covered with scales. The thing was hotter than blue blazes — *so* hot, in fact, that perspiration ran down my body and soaked my pants. In one still featuring the Sun Demon, taken after one of the fight scenes, it looks like I couldn't make it to the men's room.

In addition to creating the Sun Demon mask and costume (which ran us $500), Cassarino also worked as a set designer and he played the policeman who fights with me on the gas storage tank. (We shot all those scenes silent and added sound later.) Dick had a rubber pistol, and there's actually a shot where he fires it and you can see the gun squash up in his hand and the barrel wobble. Dick wasn't the only person working both sides of the camera. Robin Kirkman was our sound recordist and he played the cop that I hit and killed as I raced away from the mansion in the car. Ron Honthaner, our assistant editor, worked on the crew, and he *also* played a cop, the one I tackled and beat with a board in the warehouse; he was a skinny kid and we had a uniform that almost fit him. Ron later went on to work as the assistant to the producer on *Gunsmoke*, later became the show's associate producer, and did well for quite a while. Doug Menville, the boom man, played a different cop.

We also accepted whatever freebies we could get. For example, in order for Dr. McKenna to have a flashy car, I struck a bargain with a dealer in the southern part of L.A. who was importing MGs. Our arrangement

Unbelievable! Incredible!...*Incontinent?* Actually, it's just perspiration.

was that *he* would allow us the use of a car, a sporty little MG convertible, and in return *we* would give him a screen credit. Which we did. I *think*. I *hope*. [Editor's note: Nope!]

Because I produced and co-directed the picture, I'm sometimes asked why I also played the Sun Demon, instead of simply hiring a stand-in or a stuntman to take my place in those scenes. I've got a very straight answer: It just never occurred to me. I think that's pretty honest, and rather naive. I could very easily have put somebody else in the costume and nobody would ever have known the difference, and I wouldn't have had to go through all that. It would have been a very obvious and sensible thing to do. But because I was playing Dr. McKenna, I just automatically took on the responsibility of playing the Sun Demon, too. There's not a single shot in that movie where it isn't me inside that outfit.

Tom Boutross, my co-director, was a tremendous amount of help. He took pains with the picture not only during production but then later, during the editing, when he also treated it with great loving care. In one scene the Sun Demon bursts into the house, frightening his girlfriend. Tom employed a dolly shot: The camera moved in toward the door as the door opened and I entered, rushing the camera. That was Tom's pet

Gil's snazzy MG gets a windshield wipe from a gas station attendant (played by *Sun Demon* assistant director Tom Miller).

shot, and it might be the most memorable shot in the picture. It required a great deal of effort on the part of our semi-amateur crew; they had to lay track on the rough floor in order to make the shot smooth, the guy on focus had to follow-focus with the camera moving, etc. It was a very difficult shot for those guys, who were still learning the business.

Production went smoothly over the course of the 12 weekends and everyone got along nicely. In fact, the one and only time that anyone got a little bit difficult, that person was *me*. We were shooting the scene on the hospital roof, and I was wearing that hot mask and running around — I was just sweltering. We shot the scene where I jump up out of the wheelchair and run through the doorway, back into the hospital, and I was anxious to move along, to get these scenes finished up so that I could get out of that mask and costume. I looked around and everybody was just standing around, the crew and everybody, chitchatting away. I guess, if anybody ever kinda lost their temper on the picture, at that point *I* did. "Come on, you guys. We gotta break down that setup and go down and shoot in the hospital." I became upset for a few moments because I was *so* hot and they all seemed so lackadaisical. But, again, I really can't blame them at all; it was more like they were *volunteering* their efforts, because the pay was so

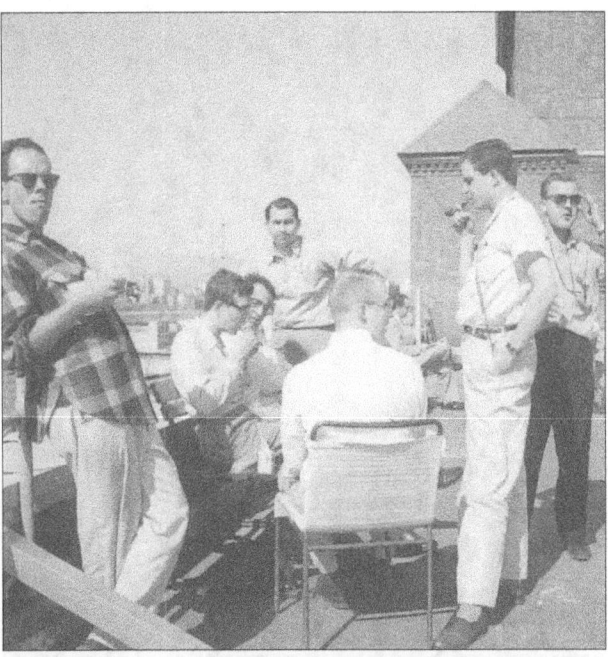

Break time atop the South Hope Street hospital with *(left to right)* Robin C. Kirkman, Doug Menville, Tom Boutross, Milt Roberts (a USC student/Cinemanor-ite who may or may not have worked on the movie), Tom Miller, Stan Follis (with pipe) and Vilis Lapenieks.

negligible: 25 bucks a day and all the hamburgers they could eat.

My brother Bill Clarke worked as a sales manager at an NBC-affiliate radio station in Amarillo, Texas, and through a friend of his, he offered me the opportunity to go to Amarillo and premiere *Sun Demon* at a drive-in. (The title was still *The Sun Demon* at that point; *Hideous* was added later.) The drive-in manager, Mr. Doyle, advertised it heavily and we had a great turnout: For five nights, we packed the drive-in, and we ended up doing $5,000 gross business in an era when admission was probably 50 cents. I was there, along with Nan Peterson, making personal appearances, and we got good publicity.

When Mr. Doyle offered to fly me in his little Piper Cub to Dallas, to show the picture to Universal, I seized the opportunity. It was a hot, hot day, and I had to lug around the 35mm print of *Sun Demon*, eight heavy reels. They ran the picture and they gave me an introduction to Universal in California, but to my dismay the people at Universal out here didn't show any substantial interest. I then had an opportunity to show it at Warner Bros., and I had high hopes that Warners might buy it because I knew they had recently acquired a Roger Corman picture called *Stakeout on*

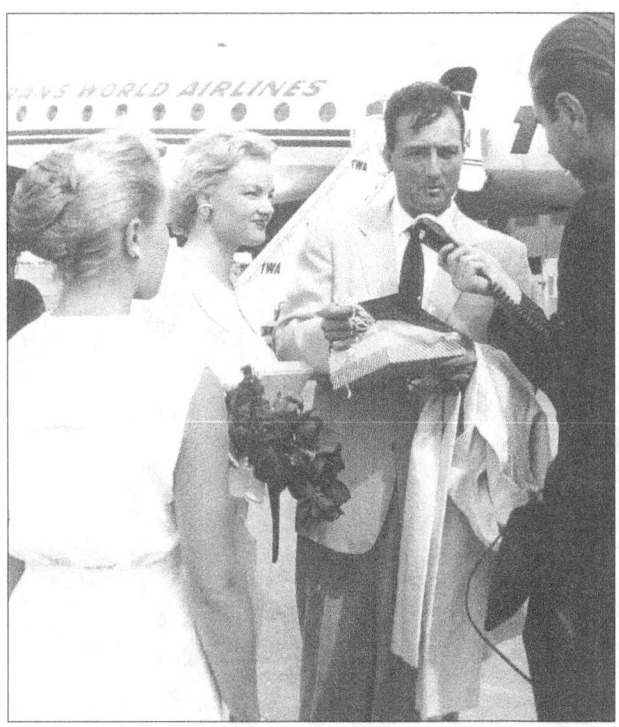

Meet the press: Clarke and Nan Peterson arrive in Texas for *The Sun Demon*'s world premiere at a local drive-in.

Dope Street (1958). But Warner Bros. passed.

Next I was introduced to Jim Nicholson, the president of American International. I went out to Nicholson's house, where I met his wife Sylvia and their three daughters, and I showed the picture there. Nicholson's daughters liked it, which I thought was a good sign, and Nicholson said, "Show it to Sam Arkoff." I left the print with Arkoff, and he ran it and got back to me. He said he liked it, but he added, "Those jiggling boobs of the gal [Peterson], as she runs down the steps toward the beach — you've got to cut *that*." (Shows you how far we've come.) Arkoff offered me a flat distribution deal, but I'd already been forewarned by Ronnie Ashcroft that I wouldn't get any money if I made an agreement like that. Too many other producers gave their pictures to companies like AIP and never made a dime — that was a well-known fact. I told Arkoff that I wanted to use *Sun Demon* as a door opener and produce other pictures, but Arkoff wasn't open to that sort of arrangement. "Oh," he said, "we've got too many producers *now*. But we'll distribute it for you." I said no thanks.

Some time later, I was on the General Service Studios lot for some reason, maybe to show *Sun Demon* to someone. It was there, in one of the offices, that I ran into Les Guthrie, the very fine production manager with whom I'd worked on *The Man from Planet X* (1951), *Sword of Venus* (1953) and other pictures. I told Les what I was up to, and it was Les who told me about a company called Miller Consolidated Pictures. A pair of guys named John Miller and Mike Miller (no relation) had started their own outfit — they wanted to be another Nicholson and Arkoff — and they were getting ready to shoot their first picture, *Date with Death*, in Roswell, New Mexico. The Millers told me that they'd be needing a companion picture for *Date with Death*, and I indicated that I might be interested in letting them have *Sun Demon* if they'd make me the right kind of deal: I told them I wanted a three-picture contract. They said, "Well, fine. If you don't require any money up front for your *Sun Demon*, we'll release that with our picture [*Date with Death*] as a double bill." They also gave me a part in *Date with Death*, a job which paid $450 or $500. I was the head of a crime syndicate and Gerald Mohr played a hobo-turned-police chief who gets the goods on me. The leading lady was Liz Renay, the girlfriend of mobster Mickey Cohen.

Through the distribution arm of their company (Pacific International), the Millers released *The Hideous Sun Demon* and *Date With Death*. *Sun Demon* didn't get very many reviews, and none of the reviews that it *did* get made it out to be any kind of gem, but they were generally fair to the film and pointed out that it would fulfill the demands of its market. In England it was released under the title *Blood on His Lips* and rated X (*another* sign of changing times).

Looking back on my acting in the film, I think I overdid it a little bit, I did too much of a "Kirk Douglas." For example, in the scene where I'm sitting on a divan and I'm very emotional over my situation ("Why should *I* be the one? Why *me*?") — that was perhaps too melodramatic. We did that scene about 14 times before I could bring myself to say, "Okay, that's a take." I kept saying, "Let's do it again" — and again, and *again* — because I had it in my mind that this would be the scene which would prove that I could act. I don't know that it proved anything, except that I could do it 14 times.

One of the things about *Hideous Sun Demon* I'm most often complimented on is the background music. I'd like to accept those compliments, but I can't: It all came from the Capitol Record Library. We paid a usage fee and John Seely, a music editor, picked music cues and edited them together. Later, after we did

Pacific International's theatrical poster shortened the title to *Hideous Sun Demon* (no *The*). Second-billed Patricia Manning isn't visually represented; instead we get artwork of a screaming Alix Talton, swiped from the poster of 1957's *The Deadly Mantis!*

the movie, I would often hear those same cues on TV shows, and I'd say to myself, "Oh. That's from the scene where…" — whatever it was. So it was funny when I would receive letters about *Hideous Sun Demon* which emphasized that the music was so great.

I am proud about two things with regard to *Sun Demon*: *One*, that we had a good story (we followed a *very* good pattern laid down by Robert Louis Stevenson) and, *two*, that the picture has *pace*. That picture never stops. It *moves*. And to this day I have people telling me that it holds up and it's still interesting and it engages their interest as an action-sci-fi-horror film. The hopes I had for it have come to a fruition, even more than I expected, because it now has its own little slot in that genre. I certainly don't mean to imply that I'm comparing it with pictures like *Invasion of the Body Snatchers* or *Forbidden Planet*, science-fiction picture that were super-great. But on the lower level of exploitation, drive-in-style sci-fi flicks, *Hideous Sun Demon* has certainly found its place of popularity, partly because it had a little more to it, it had elements that others didn't. This is what the fans tell me and I find that very flattering — particularly since that was *precisely* one of the things I set out to achieve when we made it. I was also very fortunate to join forces with all of those great guys from the USC Cinema Department, Tom Boutross and Robin Kirkman and the rest, all of them film nuts dedicated to turning out something good.

The fans tell me we did. I'd like to agree.

Left: Boutross, Clarke and Kirkman. *Right:* D.P. John Morrill looks on as Cassarino appears to be extracting a Hideous Sun Booger.

Clarke, decades after making *The Hideous Sun Demon,* with a Bob Burns-created Sun Demon mask.

NOTES ON THE SCRIPTS
by Tom Weaver

On the following pages, the first of the two reproduced scripts is *Sauros* by Phil Hiner. (See page 12 of Clarke's introductory chapter for more on Hiner.) Set in Guatemalan jungles, it features a character who becomes a reptile man in sunlight, but otherwise it bears almost no resemblance to the movie *The Hideous Sun Demon*. Hiner had to have also written a second script, *much* more like the eventual film, before USCer E.S. Seeley Jr. penned *The Sun Demon*'s Final Revised Shooting Script. But I have never found a copy of this interim script.

Notice, early in *Sauros*, the full page devoted to makeup man Jack P. Pierce. By 1957, Clarke had already encountered Pierce on various sets, knew of his makeup feats at Universal (*Frankenstein, The Mummy, The Wolf Man,* more) and hoped to get him to do the monster makeup for *Sauros*. That script page was included, Clarke told me, in hopes of making a good impression on the makeup wiz. (If Clarke ever told me whether or not he actually approached Pierce and offered him the job, I do not remember.)

Seeley's *The Sun Demon*, dated October 17, 1957, follows. To enhance your reading, consult this list of some of the differences between the Seeley script and the finished film:

✳ Gil's entire ambulance ride to the hospital, plus a page-and-a-half's worth of hospital activity, comprises the pre-credits sequence.

✳ In the movie, as Gil's ambulance speeds through city streets, we hear voiceover narration (not in the

Sun Demon crew members at work on the movie's opening scene.

script) spoken by Patrick Whyte, who plays Dr. Buckell: "Immediately after the launching of U.S. satellites #1 and #3 into outer space, newspaper headlines across the country told the world of a new radiation hazard from the sun, far more deadly than cosmic rays. An obscure scientist, my colleague, Dr. Gilbert McKenna, had already discovered this danger from the sun. This is his story…" There was a boomlet of movies with outer space monsters during that Sputnik era; perhaps this voiceover was added because Clarke wanted to make *Sun Demon* seem like it was in that subgenre. The trailer goes so far as to imply that the Sun Demon came from outer space.

✹ Like dipso Don in *The Lost Weekend* (1945), Gil (in the script) resorts to trickery to get his nips: While hospitalized for radiation exposure, he keeps a flask of gin hidden in his bedside water pitcher (page 14).

✹ In the movie, Gil begins to transform into the Sun Demon on the hospital roof and makes a simple dash back to his room. In the script (page 20), the scene is more elaborate, with the camera at Gil's heels as he runs through the corridors; patients and nurses react with horror as he passes.

✹ Pages 29-32: Ann visits Gil's hospital room to show her support, and gets the brush with the hard bristles, in a scene not in the movie. During this conversation, he identifies the house where much of the movie is subsequently set as "my father's old place."

✹ After Gil and Trudy take their high-speed cliffside drive in the movie, "problem drinker" Gil gets a decanter out of the between-seats storage compartment. In the script (page 52), he has her push a button on the dashboard and, James Bond-ishly, part of the fascia drops down to reveal a well-equipped built-in bar. (Gil: "I had it put in when I bought the car.")

✹ The movie's nighttime beach scene ends with Gil and Trudy on their feet, embracing and kissing. In the script (page 58), the climax to this scene finds them lying in the sand, making out; the camera pans down their bodies until it reaches their feet which intertwine and caress each other. The script then calls for a follow-up shot of an ocean wave crashing explosively against a pointed rock; "The spray dashes high into the air as an obvious symbol of what has just occurred between Gil and Trudy…"

✹ Gil falls asleep on the beach and wakes to see the sun in the morning sky. His over-the-speed-limit ride home is made more suspenseful in the script (pages 60-61), where he is spotted and pursued by a motorcycle cop and must take evasive action.

The Sun Demon's first beach scene was shot day-for-night but that didn't make the Pacific water much warmer for Peterson and Clarke.

✹ In the movie, after Gil receives a brutal beatdown from George and two other thugs, Trudy announces she's taking him to a hospital; as she struggles to get Gil to his feet, George and his friends saunter away ("Let's get outta here…"). In the script, Trudy says that she wants to take the semi-conscious Gil over to her place. Quite improbably, George not only accepts this, but even helps her carry Gil to her car (page 79-80).

✹ Trudy is more volatile in the script than in the movie, and comes to a violent end (pages 83-85). Fleeing the scene of her murder, the Sun Demon causes much commotion (pages 85-86).

✹ In the script, when Police Lt. Peterson is told that Gil (fleeing in his convertible) ran over a police officer, his comeback (page 96) is: "Oh great." The name of the run-over cop, Willis, is mentioned in the script but not in the movie. Only obliquely does the movie inform us that Willis dies from his injuries: Lt. Peterson tells the radio deejay, "[Gil has] killed twice," and that can only mean George and Willis.

✸ In the oil field finale, Gil (trying to stay out of view of the arriving policemen) carries Suzy around in a few shots, then allows her to run off. But in the script (page 120-21), Gil stands in the shack doorway deliberately using Suzy as a human shield to stymie the approaching policemen. Then, ignoring one cop's shouted order "Stop in the name of the Law," he runs away carrying her. He escapes into an area filled with high grass before the sun's rays cause him to collapse; only then can Suzy escape his grip.

✸ The script calls for the final chase to take place inside and atop a large stack of trolley cars not far from the shack (pages 123-26).

✸ The movie's final lines are spoken by Dr. Buckell as he, Ann and Dr. Hoffmann turn away from Gil's body at the base of the gasometer: "Don't cry, Ann. Perhaps you *should* cry. The rest of us can only hope that his life was not wasted." The lines are not well-written and cannot be well-delivered (and they're *not*!). But in the script (page 126), it's even worse: A cop bends down to examine Gil's broken body at the base of the trolley car stack, then rises, waves to grieving Ann and others (standing by a nearby car) and says, "It's okay. He's dead."

Following *Sauros* and *The Sun Demon* in the Scripts Section is the 24-page outline *Sorceress* by Arthur C. Pierce, written in 1976 when Clarke was looking to produce more sci-fi movies. Pierce was the writer of such highly derivative SF flicks as *The Cosmic Man* (1959), *Mutiny in Outer Space* (1965), *Cyborg 2087* and *Destination Inner Space* (1966), Clarke's own *Beyond the Time Barrier* (1960) and more. For additional info on *Sorceress*, see the "Fun Facts" section.

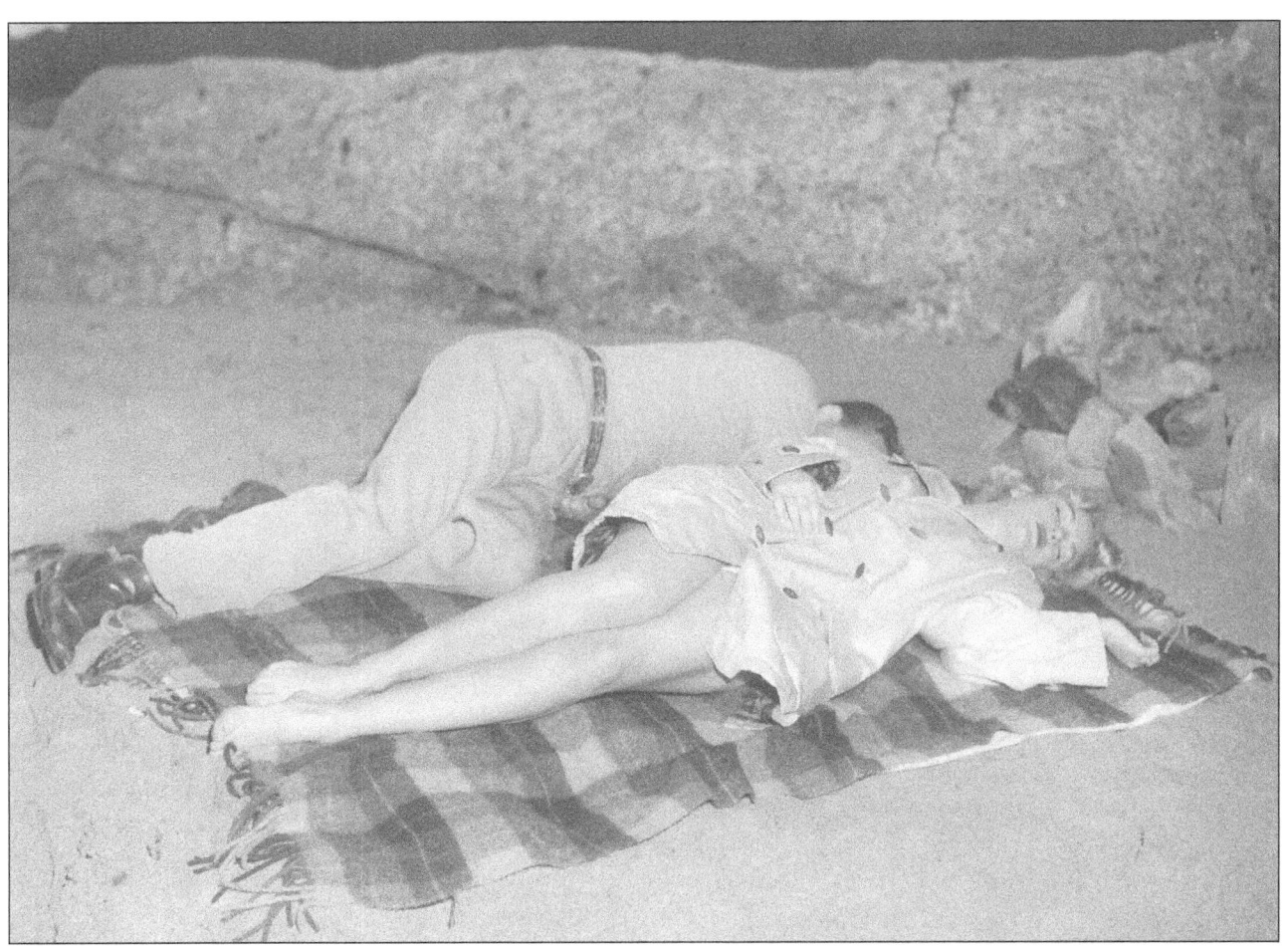

His judgment fogged by heavy breathing, Gil (Clarke) allows himself to fall asleep on the beach with Trudy (Peterson) — and awakens in sunlight.

SAUROS

S A U R O S

an original screenplay

by

PHIL HINER

from a story

by

PHIL HINER and ROBERT CLARKE

The original and bizarre
character around which this
story is woven was created and
copyrighted
         by
makeup artist

JACK P. PIERCE

S A U R O S

FADE IN

EXT. DESOLATE MOUNTAINOUS COUNTRY - DAY

1   CLOSE SHOT - A prospector, visible only from the waist down, is digging in the rocky soil with a pick. His stance is broad and his strokes are slow and deliberate. Beside him and within easy reach stands a rifle and a canteen.

　　As the prospector drives the pick into the ground for the third time, the TITLE appears superimposed over the action. The music is ominous and in rhythm with the strokes of the pick. The man continues to work as one by one the CAST CREDITS, TECHNICAL CREDITS, and the PRODUCER'S and DIRECTOR'S names appear. Each change in credits is accompanied by a downward stroke of the pick.

　　After the final credit the man pauses in his work and we see him, still but from the waist down, reach for the canteen and unscrew its cap. As the cap falls to one side on its captive chain, the motion of the man's hands freezes and we hear o.s. a rhythmic, crunching sound as of some heavy-footed creature approaching. Suddenly, the canteen clatters to the ground and the man wheels for his rifle but it too drops to the ground as something with obvious power and ferocity clutches the

(CONTINUED)

1 (CONTINUED)

        prospector. For a moment we view his legs as
he grapples desperately with an assailant that
because of the CAMERA ANGLE we cannot see

2   INSERT - of the open canteen on the ground.
Water is gushing from its spout. In the background
are the sounds of a death struggle. The sounds
build to a climax accompanied by music as the
body of the prospector is thrown to the ground
and the booted feet fall beside the canteen and
are motionless.

        The last of the water drains from the canteen,
symbolizing the ebbying life of the prospector.
In all the action we have seen neither the prospector nor his assailant, but only the lower
portion of the prospector and his booted feet
beside the canteen.

        As the last drops of water fall to the ground,
the CAMERA DOLLIES in until the words GUATEMALA
SUPPLY COMPANY are visible on the side of the
canteen. The CAMERA continues to dolly in until
only the word GUATEMALA fills the screen.

        For a moment the word GUATEMALA holds, then
the CAMERA dollies back slowly until the words
LOS ANGELES TO GUATEMALA are framed and it becomes
evident after this transition that the new words
form a portion of an airline ticket.

                    NARRATION (1)
                 (male voice)
      ... Guatemala was the last place
in the world I ever expected to
visit, yet here I was on the plane...
Los Angeles to Guatemala... 2190
miles... 7 hours and 58 minutes...
Most people are excited by a trip
in the air; I was merely impatient
to get it done with and go to work.
Geological surveys were nothing
new to me... but this time it was
uranium we were after - the new king
of the metals...

3   MED. SHOT - As the narrator speaks the airline
ticket is moved aside and we see the interior of
the plane with its twin rows of double seats. A

                                        (CONTINUED)

PH   3

3 (CONTINUED)

        stewardess moves along the isle. The CAMERA
        PANS slowly then stops to focus upon an elderly
        man in the seat beside the narrator. The man is
        white-haired, rawboned, impressive looking.
        He has a pipe in his mouth and is calmly reading.
        The entire scene is from the viewpoint of the
        narrator.

                    NARRATION (2)
        ... The Chicago Mining Engineering
        Company really thought it had some-
        thing this time. In the Altos
        country at the foot of Mount Fuego,
        geiger counters had gone crazy
        during that preliminary survey
        a year ago... This was Dr. Paul
        Jorgoson, consulting geologist
        and a vice president of the company.
        He really knew his stuff! He
        could forget more about industrial
        mining every day of his life than
        I had learned in four rugged years
        of cracking the earth's shell. He
        seemed too old for an expedition into
        the treacherous jungles of the Altos
        but the company wasn't missing
        any bets on this one...

4   CLOSE PAN SHOT - The CAMERA pans from Paul to the
        isle between the double row of seats. A pretty,
        sophisticated young lady is walking down the isle.
        She seats herself in the seat directly across
        the isle from the narrator.

                    NARRATION(3)
        ... The girl coming down the
        isle was pretty enough to draw
        a second look anywhere but at the
        moment we other passengers weren't
        feeling too kindly towards her.
        She had held up our take-off for
        twenty minutes at the Los
        Angeles International and in
        Los Angeles in August the cabin
        of an airplane feels like a
        cement kiln...

5   MED. SHOT - The stewardess speaks to the girl,

                                      (CONTINUED)

5 (CONTINUED)

smiles, and moves down the isle towards the front of the plane. The CAMERA follows her. She stops beside a rabbit-faced passenger and hands him an envelope. He thanks her profusely, his eyes lingering on her pretty face.

NARRATION (4)

... To the average male, the stewardess is the most interesting part of an airliner's equipment. This one seemed to be running a message delivery service. A few minutes ago she had delivered a radiogram to us and now she was handing out another one to the eager looking gent across the isle. We were glad to get our radiogram... but not the news that was in it... McCarthy seriously injured in automobile accident, it said. Will be replaced by his assistant, T.C. O'Conner... McCarthy was the top lawyer in our company's lease division and the company had insisted that he personally handle the legal details in leasing foreign mineral rights. McCarthy.. O'Conner.. It made no difference to me. I had already put in my beef about having a tenderfoot along and it had fallen pretty flat with the company brass. This was going to be a rugged expedition and I wasn't looking forward to nursemaiding any desk man through the wild Guatemalan jungles...

6   MED. CLOSE SHOT - The stewardess returns to the girl seated opposite the as yet unseen narrator and hands her a newspaper. They talk and smile for a moment and the stewardess leaves. The girl begins to intently read the paper.

NARRATION (5)

... The girl who had delayed our flight certainly didn't look Spanish but there wasn't any doubt about the newspaper in front of her. Either she couldn't read Spanish very well or she had stumbled across a hot piece (cont'd)

(CONTINUED)

6 (CONTINUED)

                    NARRATION (cont'd)
of news because she continued to stare intently at the same item. Then she suddenly took me by surprise by shoving the paper under my nose...

7   TWO SHOT - from the isle in front of the girl and the narrator. The opened newspaper continues to hide the narrator's face but not the girl's.

                    THE GIRL (6)
Here is the strangest story I ever read. Have you seen it?

8   INSERT - A close shot of the news item - set in Spanish type.

                    NARRATOR (7)
Sorry, Miss, Spanish or Cherokee.. it's all the same to me.

                    THE GIRL (8)
Oh, I beg your pardon. I'll translate it for you.

The Spanish language news item fades into an English version.

                    THE GIRL (9)
              (reading aloud)
Mondera, August 12. The body of an unidentified prospector was discovered at the foot of Mount Fuego in the Altos country just before dawn this morning by Miguel Jose Milla of Mondera. Cause of death was believed to be strangulation although authorities have been unable to account for numerous sharp and very deep skin lesions at the throat. The death of this prospector brings to 12 the number who have died under identical circumstances in the area during the past 10 years. Although a government investigation was conducted two years ago, none of the mysterious deaths has ever been solved.

9   TWO SHOT - As the girl reads the item we return to THE SCENE. The newspaper hides the narrator's face but not the girl's. As she finishes reading she slowly lowers the paper and for the first time we see the narrator - a rugged but good looking man in his middle thirties.

> NARRATOR (10)
> Sounds like a native superstition to me.

> THE GIRL (11)
> It doesn't sound at all like a superstition. This is a news item and the facts are undoubtedly true.

10 THREE SHOT - Paul leans towards the girl.

> PAUL (12)
> May I take a look at that item? We happen to be going to Mondera.

> THE GIRL (13)
> (handing Paul the paper)
> Oh, really! I'm going to Mondera myself.

> PAUL (14)
> Good! Then you will change planes with us at Guatemala City. Let me introduce ourselves. I am Dr. Paul Jorgeson and this is my friend, Stan Rockwell.

> THE GIRL (15)
> I'm Terry O'Conner. I'm glad to know you both.

11 CLOSE SHOT - of Paul

> PAUL (16)
> O'Conner... that name sounds familiar.

Paul frowns in thought, and slowly pulls the crumpled radiogram from his pocket. He reads aloud.

> PAUL (cont'd)
> ... will be replaced by his assistant, T.C. O'Conner... T.C. O'Conner... but that couldn't be you.

12   THREE SHOT - Terry is talking across the isle to
      Paul and Stan.

                    TERRY (17)
            I'm afraid it could be, Dr.
            Jorgeson. The T stands for
            Terry and the C for something
            that shouldn't happen to a
            cocker spaniel.

                    STAN (18)
            You mean you're taking
            McCarthy's place on this
            expedition?

                    TERRY (19)
            That's it.

Terry looks from Stan to Paul and back again,
reading the consternation on their faces.

                    TERRY (cont'd)
            Does that bother you, Mr.
            Rockwell?

                    STAN (20)
            Bother me!. It's completely
            ridiculous! We're going into
            the jungles around Mount Fuego.
            Do you have any idea what they
            are like? I don't know what
            the company could be thinking of?

                    TERRY (21)
            I'll tell you what the company
            was thinking of... Jim McCarthy
            and I spent two months studying
            Guatemalan law as well as the
            language... just for this
            expedition of yours. Then early
            yesterday morning Jim's car
            went over an embankment on Laurel
            Canyon Drive. The company had
            no choice but to send me.

                                (CONTINUED)

12 (CONTINUED)

> PAUL (22)
> (calmly)
> Do you know the legal facts as well as McCarthy?

> TERRY (23)
> I'm sure I do.

> STAN (24)
> We better revise our operations timetable! McCarthy would have been bad enough to coax through a jungle, but a woman...

> TERRY (25)
> (spiritedly)
> If you think you'll have to hold my hand every time we hear a strange noise, Mr. Rockwell, take another guess.

13   STOCK SHOT - of the airliner flying through the night skies.

> NARRATION (26)
> ... Terry and I had gotten off to a bad start. Of course it wasn't her fault she was substituting for McCarthy but this expedition meant a lot to me for personal reasons, and if she was going to be a part of it I intended to keep her on her toes every minute... Apparently, Paul, too, had personal reasons for making this trip. I had thought he was along merely because of his knowledge of uranium mining. I hadn't even guessed that there might be a deeper reason until I saw him clipping the item from the Spanish newspaper...

14   TWO SHOT - Paul finishes tearing the item from the newspaper. He removes a leather binder from an inner pocket, folds the item and carefully places it among other papers in the binder.

> STAN (27)
> (watching)
> Why this sudden interest in a simple native killing?

(CONTINUED)

14 (CONTINUED)

> PAUL (28)
> It can hardly be called a sudden interest, Stan.. or a simple native killing. As a matter of fact I've followed this story for ten years... and I've gathered enough data to fill a small trunk.

> STAN (29)
> But why, Paul? How does it affect you?

> PAUL (30)
> It's a long story, Stan... something I have a personal stake in. Some evening when we're parked in our room in Mondera with nothing to do but cut a deck of cards, I'll tell you all about it.

DISSOLVE TO

EXT. PLANE IN FLIGHT- NIGHT

15 MED. SHOT - A four-motored commercial airliner wings its way through dark, swirling clouds. The plane is dimly silhouetted by light from engine exhausts and cabin ports.

DISSOLVE TO

EXT. PLANE IN FLIGHT - DAY

16 MED. SHOT - as the plane drops through the mist and its wheels touch the concrete at the Guatemala City airport.

> NARRATION (31)
> ... It was daylight when we changed planes at Guatemala City. Apparently, Mondera was no tourist mecca because we three were the only passengers to board the single-engined job operated by a feeder line... Forty-seven minutes later we dropped our landing flaps over a strip of green that the pilot assured us was an airfield. A one-man reception committee awaited us.

17   FULL SHOT - A small, single-engined plane
      approaches the CAMERA along the runway and takes
      off directly overhead. The shot fades into a
      second view of the plane as it lands at a small,
      one-hanger, grass-covered airport in Mondera.

                                        FADE

EXT. MONDERA AIRPORT - DAY

18   CLOSE SHOT - A huskily-built native stands near
      the gate through which the passengers must pass.
      The sound of an airplane motor is in the background.
      As he stares at the plane, an unfathomable expression is engraved on his swarthy,
      glistening face.

19   MED. GROUP SHOT - as the passengers approach the
      native at the gate. Paul is walking between Terry
      and Stan. It is late afternoon, extremely hot,
      and b oth men are now carrying their coats.

                    THE NATIVE (32)
                  (stepping forward)
              Dr. Jorgeson?

                    PAUL (33)
                  (pausing)
              I am Dr. Jorgeson.

                    THE NATIVE (34)
              I am Carlos, the sobrestante of
              the La Casa Consuelo.

                    PAUL (35)
                  (extending his hand)
              I am happy to meet you, Carlos.

                    CARLOS (36)
                  (bowing)
              Senor Consuelo welcomes you to
              our village. He regrets he could
              not greet you at the airport as
              he planned but at the last
              minute.. an urgent matter.

                    PAUL (37)
              It is good of you to meet us.

                                        (CONTINUED)

19 (CONTINUED)

> CARLOS (38)
> You are to make La Casa Consuelo your home while in Mondera. It is Senor Consuelo's wish.

> PAUL (39)
> Thank you, Carlos. Allow me to present Miss O'Connor and Mr. Rockwell.

> CARLOS (40)
> (bowing)
> We were not expecting a senorita.

20   TWO SHOT - of Stan and Terry from another angle.

> STAN (41)
> Neither were we.

As he speaks Stan gives Terry a smile that manages better than words to convey his opinion of women who go along on jungle expeditions.

> PAUL (42)
> There was a last minute change in our plans. Our legal representative was seriously injured in an automobile accident and his assistant, Miss O'Conner, agreed to take his place...

> STAN (43)
> (aside to Terry so that Carlos does not hear)
> I bet they had to twist her arm.

Terry gives Stan a dirty look not seen by the others. Paul continues his conversation with Carlos.

21   TWO SHOT - of Paul and Carlos.

> PAUL (44)
> I hope the change does not inconvenience Senor Consuelo.

(CONTINUED)

21(CONTINUED)

> CARLOS (45)
> On the contrary, Senor Consuelo will be delighted to have the senorita. La Casa Consuelo is the largest estate at the foot of the Fuego. There is room for all.

Stan moves into the picture beside Paul.

> STAN (46)
> We appreciate the cooperation Senor Consuelo has given our company these past few months. But he needn't take us into his home. We can go to a hotel.

> CARLOS (47)
> If I do not bring you back, I lose my job... If you will follow me to the car please. It is a long ride and you will want to rest before dinner.

INT. DINING ROOM - NIGHT

22 FULL SHOT - of a palatial dining room with Consuelo, Carlos, Paul, Stan, and Terry seated around a large table. The food is being removed by servants and coffee and wine is being served. There is an air of geniality and contentment after a good meal.

23 CLOSE SHOT - of Senor Consuelo smiling as he raises a glass of wine and offers a toast. He is a large man with dark Spanish features, of latter middle age, and with graying hair.

> CONSUELO (48)
> I offer a toast to the success of your expedition. May it profit both your company and our own great country.

They all raise their glasses and drink the toast.

24 CLOSE SHOT - of Paul with pipe in mouth. He is calm and deliberate as usual. He speaks with slow emphasis.

(CONTINUED)

24 (CONTINUED)

                    PAUL (49)
Thank you, Senor Consuelo. As we told you in our last letter, our company is backing this expedition to the limit of its resources. If we are successful I think I can guarantee that the results will do great things for the economy of your country.

                    CONSUELO (50)
I agree. Our own government surveys indicate great natural deposits of uranium. They need only to be developed by an experienced mining concern such as yours.

                    PAUL (51)
That is right. Our preliminary geological surveys two years ago were extremely promising. If our survey shows the same results, we intend to lease land immediately.

25   GROUP SHOT - featuring Stan. He speaks rapidly, with enthusiasm.

                    STAN (52)
And within four months heavy equipment will be rolling into your town by motor caravan. Your own land, Senor Consuelo, will triple in value.

                    CONSUELO (53)
        (nodding reflectively)
This leasing of land... will you attend to the details yourselves?

26   TWO SHOT - featuring Stan as he gives Terry a special chiding smile.
                    STAN (54)
That is Miss O'Conner's department. The legal brain of our Lease Division met with an accident and his assistant, Miss O'Conner, <u>very kindly</u> agreed to accompany us.

27 ANGLE SHOT - showing a profile of Terry and featuring Consuelo in the b.g. Terry starts to glower at Stan but quickly looks pleasant again as Consuelo smiles at her.

>   CONSUELO (55)
>   If Senorita O'Conner is as efficient
>   as she is charming, the legal
>   details of your expedition are..
>   how do you say.. in the bag.
>
>   TERRY (56)
>   (warmly returning Consuelo's
>   smile)
>   Thank you, Senor. You're kind
>   words will bring me luck.
>
>   CONSUELO (57)
>   It has been a long time since we
>   entertained a young and beautiful
>   woman at La Casa Consuelo. I
>   propose a toast to the senorita.
>   (he raises his glass) To a most
>   pleasant stay in Guatemala!

28 GROUP SHOT - They all raise their glasses with the exception of Terry. She waits a moment, smiling, slightly confused, as they drink; then, raises her glass as Consuelo, noticing her hesitation, motions elaborately with his free hand and says:

>   CONSUELO (58)
>   Drink up, Senorita. You must
>   join us in this toast.
>
>   TERRY (59)
>   (raising her glass)
>   Thank you again, Senor Consuelo.

29 CLOSE SHOT - of Paul. As they lower their glasses to the table, he removes the pipe from his mouth and gazes reflectively at Consuelo.

>   PAUL (60)
>   Tell me, Senor Consuelo.. has
>   there been any uranium mining
>   around Mondera during your
>   memory?

The CAMERA ANGLE widens to include Consuelo and Carlos.

(CONTINUED)

29 (CONTINUED)

> CONSUELO (61)
> A little, senor.. but only on a small scale and on privately owned land. You see, it is only recently that our national government has taken any interest in the metal.

Consuelo snaps his fingers, remembering something that had apparently slipped his mind.

> CONSUELO (cont'd)
> But I almost forgot! Many years ago a scientist from your own country bought land a few miles from here and found rich deposits of uranium in both pitchblende and cobalt. For a time he mined great quantities. I was a young man then. I remember.. we used to talk together at the casino. His name was Walton. He was a very learned man.

> CARLOS (62)
> His son still lives in the big house his father built up in the altos country. He lives there alone.

30 ANGLE SHOT - of Stan's profile with Consuelo in the background. Stan listens with interest and sips his coffee.

> STAN (63)
> This scientist is dead?

> CONSUELO (64)
> He has been dead many years. Walton was a fine man but his son... well, there's an odd one. He is not friendly and the townspeople do not care for him. Only occasionally does he come in at night to drink at the casino.

> STAN (65)
> Isn't it strange that the son should stay here alone after his father died.. and especially, a man without friends?

(CONTINUED)

30 (CONTINUED)

> CARLOS (66)
> Many things are strange about this man Walton. His house is far back in the hills near a natural cave. They say the cave has exquisitely furnished rooms hundreds of feet beneath the ground.

> CONSUELO (67)
> It is probably only idle talk among the townspeople. Young Walton is not a friendly man but certainly he has never done anyone harm.

A sudden commotion accompanied by loud, excited voices is heard in an adjacent room. Consuelo stops talking and looks up. The others follow his glance.

31   MED. CLOSE SHOT - a native butler stands in the doorway with an excited and confused expression on his face. CAMERA PANS as the butler enters the room and rushes over to Consuelo to whisper in his ear. Consuelo listens, then nods and rises to his feet as the butler disappears o.s.

> CONSUELO (68)
> A thousand apologies to my guests but I must leave for a little while. We have just received very bad news. One of my chicleros has been missing for two days. He was found tonight in the Guandici hills - dead.

32   CLOSE SHOT - of Carlos as he comes to his feet and steps close to Consuelo. His face is tense; the guests are for the moment forgotten.

> CARLOS (69)
> Was it like the others, Senor?

33   TWO SHOT - with Consuelo talking to Carlos.

> CONSUELO (70)
> Si. Strangled!

> CARLOS (71)
> With the claw marks on his throat?

(CONTINUED)

33 (CONTINUED)

> CONSUELO (72)
> The marks were there, as always.

> CARLOS (73)
> I will go with you, Senor.

> CONSUELO (74)
> No, Carlos, you stay with our guests. They will need help packing their equipment for jungle travel. Senor Rockwell is impatient. They leave tomorrow at sun up.

DISSOLVE

INT. LA CASA CONSUELO - NIGHT

34 MED. SHOT - Paul is walking rapidly down a hallway and as he approaches the CAMERA he pauses and knocks on a door. The door opens and he passes through.

35 MED. TWO SHOT - Paul approaches Stan in the latter's room. The expression on Paul's face is troubled.

> PAUL (75)
> I want to talk to you, Stan. I waited until Terry had gone to her room for the night.

> STAN (76)
> (nodding, and indicating a seat)
> What's the trouble? You look like you just received a letter from your draft board.

> PAUL (77)
> I told you on the plane that I had personal reasons for making this trip. Do you remember?

Stan wipes his perspiring face with a handkerchief and walks towards a small, portable bar.

(CONTINUED)

35 (CONTINUED)

> STAN (78)
> Man, is it hot! I'll mix us
> both a drink. Yes, I remember.
> You said you would tell me
> about it some quiet evening.
> (He opens the window to get
> some air) You'll never find
> a quieter evening than this.
> The water hangs in the air like
> in the swamps of Australia.

> PAUL (79)
> Tonight, Consuelo spoke of
> a scientist who once lived
> here.

> STAN (80)
> (nodding)
> A man by the name of Walton...
> with a screwball son.

36   CLOSE SHOT - of Paul as he removes his tobacco pouch
and with slow, deliberate motions fills the bowl.

> PAUL (81)
> You are too young to remember,
> Stan, but James Walton was
> one of the foremost biologists
> of our times. He was a very
> good friend of mine. Back
> in the 30's he conducted ex-
> tremely advanced experiments
> on mutation in a Long Island
> university laboratory. He
> used X-Ray radiation on insects
> to change their basic chromo-
> some structure, and he derived
> some entirely new and rather
> weird species. Later, he came
> here to Guatemala and I heard
> from him occasionally. He dis-
> covered rich deposits of uranium
> in pitchblende and cobalt as
> Consuelo said, but Consuelo did-
> n't know that he was using the
> metal as a source of radiation in
> his experiments. I visited him
> here while his son was still
> quite young.

37   REVERSE SHOT - featuring Stan with Paul in the b.g. Stan has finished mixing the drinks and is showing interest. He looks up in surprise at Paul's last statement.

                    STAN (82)
            You've been here before, Paul?

                    PAUL (83)
            As I said, it was many years
            ago. I spent a few weeks with
            Walton in his big house up in
            the Guandici hills. I was
            fascinated by the progress he
            had made in his experients.
            He explained many of them to
            me and I helped him while I
            was here.

38   TWO SHOT - as Stan moves in and places the drink in front of Paul, then stands beside him looking down.

                    STAN (84)
            Did you see him again, Paul...
            I mean, after you left here?

                    PAUL (85)
            Yes. I saw him just once
            after that... years later.
            He had returned to the states
            on business and he stopped in
            to see me. I was deeply im-
            pressed by the change that had
            come over the man. He was
            morose and moody. He spoke with
            a hesitancy that he had never had
            before. He mentioned his son
            whom he had left at Mondera. I'll
            never forget what he said or the
            look on his face. Radiation had
            caused an incredible change in
            his son, he said. The change
            was so horrible he would give
            me no details. He had been able
            to only partially modify the
            change. He was very preoccupied
            and we didn't talk for long. It
            was but a few months later that
            I learned he had died in Mondera.

                              (CONTINUED)

38 (CONTINUED)

>   STAN (86)
>   Why did you want to come back
>   to Mondera, Paul? Because
>   of the son?
>
>   PAUL (87)
>   Because of the son... and
>   the strange killings in the
>   area.
>
>   STAN (88)
>   You mean, you felt there was
>   some connection between Walton's
>   son and the killings.
>
>   PAUL (89)
>   Perhaps it is foolish, but
>   I have felt that. The way
>   Walton spoke of his son, I
>   had the feeling that he was
>   the victim of a mutation due
>   to radiation... perhaps some
>   animal-like mutation. These
>   strange killings are not new,
>   Stan. I have newspaper clip-
>   pings dating back some ten
>   years. And always there has
>   been the claw-like marks on the
>   victims' throat. It's weird!
>   In recent years I have talked
>   to a number of people from
>   Mondera. There is a deeply-
>   rooted belief that some sort
>   of grotesque, unearthly monster
>   is living in the hills.
>
>   STAN (90)
>   You don't believe such non-
>   sense, Paul?

Paul shakes his head and slowly applies a match to
his pipe as the CAMERA dollies in for a CLOSE SHOT.
His drink has not been touched.

>   PAUL (91)
>   I am a scientist and I only
>   believe what can be supported
>   by facts. Yet, whenever I
>   hear of these killings I always
>   think of the look on James (cont'd)

38 (CONTINUED)

>   PAUL (91 cont'd)
> Walton's face when he spoke of
> his son. Walton was a scientist,
> too... and there were facts
> behind the horror in his eyes..

                                        FADE OUT

EXT. LA CASA CONSUELO - SUNRISE

39   GROUP SHOT - Equipment is being loaded on packs.
        It is very early morning and the sky is red in the
        east but the sun has not yet appeared. Stan, Paul,
        and Carlos are working silently. Presently, Terry
        appears dressed in slacks, boots, and leather
        jacket. She presents a very pleasing and feminine
        appearance.

40   CLOSE SHOT - as Stan stops his work and stares at
        the girl. His expression shows disapproval, yet
        undertones of forced admiration.

>   STAN (92)
> Where do you think you're
> going, Terry?

41   TWO SHOT - as Terry approaches and eyes Stan coolly.

>   TERRY (93)
> Wherever the rest of you go.
> I was under the impression we're
> here to make a mineralogical
> survey.

>   STAN (94)
> You're not actually thinking of
> tramping through the jungle
> with us?

>   TERRY (95)
> And why not? I'm young and
> in reasonably good shape.

>   STAN (96)
> It's not going to be any
> sorority garden party, Terry.
> This is rough country.

                                        (CONTINUED)

41 (CONTINUED)

                    TERRY (97)
I'm sure it is. McCarthy and I made a careful study of the terrain during the past two months. It was part of our job. And incidentally, Mr. Rockwell, the jungle beneath the Guandici Hills is snake country.. and of the poisonous variety, too. Those ankle boots you are wearing will not do at all.

                    CARLOS)98)
            (joining the two)
She is right, Senor. You must wear special boots in the jungle country. Come with me and I will find you a pair to fit.

Carlos leads Stan out of the picture. The CAMERA PANS slightly as Terry turns to Paul who continues to load supplies.

                    TERRY (99)
Your Mr. Rockwell does not seem to approve of me.

                    PAUL (100)
            (turning with a half smile)
It is nothing personal. Stan did not approve of having McCarthy accompany us, either, and then when a switch was made for a woman... well, you can hardly blame him.

                    TERRY (101)
And just what is his objection to women?

                    PAUL (102)
Well, I hardly think he objects to women in a broad sense.. but he feels that a woman will handicap the expedition.

                    TERRY (103)
I suppose he thinks that he'll have to carry me over streams... and hold my hand whenever a monkey chatters in a tree overhead.
                        (CONTINUED)

41 (CONTINUED)

>   PAUL (104)
>   (smiling)
>   Perhaps. It may be rougher
>   than you think, Terry.

42   CLOSE SHOT - of Terry as she talks earnestly with
        Paul.

>   TERRY (105)
>   Do you mind having me along, Dr.
>   Jorgeson? I wouldn't bother
>   you if it weren't necessary.
>   But I do know that McCarthy
>   planned to rough it with the
>   rest of you and I honestly can't
>   see how I can prepare leases
>   without being on the spot to see
>   the land and appraise its value
>   and to see the owners and
>   discuss terms.

43   TWO SHOT - of Paul and Terry.

>   PAUL (106)
>   You're right about that of
>   course. You can't lease land
>   while parked in your room at
>   the La Casa Consuelo.

>   TERRY (107)
>   I might as well be back on
>   Sunset Boulevard... I'm tough-
>   er than I look, Dr. Jorgeson.
>   I'll make it all right. Don't
>   you worry for a minute.

Paul smiles and lays a friendly hand on her shoulder.

>   PAUL (108)
>   I've been judging human nature
>   for a good many years, Terry.
>   You'll make it all right...
>   and maybe with a little to spare.

>   TERRY (109)
>   (smiling up at Paul)
>   Thank you, Dr. Jorgeson.

                                           (CONTINUED)

43 (CONTINUED)

> PAUL (110)
> Let's drop the formalities in the jungle. (He points down the trail which they will soon take) From this trail on, I'm Paul. Remember that!

> TERRY (111)
> Thanks, Paul. You've made me feel a lot better. I won't let you down.

> PAUL (112)
> Just one word of advice.. or rather, warning before we start. We're heading into mystery country whether we like it or not and we can't take chances with you. These strange killings like the one that upset Consuelo last night... they are not new. For ten years they have been haunting these hills and not a single one has ever been solved. Keep close to Stan or myself. Don't wander off!

EXT. JUNGLE - DAY

44 TRUCKING SHOT - showing the four trudging along a path, single file. Stan is leading the way, followed by Terry, Paul, and Carlos. The path ends abruptly at a rocky ledge. Stan climbs up and silently gives Terry a hand. She slips once and then with Paul's help from behind, she gains footing and without a word being spoken, they trudge on around the ledge.

DISSOLVE TO

45 FULL SHOT - of another jungle view. The four approach the CAMERA along a narrow path. It is obvious that the pack on Terry's back is becoming heavy but she moves along gamely. They reach a spot where a large tree has fallen across the path. The doctor, too, portrays weariness.

> PAUL (113)
> Let's take five.

They sit down on the log, all but Stan who is young and virile. He paces impatiently.

46   MED. SHOT - of tree foliage above Terry becoming a CLOSE SHOT as the CAMERA dollies in to view a large, venomous snake directly above the girl. She does not see the snake. The snake coils downward so that it's head almost touches Terry's face.

47   CLOSE SHOT - of Stan pacing, then of his face suddenly coming alive as he sees the snake.

48   REVERSE SHOT - Terry observes the change in Stan's expression as he freezes.

>   TERRY (114)
> What's the matter, Stan?

49   CLOSE SHOT - of Stan eyeing the snake.

>   STAN (115)
>   (in a low, commanding voice)
> Don't move, Terry. Don't move
> a muscle!

50   CLOSE SHOT - of the snake coiling downward.

51   MED. SHOT - With a sudden, imperceptible whirl of movement, a gun is out of Stan's belt holster and he is firing from the waist, crouching slightly.

52   REVERSE SHOT - as the third shot crashes the CAMERA SPOTS the snake. With its head shattered by lead, it uncoils from the branches and drops across Terry's lap and to the ground. Terry jumps up and stifles a scream as she realizes the peril from which his shooting has saved her. CAMERA ANGLE WIDENS as Stan walks over and raising the snake with one hand, casually studies it.

>   STAN (116)
> As you said, Terry, this is
> snake country.

53   CLOSE SHOT - Terry turns slowly to face Stan. The struggle within her can be seen on her face as she attempts to shake off the horror and show no fright. She swallows and her jaw tightens as she reaches for her pack.

>   TERRY (117)
> Well, let's move. We'll never
> find uranium sitting here.

                              DISSOLVE TO

EXT. JUNGLE - TWILIGHT

54 MED. SHOT - The group trudge wearily along a path towards the CAMERA until Stan becomes a CLOSE SHOT as he pauses and his eyes narrow as he scans the terrain ahead.

> STAN (118)
> This clearing looks okay for one night.

55 TWO SHOT - as Carlos steps up beside Stan.

> CARLOS (119)
> I have camped here before. It is a good spot.

> STAN (120)
> How far are we from the hills?

> CARLOS (121)
> (reflecting, staring ahead)
> We reach the altos before noon tomorrow.

> STAN (122)
> Good! Then we start to work.
> (He turns to the others).
> This is it, folks. Let's make camp.

56 REVERSE SHOT - of Terry who is almost exhausted. She drops to a sitting position on a rock without even removing her pack.

57 CLOSE SHOT - Stan pauses to stare down at Terry. His expression is one of amusement and indulgence, yet he has no intention of "letting up" on her. The CAMERA PANS as he moves to her side and taps her briskly on the shoulder.

> STAN (123)
> It's not siesta time yet, young lady. We have four empty stomachs to fill.

58 CLOSE SHOT - of Paul as he watches Stan. From his expression it is obvious that he feels a little sorry for the girl. He moves as though to intercede, then thinks better of it and remains silent.

59   TWO SHOT - Terry glances up, then wearily slips
      her pack from her shoulder and lets it drop. She
      returns Stan's look with a slight grimace.

                    TERRY (124)
              If you needed a cook you should
              have brought one - instead of
              a lawyer.

                    STAN (125)
                  (giving her a hand and pulling
                      her to her feet)
              Maybe we've got both in one
              package.

                                    DISSOLVE TO

60   GROUP SHOT - The four are busy pitching camp

                    CARLOS (126)
              I will gather fire wood.

                    STAN (127)
              I'll help. It will take plenty
              of wood to keep the fire going
              all night.

      Stan and Carlos disappear o.s. leaving Paul and
      Terry alone.

61   TWO SHOT - featuring Paul as he watches Terry
      wearily going through the motions of work.

                    PAUL (127)
                  (kindly)
              You're all in, aren't you?

                    TERRY (128)
              I could sleep on a cactus bed.

                    PAUL (129)
              Confidentially, I'm done
              in myself.

                    TERRY (130)
              Don't let Stan know - or he'll
              tie an apron around you, too.

                    PAUL (131)
                  (smiling with amused
                      indulgence)
              Stan likes people to be (cont'd)

                                    (CONTINUED)

61 (CONTINUED)

> PAUL (cont'd)
> rugged.. like himself. Just don't let him think you're soft and you'll get along fine.

> TERRY (132)
> Don't worry. I'll stick it out if I have to finish on my hands and knees.

62 CLOSE SHOT - Terry, kneeling, opens a pack that contains cooking utensils. The CAMERA ANGLE widens slightly to form a TWO SHOT as Paul moves into the scene and with slow deliberation drops on a rock beside her. His pipe is between his teeth. He helps her sort the articles.

> PAUL (133)
> Stan is a fine fellow, Terry. You'll like him when you get to know him.

> TERRY (134)
> (with slight sarcasm)
> You want to bet?

> PAUL (135)
> (smiles)
> I've known Stan for quite a number of years. For the past four years we've placed him in charge of all our foreign surveys. He gets results, too.

> TERRY (136)
> (looking suddenly grim)
> I'm sure he does...

Terry picks up a utensil, studies it thoughtfully, then lays it aside.

> TERRY (cont'd)
> Have you two made trips together before?

> PAUL (137)
> No. This is the first. When I was a young man I headed many expeditions such as this but that was many years ago. (cont'd)

(CONTINUED)

62 (CONTINUED)

>   PAUL (cont'd)
> I thought my adventuring days
> were over but then we got
> financial backing for large
> scale uranium mining and it was
> important that I come along...
> for several reasons.
>
>   TERRY (138)
> Paul. Do you really believe
> we are in danger from.. from
> something that is killing
> miners and ranch hands in
> the altos?
>
>   PAUL (139)
>   (shaking his head)
> I don't know, Terry.. No one
> really knows. Uneducated
> peoples always exaggerate
> their fears and superstitions
> as you know; yet we have facts.
> Men have been killed.. many
> men.. over a period of
> ten years...

                                        DISSOLVE TO

EXT. JUNGLE - NIGHT

63   CLOSE SHOT - of a blazing campfire. A hand with
      a twig moves into view, the twig ignites, and the
      hand and twig withdraw to the bowl of a pipe as
      the CAMERA FOLLOWS. The pipe lights and is withdrawn
      from the owners mouth as a voice begins:

>   PAUL'S VOICE (140)
> Over a period of ten years many
> men have died in the Guandici
> hills... and under similar cir-
> cumstances. There is no doubt
> a logical explanation - when it
> becomes known.

64   GROUP SHOT - The CAMERA is below and to the left
      of the campfire so that we have an angle shot of
      Carlos, Stan, and Paul with the pipe in his mouth
      while lapping tongues of flame are visible in the
      corner of the picture.

                                        (CONTINUED)

64 (CONTINUED)

> PAUL (141)
> ... But of one thing you can be sure... the killings are not coincidents.

> CARLOS (142)
> No, Senor Jorgeson, they are not coincidents. With my own eyes I have seen two of the victims. I have talked with others who have seen. Always, they died the same.

> STAN (143)
> Tell us, Carlos, exactly what happened to these men?

65 CLOSE SHOT - of Carlos as he replies to Stan.

> CARLOS (144)
> Have you ever seen the victim of a strangler, Senor? The throat is swollen and bruised, but the skin is not torn. These men were strangled but the marks on their throats were like the claw marks of an animal - not like the bruise marks of human fingers. Do you know an animal that strangles it prey?

66 GROUP SHOT - featuring Stan and Carlos.

> STAN (145)
> (with a short laugh)
> No, I have never seen such an animal.

> CARLOS (146)
> Neither have we in our country. That is why the townspeople are afraid, and only the foolish go into the Guandici hills alone.

> STAN (147)
> Can you describe the marks on the victims, Carlos?

(CONTINUED)

66 (CONTINUED)

> CARLOS (148)
> I can describe them, Senor, but you will not believe me. I saw poor Pedro when they brought him into town last night. The claw marks on his throat were deep, yet sharp and clean so that they drew but little blood.

> STAN (149)
> Couldn't they have been caused by human nails?

> CARLOS (150)
> Human nails scratch and tear the skin but they do not pierce deeply. With Pedro it was as though a big cat with knife-like talons had reared up on its hind legs and strangled him with its fore paws.

67 CLOSE SHOT - of Terry with the CAMERA above the fire and angling down at her as she sits by the side of Carlos. She is listening avidly to the conversation, lips slightly parted.

> TERRY (151)
> Do the people believe that a monster of some sort is living in the Guandici hills?

The CAMERA moves slightly to make a TWO SHOT showing Terry and Carlos.

> CARLOS (152)
> The people of our village are not superstitious, Senorita. But when men have died without reason for so many years, who can blame them for being afraid. The few who lived in this area have moved away.

> TERRY (153)
> No one lives in these hills?

> CARLOS (154)
> (shaking his head slowly)
> The last chiclero loaded up his wagon and moved out five years ago.

68   ANGLE SHOT - featuring the profile of Paul with a frontal view of Carlos in the immediate b.g.

> PAUL (155)
> Not the last man, Carlos. You have forgotten one.
>
> CARLOS (156)
> (showing surprise)
> I have? Who is that, Senor?
>
> PAUL (157)
> Walton, son of the American scientist. He still lives in the big house his father built at the foot of the altos.
>
> CARLOS (158)
> (laughing suddenly)
> You are right, Senor. I had forgotten Walton. We see him but seldom in the town and we do not think of him as one of us.

69   MED. SHOT - showing Stan, Carlos, and Terry. Terry is staring up at Carlos.

> TERRY (159)
> Isn't Walton afraid?
>
> CARLOS (160)
> (laughing)
> Who knows, Senorita... but they say his place is barred with irons an inch thick and that he travels only at night and in a fast car.
>
> STAN (161)
> At least he hasn't run away.
>
> CARLOS (162)
> He would have to be very badly frightened to run away. He has inherited great tracts of land from his father... land rich in minerals.

(CONTINUED)

69 (CONTINUED)

> STAN (163)
> As a matter of fact the preliminary survey made two years ago indicates that his land has very good uranium possibilities. We shall probably be talking with Senor Walton.

> CARLOS (164)
> We are on the edge of his land now, Senor.

70   GROUP SHOT - featuring Paul as he rises stiffly to his feet and stirs the fire.

> PAUL (165)
> It's time we turn in; we have a hard day ahead of us.

> CARLOS (166)
> (climbing to his feet)
> We will take turns sitting watch tonight. We take no chances in this part of the country.

> STAN (167)
> (joining Carlos and Paul)
> Right. There are four of us. We can split the time - two hours for each person.

> CARLOS (168)
> (looking startled)
> But the senorita cannot sit watch.

> STAN (169)
> And why not? She's young and healthy. Give her the first watch, before she gets drowsy.

71   CLOSE SHOT - showing Terry looking surprised and grim. Then she smiles, determined to go along with whatever hardships Stan may have in store for her. She hops briskly to her feet.

> TERRY (170)
> Of course I can sit watch. My eyes are 20-20. Just give me the rifle and you fellows can drop off to sleep and feel completely protected.

72   TWO SHOT - as Stan approaches Terry and hands her the rifle.

>   STAN (171)
>   (with light sarcasm)
>   You know where the trigger is?

Terry snatches the rifle from Stan's hand and disdains to answer. She walks to a large rock a few feet from the campfire and as the CAMERA FOLLOWS, perches atop it with the rifle across her knees. She stares grimly into the black jungle.

73   GROUP SHOT - Paul and Carlos spread out their sleeping bags and turn in. Stan moves about restlessly. He is concerned about Terry but doesn't want to show it.

74   CLOSE SHOT - of Terry as she eventually turns and looks at Stan. She senses his concern and her face shows a little smug satisfaction in the knowledge.

>   TERRY (172)
>   If you don't turn in and get
>   some sleep I'll have to sit
>   your watch as well as mine.

75   ANGLE SHOT - showing a profile of Terry with Stan moving about in the b.g. He places several logs on the fire and it begins to brighten.

>   STAN (173)
>   This fire should be built
>   up a little.

>   TERRY (174)
>   You needn't bother, Stan. I
>   know how to drop a log on a
>   fire.

>   STAN (175)
>   Call me in two hours.

76   CLOSE SHOT - of the campfire as it continues to blaze brighter.

                              DISSOLVE TO

77   CLOSE SHOT - of the same view of the fire which has now died down, indicating substantial passage of time. The CAMERA PANS slowly from the dying fire to the sleeping figures on the ground, and then back to Terry with the rifle across her knees.

                              (CONTINUED)

77 (CONTINUED)

    She is obviously tense and nervous, feeling very much alone. All around are the strange night sounds of a jungle. She straightens suddenly, intensely alert, as a distinct sound of movement comes from the thick jungle foliage close to the rock on which she is sitting.

78   MED. SHOT - of the black jungle foliage as the sound is repeated.

79   CLOSE SHOT - Terry listens and again hears the movement. She comes slowly to her feet, almost paralyzed with fright. The sound is repeated, but louder, and she turns and runs.

80   TWO SHOT - Terry bends over the sleeping Stan and shakes him roughly. He sits up, blinking his eyes, but almost instantly alert.

              STAN (176)
        What's the trouble, Terry?

              TERRY (177)
        (pointing)
        Something is moving in those
        bushes. You better come
        and look.

Stan reaches for his rifle and flashlight and climbs to his feet.

              *STAN (178)
        Sure it's not your girlish
        imagination?

Terry disdains to answer and follows him towards the rock on which she had been sitting.

81   TWO SHOT - as Stan and Terry approach the CAMERA. They stop at the rock and stare straight ahead into the jungle brush. Stan listens intently a moment. He hears nothing. He flashes the light into the brush. Slowly and methodically he pans the light until there is sudden movement, then he spots the object and holds it in his light beam. At the same moment he raises the rifle and stands in readiness.

82   CLOSE SHOT - of a large, peaceful-looking rabbit as it stares balefully into the beam of light.

83   TWO SHOT - Terry looks up at Stan as he turns in amusement and disgust. Slowly, he lowers the gun.

> STAN (179)
> There's your monster, Terry.
> Pretty gruesome, isn't it!

Stan turns and walks briskly towards the spot where he had been sleeping.

> STAN (cont'd)
> (calling over his shoulder)
> Next time a rabbit makes a pass
> at you, try to reason with it
> before waking me up, will you?

> TERRY (180)
> (calling back)
> I wouldn't ask your help again
> if a dozen wildcats stampede
> this camp.

Terry turns and slowly reseats herself on the rock. Her face is drawn up in a half pout. She snaps a cigarette lighter and looks at her watch. She lays the rifle across her knees and once more begins the lonely watch.

84   STOCK SHOT - showing the moon (not full) rising above the rim of the jungle.

DISSOLVE TO

85   STOCK SHOT - showing the moon much higher in the sky (indicating passage of time)

DISSOLVE TO

86   CLOSE SHOT - Terry is slowly pacing near the low burning fire. The rifle is clenched tightly in her hand. She pauses to listen. Above the background of jungle sound, a more distinct sound, like the cautious movement of a body in the underbrush, comes from the outer perimeter of the clearing. Terry stands motionless, lips slightly parted. The sound is repeated. She casts an anxious glance towards the sleeping Stan, but does not move in his direction. As the sound is repeated a third time, the scene DISSOLVES TO:

87   INSERT - showing a pair of heavy boots walking with rhythmic tread along the jungle ground.

88   CLOSE SHOT - of Terry with the rifle. She faces the underbrush and stares frightened and alert. The sound of movement becomes louder. Her eyes suddenly widen and the rifle comes up against her shoulder. She holds that position for a moment, then fires.

89   GROUP SHOT - showing Stan, Paul, and Carlos asleep around the smoldering campfire. In the quiet of the jungle night, the rifle shot carries the impact of a 75 mm. howitzer. The three men leap from sleeping bags and look about in a dazed, sleepy fashion. Stan spots Terry first and leads the others in her direction.

90   TWO SHOT - of Terry as Stan rushes up to her side. Terry stands as though in a trance, slowly lowering the smoking rifle.

>   STAN (181)
>   What's the matter, Terry?
>   What are you shooting at?

Terry turns and looks at him without speaking. She points into the underbrush. Stan's gaze follows along her arm but he sees nothing.

>   STAN (cont'd)
>   Did you finally get the rabbit that's been stalking you?

Paul and Carlos rush into the scene beside Terry. Carlos has a glowing flashlight in his hand. Stan reaches for the light and pans the underbrush ahead of him. Suddenly he stops panning and his eyes widen in surprise.

91   INSERT - A large, vicious looking cat lies in the center of the pool of light on the outer edge of the underbrush. It is dead, dropped by the bullet from Terry's rifle.

92   GROUP SHOT - The four stare at the body of the cat

>   PAUL (182)
>   It's no rabbit!

>   CARLOS (183)
>   (wonderingly)
>   An altos puma!

(CONTINUED)

92 (CONTINUED)

    Stan moves forward cautiously, a pistol in his outstretched hand. He drops on his knees beside the cat.

                  STAN (184)
        It's dead all right. A clean
        shot... right between the
        breast bones!

93   CLOSE SHOT - of the boots approaching with the same, measured tread.

                STRANGE VOICE (o.s.) (185)
        An excellent shot!

94   CLOSE SHOT - of Stan as he stares at the cat and sees instead the pair of strange boots beside the cat's body. The CAMERA PANS from the cat to the boots and slowly along the man's body to his face. The man is dressed in excellent jungle attire. A fancy pistol is slung on a holster at his belt and a rifle is in his hand. Stan comes warily to his feet, gun still in hand.

                  STAN (186)
         (mocking voice)
        I don't believe I've had
        the pleasure.

                  WALTON (187)
         (smiling affably)
        Walton is the name. I saw
        your campfire and was coming
        over to investigate when this
        pretty young lady nearly shot
        me.

95   CLOSE SHOT - of Terry staring at the newcomer. The rifle is in her hand but lowered and held unconsciously.

                  TERRY (188)
        I'm sorry. I was shooting
        at the cat.

96   GROUP SHOT - of Terry, Stan, and Paul facing the newcomer, Walton.

                            (CONTINUED)

96 (CONTINUED)

>WALTON (189)
>That's all right. Actually, you didn't come close at all... only startled me. These mountain cats can be quite nasty. That was mighty fine shooting, Senorita.

Paul steps forward and speaks to Walton.

>PAUL (190)
>You bear a great deal of resemblance to your father, Mr. Walton.

97   CLOSE SHOT - of Walton. As Paul mentions his father Walton looks distinctly startled for a moment, but the friendly smile quickly returns.

>WALTON (191)
>You knew my father?

98   TWO SHOT - of Walton and Paul.

>PAUL (192)
>Yes, and I knew you... although I'm sure you were too young at the time to remember me. I am Paul Jorgeson, a geologist. Your father and I were very good friends... Let me present the others. The young lady with the rifle is Miss O'Conner, a lawyer with my company. This is Stan Rockwell, a geologist like myself; and Carlos, the sobrestante of La Casa Consuelo.

Walton bows acknowledgement.

>WALTON (193)
>It is a pleasure. Senor Carlos and I have met before at the Casino in the village.

>PAUL (194)
>I would like some coffee. How about you, Mr. Walton? Stay with us and talk for a while. We will build up the fire.

(CONTINUED)

98 (CONTINUED)

> WALTON (195)
> That's very kind of you. Yes, I would like some coffee, but I cannot stay long. I must reach my home tonight.

DISSOLVE TO

EXT. CAMPFIRE - NIGHT

99   GROUP SHOT - featuring Walton with Stan on one side and Paul on the other. Terry and Carlos are sitting close by. They are drinking coffee from tin cups. Walton is talking.

> WALTON (196)
> I saw the light of your campfire from a rise some miles away and was curious. You see, I manage to make a survey of my land once each year and that means ten days of hard traveling. Now the survey is finished I'm happy to say and I intend to reach my home before sun up.

> PAUL (197)
> We are probably trespassing on your land now.

> WALTON (198)
> (spreading his hand in an expansive gesture)
> It is wild country and you cannot harm it. (He laughs) You are the ones who must be careful.

> PAUL (199)
> True enough... as evidenced by this mountain cat.

> WALTON (200)
> (nodding, and glancing towards Terry)
> Your young lady is truly amazing. Such nerve and such night shooting!

100   CLOSE SHOT - of Terry. She is a little embarassed at the praise.

(CONTINUED)

100 (CONTINUED)

> TERRY (201)
> I'm afraid it was all luck. I just closed my eyes and squeezed.

101   CLOSE SHOT - of Walton. He laughs at Terry's words.

> WALTON (202)
> Then I shall try it myself next time. It is a good system.

Walton lowers his coffee cup and climbs reluctantly to his feet. He looks in Paul's direction.

> WALTON (cont'd)
> I have enjoyed your company but I'm afraid I must be on my way. It is late and night travelling is difficult in the jungle. (he pauses as though remembering something) Oh, yes, I almost forgot to ask... what are you doing here? You are obviously on some sort of expedition.

CAMERA ANGLE WIDENS to include Paul as he also rises to his feet.

> PAUL (203)
> Uranium, my friend. The metal has become very important during the last few years.

> WALTON (204)
> Then you are in Guatemala to lease land for mining?

> PAUL (205)
> We represent one of the largest engineering mining companies in the world. We want to lease mineral rights.

> WALTON (206)
> I have expected it for a long time. The land is very rich in pitchblende.

(CONTINUED)

101 (CONTINUED)

                    PAUL (207)
          Have you seen evidence of
          it yourself?

                    WALTON (208)
            (smiling as he remembers)
          In one part of my land at the
          foot of the altos I have seen
          a pitchblende vein five hundred
          feet wide and with a uranium
          assay of 60 percent. The
          supply is inexhaustable.

                    PAUL (209)
          It sounds incredible.

                    WALTON (210)
          There are many such veins.

                    PAUL (211)
          We shall be back in Mondera
          by Saturday. Could we meet
          you some place and discuss
          a detailed survey of your
          land?

102   CLOSE SHOT - of Walton as he answers Paul.

                    WALTON (212)
          I am interested in neither
          uranium nor great wealth but...

Walton looks beyond Paul to whom he is talking.

103   REVERSE SHOT - We see Terry seated with a coffee
       tin in her hand and it is evident that Walton's
       interest lies with her more than uranium.

                    WALTON'S VOICE (cont'd)
          ... there is no harm in talking.

104   CLOSE SHOT - of Stan as he notices Walton's interest
       in Terry. The CAMERA PANS with Stan as he climbs
       to his feet and faces Walton.

                    STAN (213)
         Why not meet us for cocktails
         Saturday at the Casino... 5
         o'clock?

                            (CONTINUED)

104 (CONTINUED)

>   WALTON (214)
>   (shaking his head)
>   Five o'clock is much too early
>   for me. Let us say 10 o'clock
>   for a late dinner at the Casino.
>   You will be my guests... the
>   three of you.

>   PAUL (215)
>   That is very kind of you,
>   Mr. Walton. Saturday at ten,
>   if you wish.

>   WALTON (216)
>   It is settled then. Goodnight,
>   gentlemen... Goodnight,
>   Senorita.

105   CLOSE SHOT - of Terry. She looks up and smiles as
        Walton speaks to her.

>   TERRY (217)
>   Goodnight, Mr. Walton.

Terry sets her coffee cup down by the fire and
picks up the rifle. The CAMERA PANS with her as
she rises to her feet and walks slowly towards
Stan and Paul who are returning to the circle
around the campfire. She stops in front of Stan
and looks up cockily.

>   TERRY (218)
>   So now we have a dinner date.
>   Looks like I'm going to use
>   that evening gown I packed
>   after all.

106   THREE SHOT - with Stan, Paul, and Terry standing
        beside the fire.

>   PAUL (219)
>   I hope it's a nice gown. I
>   must admit that Walton seems
>   more impressed by you than
>   by our offer to make him
>   money.

As Paul talks he seats himself beside the fire and
begins to fill his pipe.

                                        (CONTINUED)

106 (CONTINUED)

                    STAN (220)
          What can we expect! The
          poor fellow probably hasn't
          seen an American girl in
          years.

The remark sounds as if Stan thinks that undoubtedly
Walton would be impressed with a wheelbarrow if
it wore a skirt. Terry glowers. She shoves the
rifle at Stan with both hands.

                    TERRY (221)
          Here, fellow, it's your turn
          to scare away the rabbits.
          I'm turning in for some sleep.

Terry strides o.s. while the CAMERA moves in
for a CLOSE SHOT of Stan as he holds the rifle and
stares after her. A half smile appears on his
face.

                    STAN (222)
            (almost under his breath so
             that no one but the
             audience hears)
          Touché.

107   CLOSE SHOT - of Paul seated by the fire, smoking.

                    PAUL (223)
            (speaking aloud, yet to himself)
          It's amazing. That Walton is
          the splitting image of his
          father 20 years ago - except
          for the eyes - there's some-
          thing different about the
          eyes...

                STAN'S VOICE (o.s.)(224)
          Turning in, Paul?

                    PAUL (225)
          Soon, Stan... soon.

Paul continues to smoke in silence as the scene

                                  DISSOLVES TO

INT. UPPER HALLWAY - LA CASA CONSUELO - NIGHT

108 MED. SHOT - Stan approaches the CAMERA along a wide hallway and stops before a closed door. He raps sharply.

                      TERRY'S VOICE (226)
                  (from behind the closed door)
Yes?

Without answering, Stan pushes open the door and walks through.

109 MED. SHOT - from Stan's point of view. Terry is standing in front of a full length dressing mirror so that we see both her back and the reflection of her front in the mirror. She is wearing an evening dress that has not yet been zipped up the back. Terry glances up as Stan enters and regards him through the mirror. Her expression shows no embarassment, only slight annoyance.

                      TERRY (227)
I don't remember saying,
Come in.

Stan appears slightly confused as he walks into the PICTURE and then pauses.

                      STAN (228)
I'll go out and knock again.

                      TERRY (229)
                  (watching him through the
                    mirror)
Never mind, Stan. Since you're already in, would you zip up this dress? It's so hard to reach.

110 REVERSE SHOT - of Stan as he approaches Terry. The CAMERA ANGLE is across Terry so that a CLOSE UP front view of her face appears on the left side of the screen. Stan looks slightly confused, then smiles.

                      STAN (230)
Okay. Guess I can handle
a zipper.

                              (CONTINUED)

110 (CONTINUED)

>   TERRY (231)
>   My arms are so sore from haul-
>   ing that pack around I'm
>   afraid I could never reach
>   it.

Terry picks up the hairbrush and begins to brush her hair as Stan reaches for the zipper.

>   STAN (232)
>   Hold still if you want me
>   to work this thing.

111   TWO SHOT - from a different angle. Stan takes ahold of the dress and zipper, a little clumsily, and pulls. Halfway up, the zipper catches some material and jams. Stan works a moment to free it, but with no luck. Terry squirms impatiently.

>   STAN (233)
>   Hold still. I'm afraid it's
>   caught.

112   REVERSE SHOT - from the mirror, showing a CLOSE UP of Terry with Stan appearing over her shoulder.

>   TERRY (234)
>   (with slight sarcasm)
>   I thought you said you could
>   handle a zipper?

>   STAN (235)
>   Don't panic. It's very easy
>   for a zipper to catch material...
>   especially with lower priced
>   dresses.

>   TERRY (236)
>   Lower priced! Evidently,
>   you can't judge material any
>   better than you can work a
>   zipper. All this dress left
>   of a week's salary was park-
>   ing meter change.

113   MED. SHOT - of the open doorway as Paul enters the room from the hallway. He stares a moment at the two standing in front of the mirror and breaks

(CONTINUED)

113 (CONTINUED)

into a broad smile.

>PAUL (237)
>Have you two declared a truce?

114   MED. TWO SHOT - from another angle, showing Stan and Terry with Paul approaching them.

>TERRY (238)
>Not on your life. Stan caught my zipper. I think he did it on purpose.

>STAN (239)
>(looking up)
>If I had done it on purpose, I couldn't have done a better job.

>PAUL (240)
>Stan, I was wondering... would you have time to go over some reports with me?

>STAN (241)
>We don't have much time. We meet Walton in two hours.

>TERRY (242)
>Do you think I'll be loose by then?

>PAUL (243)
>Maybe I can help.

Paul moves in and studies the offending zipper.

>PAUL (cont'd)
>I think we should get a razor blade and cut the material where it is caught.

115   REVERSE SHOT - with the CAMERA behind the three people and the mirror in the b.g. A front view of Terry reflects from the mirror.

(CONTINUED)

115 (CONTINUED)

> TERRY (244)
> Oh, no you don't

Terry twists away from the two men and turns so that she faces them. She reaches behind her and finds the zipper.

> TERRY (cont'd)
> I'll handle this little problem myself.

She pulls the zipper downward, twists gently, and gives another pull. The zipper comes loose and is quickly fastened.

> TERRY (245)
> (disgustedly)
> Men! No wonder the world's in such a mess!

She turns her back to them to face the mirror and again picks up the hairbrush. Stan begins to laugh and the others join in.

116 TWO SHOT - featuring Stan with Paul.

> PAUL (246)
> This girl has a magic touch. We may be glad we brought her along yet.

> STAN (247)
> Maybe she can use the magic touch on Walton. Consuelo seems to think that he's impossible to deal with.

> PAUL (248)
> I'm afraid Consuelo's right. A few years ago Consuelo wanted to buy some of Walton's land to cultivate sapote trees. The man wouldn't even consent to talk about it.

> STAN (249)
> I'll give you odds that we run into the same trouble. Walton seemed friendly enough but when he said he had no interest in money or uranium I got the impression he wasn't bluffing.

(CONTINUED)

116 (CONTINUED)

> PAUL (250)
> And no son of James Walton is any fool. If his mind is made up it wouldn't be easily swayed.

117 CLOSE SHOT - of Terry in front of the mirror. She drops the hairbrush and turns to face the two men. She presents a very fetching appearance.

> TERRY (251)
> If you two gentlemen have any trouble with Walton, just turn him over to me... I'll use my "magic touch". And now, if you will excuse me, I would like to finish dressing.

DISSOLVE

INT. CASINO - NIGHT

118 FULL SHOT - of a small, native rumba band as it plays a lively dance number. The CAMERA PANS slowly away from the band, showing first the crowded bar and then the closely-grouped tables and the noisy, carefree natives. The CAMERA focuses at last on a single table with four people around it, and dollies in for a GROUP SHOT featuring Terry as she laughs up into Walton's face.

> WALTON (252)
> I still insist that it is a shame to spend the whole evening discussing business when a beautiful lady is present.

> STAN (253)
> Perhaps we should have left the beautiful lady at home tonight.

> TERRY (254)
> (looking at Stan)
> You certainly did you best to keep me home.

(CONTINUED)

118 (CONTINUED)

>   WALTON (255)
>   If she had not appeared I would
>   have gone after her myself.
>
>   TERRY (256)
>   Thank you, Mr. Walton.
>
>   WALTON (257)
>   May I beg another dance,
>   Senorita?

119 TWO SHOT - Terry nods, smiling. Walton rises and pulls her chair back from the table. He glances at Stan and Paul who remain sitting.

>   WALTON (258)
>   Would you gentlemen excuse
>   us, please?
>
>   DISSOLVE TO

120 TRUCKING SHOT - as we follow Terry and Walton dancing to slow music. The dance floor is of medium size and reasonably crowded.

>   TERRY (259)
>   (looking up at Walton)
>   You are a very good dancer.
>
>   WALTON (260)
>   Does that surprise you?
>
>   TERRY (261)
>   A little. I hear that you
>   seldom visit the Casino.
>
>   WALTON (262)
>   There are other towns and
>   other casinos.
>
>   TERRY (263)
>   Of course there are. But a
>   long distance from Mondera.
>
>   WALTON (264)
>   Not so far! (taking her hand)
>   Let me show you something.

                              (CONTINUED)

120 (CONTINUED)

    The CAMERA FOLLOWS as Walton leads Terry to a small square window at the edge of the dance floor. He points through the window and she brushes aside the curtain and presses her head against the small opening.

121   FULL SHOT - of the outside from Terry's viewpoint. A long, impressive-looking, convertible sedan is parked beneath a tree.

          WALTON'S VOICE (265)
        (as we continue to view the sedan)
    It's a Daimler... custom built to my own specifications. In it, even Guatemala City is only two hours distant.

122   CLOSE SHOT - of Terry. She looks impressed

          TERRY (266)
    It's beautiful. I'll bet its fast and powerful, too.

123   TWO SHOT - Walton and Terry face each other in front of the square window at the edge of the dance floor. Dancing couples glide by in the b.g.

          WALTON (267)
Tonight, I want to take you for a ride in the Daimler. You must see Mount Fuego at night.

          TERRY (268)
The volcanic mountain?

          WALTON (269)
        (nodding)
Fuego is spilling over again. There is a rise halfway to my place that faces Fuego from the east. When the molten lava flows at night it is the most beautiful sight in the world. Can you imagine fiery fingers of red and yellow as they snake a path down mountain crevices.

          (CONTINUED)

123 (CONTINUED)

> TERRY (270)
> I'd love to see Mount Fuego.
> Will it take long?

> WALTON (271)
> Not long. We can be on the
> rise in an hour if we start
> right away.

>> DISSOLVE

124   MED. SHOT - as Terry and Walton approach the table, Stan and Paul start to rise but Terry stops them.

> TERRY (272)
> Don't get up. Mr. Walton
> is taking me for a ride in
> his new Daimler. Isn't that
> nice?

> STAN (273)
> We mustn't put Mr. Walton
> to any trouble, Terry.

> TERRY (274)
> (annoyed)
> Mr. Walton asked me to ride
> with him to see the volcano.

> WALTON (275)
> (interrupting)
> I'll assure you it's no trouble.
> A view as beautiful and awesome
> as Mount Fuego at night is
> meant to be shared.

125   CLOSE SHOT - of Stan seated at the table.

> STAN (276)
> If you like, Paul and I will
> wait here and we can continue
> our discussion when you get
> back.

> WALTON (277)
> No, please don't wait. I've
> heard your proposition and I
> think the terms are very fair.
> But the fact is, I'm simply not
> interested in leasing any land
> for exploitation.

126   ANGLE SHOT - showing a side view of Paul with
        Terry and Walton in the immediate b.g.

                    PAUL (278)
            Exploitation of your undev-
            eloped resources will do
            a lot for your country as
            well as for yourself, Mr.
            Walton. Why not mull it
            over in your mind for a few
            days before giving a defin-
            ite answer.

                    TERRY (279)
            Paul is right. Think it over
            for a couple of days, then we
            can meet here at the Casino
            again.

                    WALTON (280)
            If you like, Senorita. But
            one day will be enough. I'll
            meet you here again tomorrow
            night at ten.

        Walton's manner gives the impression that he is
        willing to meet with them again more out of interest
        in Terry than any interest in mining.

                    WALTON (cont'd)
            Goodnight, gentlemen.

        Terry smiles brightly and waves as she and Walton
        disappear o.s.

127   TWO SHOT - Stan and Paul, still seated at the table,
        turn and look at each other.

                    STAN (281)
            That girl's going to give
            us trouble yet.

                    PAUL (282)
            Walton seems more interested
            in her than in our propos-
            ition.

                                            (CONTINUED)

127 (CONTINUED)

>   STAN (283)
> Yeah. Depend on a woman to turn a business trip into a weekend at the Waldorf. Already, I'll bet she can't remember why she's making this expedition.

>   PAUL (284)
> That isn't what worries me, Stan.

>   STAN (285)
> What does worry you?

>   PAUL (286)
> I don't think Terry should be out alone with Walton.

>   STAN (287)
> Why not? Surely, you're not taking that business seriously about Walton's radiation experiments and something or other that may have happened to his son as a result.

>   PAUL (288)
> Stan, I've given a great deal of thought to Walton and the experiments I saw his father perform. There are several possible theories but there is only one theory that can account for both the experiments and the things Professor Walton hinted at when he talked to me twenty years ago in Chicago... and that theory is too heinous to even think about... We should have kept Terry with us.

>   STAN (289)
>   (disgustedly)
> And how would you do that — put a leash on her?

(CONTINUED)

127 (CONTINUED)

> PAUL (290)
> (smiling)
> Unfortunately, the girl is of age and seems to have a mind of her own.

> STAN (291)
> Stop worrying, Paul. This fellow Walton appears perfectly normal.

> PAUL (292)
> Exactly. He appears normal... Stan, you can have no conception of what I am talking about since you do not know the nature and the inherent dangers of radiation experiments... if anything should happen to Terry, I'll never...

FADE OUT

WINDING MOUNTING ROAD - NIGHT

128   LONG SHOT - The twin glow of distant headlights as they wind around a twisting mountain road.

DISSOLVE TO

129   LONG SHOT - from a different ANGLE - as the headlights curve about a U in the road and approach the CAMERA.

DISSOLVE TO

130   TWO SHOT - as Terry and Walton, seated in the front seat of the Daimler, glide rapidly over the mountain road. Terry looks at her watch in reflected dash light.

> TERRY (293)
> We have been gone almost an hour. How much farther is it to the rise?

> WALTON (294)
> We will be there any minute now...

(CONTINUED)

130 (CONTINUED)

      TERRY (295)
Is there any danger from the volcano?

      WALTON (296)
None at all. It has been years since we have had a dangerous eruption... ah, you can see in the headlight beam, the next bend in the road. That is it.

The Daimler pulls to the side of the road and stops. Terry looks all about in a kind of wonderment. Walton watches her, pleased with the reaction, then he turns and points across the hood of his car.

      WALTON (cont'd)
There is our Fuego - one of nature's masterpieces. Take a good look and remember what you see for no where in this world is there a sight to compare with it.

131 LONG SHOT - of the dimly outlined volcano. Glowing lava streams, blood-red with fiery orange fingers, snake slowly down the flanks of the mountain while low lying clouds of steam hover above and reflect the dancing light. From the crater rise billowing clouds of steam and smoke.

      TERRY (297)
  (awed, staring with a half smile)
It is the most beautiful thing I have ever seen. I could stay here forever.

      WALTON (298)
I have seen it a thousand times, yet tonight is the first time I ever thought it really beautiful. Like I said at the Casino.. it is a sight to be shared.

      TERRY (299)
Yes. It is indeed...

         (CONTINUED)

131 (CONTINUED)

> Walton turns in his seat and faces Terry. He drops his hand over the back of the seat so that it just touches her shoulder.

>> WALTON (300)
>> I have seen you only twice.. once in the jungle and again tonight... yet, I can think of no one I would rather share it with.

>> TERRY (301)
>> That's very flattering, Mr. Walton.

>> WALTON (302)
>> I am not trying to flatter you. I mean what I say. In many ways you are like the volcano... mysterious... beautiful..

> Terry turns to look at Walton. She sees the fervent expression in his eyes and laughs softly, attempting to return the conversation once more to a safe, breezy plane.

>> TERRY (303)
>> In Los Angeles I am considered very plain and ordinary. It has been too long since you have seen an American girl, I'm sure.

>> WALTON (304)
>> That is not true, Senorita. I see American girls every week... many of them in Guatemala City. I am not as impressionable as you may believe.

> For Walton the spell is broken. He is slightly annoyed. He turns the key and pushes the starter. The motor fires immediately but when he presses the accelerator nothing happens. He tries again with no better luck, then looks down towards the accelerator.

132   CLOSE SHOT - of the accelerator pedal with Walton's foot pressing it impatiently several times while the b.g. sound continues to be only the sound of an idling motor rather than the sound of a racing motor.

133   TWO SHOT - featuring Terry. She watches Walton rather anxiously as he attempts to make the motor accelerate.

> TERRY (305)
> What is wrong?

Walton shuts off the ignition and sits back disgustedly.

> WALTON (306)
> This would have to be the night it breaks.

Walton reaches down and pulls a demoutable flashlight from the steering column, checks it.

> WALTON (cont'd)
> You see, I noticed a couple of months ago that a push rod between the accelerator and the carbureator had been rubbing against the frame of the car and was almost worn in two. I ordered a new one from the factory and it came last week. The package is in my garage.. unopened.

> TERRY (307)
> How far are we from your place?

> WALTON (308)
> Ordinarily it is only an hour's ride. And it would take only fifteen minutes to install the new push rod... if we could get there.

> TERRY (309)
> Can't we tie it up with wire or something - temporarily?

Walton glances anxiously towards the sky in the east.

134 INSERT - of the eastern sky. It is beginning to lighten noticeably.

135 MED. SHOT - of the side of the car as Walton opens the door and steps out.

> WALTON (310)
> We'll take a look. We can't sit here all night. Daylight comes very early this time of year.

136 CLOSE SHOT - of the motor as the hood comes up. The CAMERA FOLLOWS inside the motor as Terry holds the flashlight and Walton examines the broken push rod.

137 TWO SHOT - of Terry and Walton staring at each other across the opened motor.

> WALTON (311)
> I have some wire and tools in the trunk. I will tie one end of a piece of wire here and run the other end through a hole beneath the dash, then we can accelerate the motor by hand... Do you drive?
>
> TERRY (312)
> Yes, I drive.
>
> WALTON (313)
> (smiling)
> Then we will have no trouble at all. You will drive to my place while I hold the wire and accelerate.

138 CLOSE SHOT - Walton straightens up and again glances anxiously at the eastern sky, then down at the watch on his wrist.

> WALTON (cont'd)
> We'll have to hurry. It will soon be light...

DISSOLVE TO

139 ANGLE SHOT - of modernistic metal garage doors. In the b.g. is the sound of a car motor approaching. Slowly, as though actuated by an electron

(CONTINUED)

139 (CONTINUED)

    eye, the doors rise from the ground. When they are just high enough for a car to pass beneath, the Daimler enters and the doors slowly close.

140   TRUCKING SHOT - Walton opens the car door for Terry, she steps out, and the CAMERA FOLLOWS as they walk silently side by side down a long stairway in semi-darkness. At the foot of the stairway, Walton opens a door and they pass through the doorway, into a large beautifully furnished room.

141   MED. TWO SHOT - from inside the room, facing the doorway. Terry glances slowly about the room, a look of amazement and rapture on her face as she views the elaborate furnishings. Walton closes the door and steps to her side, watching her expression as she stares.

> TERRY (314)
> What a beautiful, exotic place. To think that you have built all this in the middle of a jungle.
>
> WALTON (315)
> Would you like to live in a place like this?
>
> TERRY (316)
> I don't know. It's so far away from everything... so lonely.
>
> WALTON (317)
> (very intense, anxious to drive home his point)
> But that is just the point. Here, one is alone... away from the miserable snarling pack of humans one finds in every corner or the globe.
>
> TERRY (318)
> I never think of people in that way.
>
> WALTON (319)
> Of course you don't. You have always lived among them - like a single lamb in a great (cont'd)

(CONTINUED)

141 (CONTINUED)

>   WALTON (cont'd)
>   herd. You have come to accept
>   their selfish, egocentric ways.
>   I was born in this house and
>   have lived here alone for most
>   of my life. I see people with
>   a perspective and detachment
>   that is possible for only a few.
>
>   TERRY (320)
>   (looking at her watch)
>   I'm afraid Stan and Paul will
>   worry about me. We better
>   hurry.
>
>   WALTON (321)
>   You're right. It is already
>   daylight.

Walton turns and points to the bar behind Terry.

>   WALTON (conti'd)
>   I will fix the car while you put
>   on some coffee. You will find
>   everything you need on the bar
>   behind you.

142   MED. SHOT - as Walton disappears o.s. and Terry begins to prepare coffee. She quickly finds what she needs, puts the coffee on to brew, and begins absently to inspect the place.

143   TRUCKING SHOT - as Terry wanders through an open doorway into a second room filled with laboratory equipment. Fascinated, she walks slowly, picking up and examining objects. She wanders through a second door and into a long tunnel-like corridor. The music assumes an ominous mood.

144   REVERSE SHOT - from Terry's viewpoint of the strange corridor that projects almost 300 feet into the distance.

145   CLOSE SHOT - Terry stares ahead. Intrigued, she moves slowly along the corridor.

146   CLOSE SHOT - of Walton finishing with the car repair and dropping the hood. He turns, listening a moment as though he hears a sound and is alarmed, then quickly starts down the long stairway.

147 MED. SHOT - of Terry as she continues to move along the long, dimly lightly corridor, curiously inspecting details.

148 ANGLE SHOT - pointing up at Walton as he burst into the open doorway of the large room at the foot of the stairway and pauses for a CLOSE SHOT of his strained, anxious face. He glances in all directions but sees no sign of Terry.

149 REVERSE SHOT - Walton runs across the room and through the open door at the opposite side of the room.

150 CLOSE SHOT - of Terry's face as she comes to the end of the long corridor and looks up.

151 MED. SHOT - from Terry's viewpoint of the end of the corridor. The corridor is terminated by a huge sliding concrete and rock panel.

152 LONG SHOT - of Walton as he approaches silently along the corridor from a great distance. He looks in all directions as he approaches the CAMERA, obviously searching for the girl.

153 MED. SHOT - of Walton from another angle as he nears the end of the corridor.

154 CLOSE SHOT - A three quarters view of Terry as she moves along the end of the corridor with her hands feeling along the concrete panel.

155 INSERT - of Terry's hands as they approach and feel for a button at the side of the panel on the tunnel wall.

156 CLOSE SHOT - of Walton as he runs forward and stops short, panting, then spots Terry with her finger against the button.

　　　　　　　　　　　WALTON (322)
　　　　　　No! No! Don't press it!

157 INSERT - of Terry's fingers and the adjacent panel as simultaneously with Walton's cry her finger releases the button and the panel begins to move upward. A whirrling sound of the hidden motor drowns out his words. Gleaming shafts of sunlight enter the tunnel from beneath the rising panel.

158   BACK TO SCENE: For a moment Walton watches, a
        look of panic on his face, then he turns and starts
        to run back in the direction from which he had
        come.

159   MED. REVERSE SHOT - A rear view of Walton as he
        runs. He stops short as a second panel drops
        from the ceiling of the corridor and blocks his
        retreat.

160   FULL SHOT - of the corridor entrance with the
        concrete and rock panel almost completely raised.
        A bright sun gleams over the crest of a distance
        mountain. Terry walks into the side of the
        PICTURE and looks out into the sunrise. She turns
        to glance back into the tunnel entrance and with
        a climatic crash of music her face becomes a
        reflection of complete horror and she sinks to-
        wards the ground.

161   FULL FRAME CLOSE SHOT - of the monster's eyes (only).
        Slowly, the monster retreats into the darkness of
        the cave so that as the outline of his head and
        upper body grows complete on the screen, revealing
        more of the hideous details, it also grows
        indistinct. (only the monster's reptile-like eyes
        are shown clearly; the rest of his body is im-
        perfectly detailed in the shadowy light)

                                FADE

INT. LA CASA CONSUELO - PAUL'S ROOM - DAY

162   MED. SHOT - with Paul seated in a leather lounge
        chair, pipe in mouth; and Stan pacing slowly back
        and forth in front of him. Stan pauses and
        looks at his watch.

                    STAN (323)
                They've had time to drive to
                Guatemala City and back.

                    PAUL (324)
                Yes. I think we better talk
                with Consuelo. He will know
                how to handle this.

                    STAN (325)
                They may have had car trouble...
                or an accident.

                                        (CONTINUED)

162 (CONTINUED)

>   PAUL (326)
>   ... or it could be something
>   much worse. In any event,
>   we can't delay any longer.

Paul rises to his feet and starts towards the door. Stan walks by his side.

163 REVERSE SHOT - Terry stands motionless in the doorway. She looks worn and bedraggled; her eyes are glazed with weariness. Stan and Paul walk into the side of the PICTURE and for a moment the three stare at each other.

>   STAN (327)
>   (sarcasticly)
>   This is a fine time to be
>   dragging in. Ran out of gas,
>   I suppose.
>   PAUL (328)
>   What happened, Terry?

Terry doesn't answer. She continues to stare at the two men for a silent moment, then walks listlessly into the room as the CAMERA FOLLOWS, and drops into the leather chair Paul has just vacated. Stan and Paul follow.

164 CLOSE SHOT - Terry still doesn't speak but sits quietly, staring, as though in a trance.

>   PAUL'S VOICE (329)
>   (worried)
>   Is everything all right, Terry?

165 TWO SHOT - as Terry turns her head slowly until she is looking at Paul. She nods. Stan moves into the PICTURE from the b.g. He stops beside Paul.

>   STAN (330)
>   Is something the matter with
>   your voice, Terry? Can't
>   you talk?
>
>   TERRY (331)
>   Yes, I can talk.

>   (CONTINUED)

165 (CONTINUED)

> STAN (332)
> Then why don't you? Do you realize that we sat up all night worrying about you? Couldn't you have let us know where you were... or something?

Terry removes a hair brush from her purse and slowly runs it through her tangled hair.

> TERRY (333)
> (sarcasticly)
> Of course. I fully intended to send a wire... but I've been so absentminded lately.

> STAN (334)
> If that's supposed to be funny, it isn't.

> TERRY (335)
> And what happened last night wasn't funny, either.

> STAN (336)
> I suppose you had car trouble?

> TERRY (337)
> (angrily)
> As a matter of fact, we did have car trouble.

166 CLOSE SHOT - of Paul. A half smile of amusement appears on his face. He looks from Terry to Stan.

> PAUL (338)
> I think we better grab a few hours sleep. It will do us all good.

167 MED. CLOSE SHOT - of Stan as he starts for the door.

> STAN (339)
> We've lost enough time. I'm going to pick up those supplies we ordered.

Stan turns and pauses in the doorway.

(CONTINUED)

167 (CONTINUED)

> STAN (cont'd)
> Better put a ball and chain around that girl's ankle, Paul.

Stan closes the door behind him.

168 TWO SHOT - as Paul paces thoughtfully in front of Terry

> PAUL (340)
> What really happened last night, Terry?

> TERRY (341)
> I told you... we had car trouble.

> PAUL (342)
> Was that all that happened, Terry. Did that keep you away all night?

169 CLOSE SHOT - of Terry as she starts to answer, then hesitates and bites her lip.

> TERRY (343)
> Paul, if I tell you what really happened last night, you won't believe me... not in a million years.

DISSOLVE TO

EXT. VILLAGE STREET - DAY

170 TRUCKING SHOT - Paul is striding rapidly along a narrow street, crowded with natives in Guatemalan dress. His expression is strained and worried. He pauses to look into an open store front as though searching for someone, then moves on.

DISSOLVE TO

171 SECOND TRUCKING SHOT - as Paul continues along the street and stares into another store. He sees Stan inside, gathering supplies, and attracts his attention by motioning. Stan speaks to the proprietor and walks out to meet Paul.

172   TWO SHOT - of Stan and Paul

                    PAUL (344)
          Something very strange has
          just come up, Stan. I want
          to talk to you right away.

                    STAN (345)
              (wiping his face with
               a kerchief)
          Okay. There's a bar just across
          the street. We can talk over
          a cold drink while this fellow
          gets my stuff together.

                              DISSOLVE TO

INT. LOCAL BAR - DAY

173   TWO SHOT - Stan and Paul face each other across
       a small table beside a window. It is very hot
       and their faces and open necks glisten with
       perspiration. Beer mugs stand on the table in
       front of them.

                    STAN (346)
          The girl must be off her
          rocker.

                    PAUL (347)
          Walton told her the same
          thing - but in a nice way.
          He called it a hallucination.

                    STAN (348)
          What did he do with her?

                    PAUL (349)
          She said he carried her back
          into a room in the cave and
          made her rest an hour before
          driving into town.

                    STAN (350)
          She drove?

                    PAUL (351)
          She drove his Daimler back
          by herself. Walton said he
          would pick up the machine to-
          night at the Casino.

                              (CONTINUED)

173 (CONTINUED)

> STAN (352)
> Give me a straight opinion, Paul. Do you think she actually saw anything?

> PAUL (353)
> I'm convinced that she saw something. In fact, I'll go along with her story. I think she saw exactly what she said she saw.

> STAN (354)
> But that's impossible!

Paul carefully packs tobacco into his pipe and lights it with the slow deliberation of an older man.

> PAUL (355)
> You're young yet, Stan. But you're old enough to know that while a scientist often uses the word "improbable" he never uses the word "impossible". You must remember from your study of genetics that once in a great while - perhaps once in a hundred million births - a genuine throwback occurs. Such a newborn creature may not resemble its own species at all but may instead resemble some creature that preceeded it along the evolutionary chain by millions of years. We call these creatures mutations.

> STAN (356)
> Have you actually seen a human mutation?

> PAUL (357)
> I have and I'll assure you it is a most disturbing sight.

> STAN (358)
> Can you describe what you saw, Paul?

(CONTINUED)

173 (CONTINUED)

> PAUL (359)
> It was at the laboratory on Long Island a number of years ago. I saw a human with feet that were almost reptilian, complete with scales and claws. The poor creature lived only a few hours after birth. And at the university where I taught, I saw a human embryo partially covered with feathers - actual, perfectly formed feathers.

> STAN (360)
> But Walton could be nothing like that. We've seen the man. He's a normal, physical speciman.

> PAUL (361)
> The man appears quite normal. Granted. But why is he seen only at night? Ask any native of Mondera. He has never been seen in the daylight.. by anyone! There has to be some explanation for that.

> STAN (362)
> Then he sent Terry back alone in his car because it was daylight?

> PAUL (363)
> Perhaps. Dr. Walton told me years ago that something was terribly wrong with his son. And it is not something that is obvious. I've been trying to recall the doctor's exact words. It's entirely possible that Dr. Walton's own chromosome structure was affected by radiation from uranium experiments so as to cause (cont'd)

(CONTINUED)

173 (CONTINUED)

> PAUL (cont'd)
> his son to be born a mutate.
> It is also possible that these
> mutations appear only when
> the man is subjected to
> radiation.

> STAN (364)
> Such as cosmic ray radiation
> that accompanies the rays
> of the sun?

> PAUL (365)
> That is a possibility.
> High-energy cosmic rays constantly bombard the earth but
> under normal conditions only
> a small percent penetrate
> the atmosphere and reach the
> surface of the earth. However, I noticed a peculiar
> phenomenon the other day when
> we were measuring radiation
> in the altos. The radiation
> level was extremely high,
> but only for as long as the
> sun was shining. When the sun
> sank, radiation dropped to an
> almost negligible background
> count on the geiger counter.
> I can't begin to explain it.

> STAN (366)
> Then it is possible that the
> man changes into the creature
> Terry described when subjected
> to the sun's rays?

> PAUL (367)
> It is not only possible...
> I believe it is the answer.

> STAN (368)
> (jumping suddenly to
> his feet)
> I think it's time we pay
> Walton a visit... by daylight!

EXT. ROCKY JUNGLE ROAD - BRIGHT DAYLIGHT

174 MED. SHOT - A jeep approaches along a rocky road and stops just short of the CAMERA. Stan jumps to the road from the driver's seat while Paul, rifle in hand, steps down from the other side, then pauses to give Terry a hand as she jumps to the ground. The three are attired for jungle travel.

> STAN (369)
> You're sure this is the right spot?

> TERRY (370)
> (nods and points ahead)
> Up there... high on the hill, is the house. The cave entrance is below. I think I can find it.

Stan starts uptrail and then pauses.

> STAN (371)
> Bring the geiger counter, Paul. I'd like to get a background count up here.

175 CLOSE SHOT - Paul lifts the geiger counter from the jeep, then turns and shades his eyes to stare in the direction of the house.

> PAUL (372)
> Not a sign of life anywhere...

Paul quickly places the geiger counter on the ground and begins to unbuckle the gun belt from around his waist.

> PAUL (cont'd)
> Come here, Terry.

176 TWO SHOT - as Terry approaches Paul, puzzled at what he is doing.

(CONTINUED)

176 (CONTINUED)

> PAUL (373)
> (extending the gun and belt)
> Put this on, Terry... you'll feel safer.

Terry takes the belt and buckles it around her waist.

> TERRY (374)
> I thought you didn't believe what I told you this morning.

> PAUL (375)
> I've done a lot of thinking, Terry... since we talked this morning. I'm convinced there is something devilish and unhealthy up in these hills. Look around! The place is completely desolate! Surely, it would take more than native superstition to drive away every last human.

Paul picks up his rifle and slings the geiger counter strap over his shoulder.

> PAUL (cont'd)
> Stick close to Stan and myself.

DISSOLVE TO

177 TRUCKING SHOT - The three are walking carefully along a rough, rock-strewn, uphill trail, all the time keeping an anxious lookout for signs of danger. Terry stops and shades her eyes with her hand as she peers into the distance.

> TERRY (376)
> We're closer to the house but I still can't see the cave.

> STAN (377)
> Take a look through these glasses.

(CONTINUED)

PH   73

177 (CONTINUED)

                              TERRY (378)
                         (using the glasses)
                    There's no sign of life...
                    Yes, I think I see the cave..
                    This trail should lead
                    right to it.

        Terry returns the glasses and they continue
        on the trail.

178   MED. SHOT - Terry, in the lead, approaches a rock
        that blocks the trail. She scrambles over the
        rock and continues o.s. The others follow.

179   CLOSE SHOT - of Terry with the field glasses held
        before her eyes. She lowers the glasses.

                              TERRY (379)
                    It's the cave entrance all
                    right. I couldn't forget
                    it.

                                        DISSOLVE TO

180   MED. CLOSE SHOT - viewing the mouth of the cave
        with the huge rock door blocking the entrance.
        The three walk into the left side of the
        PICTURE and stand, silently, staring up at
        the cave entrance.

181   CLOSE SHOT - of Terry as she stares at the cave.
        Her eyes are a little frightened. She turns
        towards Paul and Stan as the CAMERA ANGLE WIDENS.

                              STAN (380)
                    It looks like solid rock.
                    How did you get out?

                              TERRY (381)
                    When I pressed the button the
                    rock rose straight up inside
                    the cave.

                              PAUL (382)
                    It must weight many tons.

                                        (CONTINUED)

181 (CONTINUED)

>   STAN (383)
> If a button opens the cave from the inside, another button must open it from the outside. Let's look around.

182 MED. SHOT - The three begin cautiously to examine the outer surface of the cave but find nothing. After a few moments Paul picks up the geiger counter which he had placed on the ground and energizes it.

183 INSERT - of the geiger counter. A rapid clicking is audible.

184 TWO SHOT - Stan turns and stares at Paul as he operates the instrument.

>   PAUL (384)
> Listen to that count! There's something very strange about this area.

>   STAN (385)
> We must be close to a source of radioactivity.

>   PAUL (386)
> I don't think so. Remember, I told you before... I checked the background count early one morning on the altos just as the sun was coming up. It was like this. But when I checked the same spot at night, the count was low. If we were close to a source of radioactive ore, the count would not change.

>   STAN (387)
> Perhaps a combination of extreme cosmic ray activity from the sun's rays and the thin atmosphere at this altitude is the answer.

185   CLOSE SHOT - of Paul as he turns the counter off
      and looks up at Stan.

                    PAUL (388)
          Yes, I had thought of that.
          It may be the sun's rays that
          effect the change in Walton...
          if it was actually Walton
          that frightened Terry.

                    STAN (389)
          Is there any real scientific
          possibility of such a
          change, Paul?

                    PAUL (390)
          Such a change is scientifically
          possible. But the math-
          ematical probability of
          its actually happening is
          something like one in a
          hundred million.

                    STAN (391)
          Hardly betting odds...

                                    DISSOLVE TO

186   MED. GROUP SHOT - Stan turns to Terry who is
      still staring at the stone entrance to the cave.

                    STAN (392)
          There's nothing we can do
          here. Let's go on up to
          the house.

      Terry turns quickly, eyes widening.

                    TERRY (393)
          Oh no, Stan! Let's go back!

                    STAN (394)
          Go back! We've got to get
          to the bottom of this or we'll
          never mine any uranium ore.
          As it is now, we can't get a
          native within five miles of
          the area.

                                    (CONTINUED)

PH

186 (CONTINUED)

> TERRY (395)
> I'm frightened, Stan. You didn't see what I saw here or you wouldn't blame me for being frightened.

> PAUL (396)
> Just where were you standing, Terry, when you saw.. ah, this thing?

187   CLOSE SHOT - of Terry as she stares at the cave. Her eyes reflect a little of the horror she felt when she stood at the cave entrance and saw the monster.

> TERRY (397)
> I stood right on that spot. (pointing) The sun had just come over the top of those hills and was glaring down in my face. Then I turned...

Terry turns. She stops talking. Her mouth drops open and her eyes widen in new horror as with a startling crash of background music the scene changes to:

188   MED. LONG SHOT - from Terry viewpoint. High on a knoll, gleaming like silver in the sunlight, stands the monster, staring down at the three intruders. From the waist down it is human; from the waist up it is reptilian. The head is like that of a mammoth lizard, the flesh like alligator leather, and the hands are scaly with sharp claws. Half man; half reptile!

189   GROUP SHOT - The three stand a moment, frozen to the spot; then Stan reacts. He whips the pistol from its holster. Motioning for the others to follow, he runs towards the knoll.

190   LONG SHOT - as the monster watches Stan approach for a moment, then turns and disappears beyond the opposite side of the knoll.

PH   77

191   TWO SHOT - Paul grabs Terry by the hand and the
        two follow Stan in the direction of the knoll
        and the monster.

192   LONG SHOT - from the top of the knoll. The
        monster is running in the distance (away from
        the CAMERA) with Stan in pursuit. Terry
        follows a good distance behind Stan. Paul,
        being much older, lags far behind.

193   MED. SHOT - A rear view of the monster as he
        scrambles onto a rock and disappears over the
        other side. Stan comes into the PICTURE,
        pistol in hand, and scrambles over the same
        rock.

194   REVERSE ANGLE SHOT - from the side of the same
        rock as Terry approaches along the path and
        scrambles up onto the rock, and over the
        other side.

195   LONG SHOT - from Stan's point of view. The
        monster pauses at the top of a hill, looks
        back, then turns and runs on.

196   CLOSE SHOT - of the monster's back as he runs
        along a path and suddenly darts over a fallen log
        at the side of the path and disappears in
        the underbrush. The shot holds until Stan
        appears and runs on along the path, past the
        log where the monster disappeared, making
        it obvious that the monster has eluded him.

197   MED. SHOT - The monster comes out of the
        underbrush, moving towards the CAMERA and
        away from the path where he eluded Stan.
        He looks cautiously in all directions, then
        follows another trail, apparently backtrack-
        ing towards the cave entrance.

198   CLOSE SHOT - Paul is alone. He stops running
        and leans on his rifle, gasping to catch
        his breath. He sits down on a rock to
        rest and lays his rifle on the ground beside
        him.

199   CLOSE SHOT from another ANGLE - of Paul sitting
        on the rock, breathing hard. The sun is

                                                    (CONTINUED)

199 (CONTINUED)

shining brightly. A shadow crosses Paul and he looks up startled at something out of CAMERA RANGE. A look of horror sweeps his features.

DISSOLVE TO

200   TRUCKING SHOT - of Stan walking wearily back along the trail. His face and clothes are dirty and from his discouraged look it is apparent that he was unable to find any trace of the monster. Suddenly he stops walking and stares ahead, squinting, as though not quite sure of what he sees.

201   LONG SHOT - from Stan's viewpoint. The figure of a girl lies face downward across the trail.

202   TWO SHOT from a REVERSE ANGLE - as Stan races along the path and stoops beside the girl. He turns her over. The face is Terry's; the eyes are closed. Quickly, Stan opens his canteen, pours water on a handkerchief, and dampens her face. Then he pours water on her forehead and she squirms and her eyes open.

203   TWO SHOT - from another ANGLE of Stan bending over Terry.

                   STAN (398)
             You all right, Terry?

She winces and struggles to sit up. Her eyes close and she falls back in Stan's arms. He holds her tight against his chest.

                   STAN (cont'd)
            If anything happens to you, I'll...

204   CLOSE SHOT - of Terry's face against Stan's jacket as one eye comes open and looks up at him.

(CONTINUED)

204 (CONTINUED)

                TERRY (399)
     You'll what...?

205   TWO SHOT - as Stan holds Terry out to look at her.

                STAN (400)
     Why you little faker...
     Just for that...

Stan bends over and kisses her. Terry submits without resistance, almost smugly. As she catches her breath, she looks up at him.

                TERRY (401)
     Could be you're human after all?

                STAN (402)
     Where you're concerned... could be!

                TERRY (403)
     I thought you didn't like me?

                STAN (404)
     I tried not to like you...
     I'm afraid I failed miserably.

In a sudden change of mood, Terry looks about anxiously.

                TERRY (405)
     Where is Paul?

                STAN (406)
     I thought he was with you.

                TERRY (407)
     No. He was behind me. I tripped and fell as I was running and that's the last I remember until (brushing water from her face) you tried to drowned me.

                        (CONTINUED)

205 (CONTINUED)

>Stan steps to his feet and helps Terry to hers. His arm remains around her.

>>STAN (408)
>>Then he must be behind you. He wouldn't pass and leave you lying here... Come on, we'll find him.

>>>DISSOLVE TO

EXT. THE JUNGLE - DUSK

206 MED. SHOT - Terry is standing alone beside the jeep. She hears footsteps in the underbrush and she raises the rifle to her shoulder. Her face is strained, alert, and she moistens her lips as she waits.

207 REVERSE SHOT - The sound of footsteps becomes louder, then Stan walks out of the underbrush and quickly approaches.

208 TWO SHOT - Stan steps wearily to Terry's side and drops his rifle across the seat of the jeep.

>>STAN (409)
>>I pounded on the door until I nearly broke my fist, but no answer and no sign of life.

>>TERRY (410)
>>What can we do? It's getting dark and there isn't another house within miles.

>>STAN (411)
>>There's only one thing we can do now - hurry back to Consuelo's for help.

>>TERRY (412)
>>It's terrible to leave Paul out here by himself.

>>>(CONTINUED)

208 (CONTINUED)

>Stan puts his arm around Terry. She leans against him. For a moment he is silent, thinking.

>>STAN (413)
>>Something has happened, Terry; or we would have found him. We might as well face it. We've hunted all afternoon and not a trace. The best thing we can do for Paul now is to get back to Mondera as fast as we can.

>>DISSOLVE TO

INT. TERRY'S ROOM - NIGHT

209 MED. SHOT - Terry is sitting glumly in her rocking chair while Stan paces back and forth in front of her.

>>STAN (414)
>>Consuelo is doing the best he can. He has found ten men who are willing to go out tonight. We are going to build a big brush fire near the entrance to the cave so that if Paul is anywhere around he can follow its light. There isn't much else we can do until morning.

>>TERRY (415)
>>Stay here, Stan... at least until morning. The men know how to find the cave. There's nothing you can do.

>>STAN (416)
>>I can't just sit here and wait. Consuelo expects me to go with his men.

>>(CONTINUED)

PH

209 (CONTINUED)

> TERRY (417)
> But we were supposed to meet Walton tonight at the Casino. Had you forgotten?
>
> STAN (418)
> (stops pacing)
> Yes, I had. Anyway, he won't show.
>
> TERRY (419)
> I think he will.

210 CLOSE SHOT - of Stan and Terry from another CAMERA ANGLE. Stan gives Terry a long, speculative look.

> STAN (420)
> Maybe you're right. What's on your mind, Terry?
>
> TERRY (421)
> I think Walton found Paul this afternoon and I'm afraid to even think what he might have done with him. That's why I think we should wait for Walton at the Casino tonight.
>
> STAN (422)
> But what makes you think he'll show?
>
> TERRY (423)
> If for no other reason... to appear innocent of whatever happened this afternoon.

211 CLOSE SHOT - of Stan, frowning in thought.

> STAN (424)
> You're right... absolutely right!

212 TWO SHOT - Stan turns suddenly towards Terry. He appears excited.

(CONTINUED)

PH   83

212 (CONTINUED)

                         STAN (cont'd)
              Terry, do you have a key to
              Paul's room?

                         TERRY (425)
              Yes, I'm sure I do. Why?

                         STAN (426)
              Then find it and come along.
              There's something in Paul's
              room I must have, if we're
              to meet Walton tonight at
              the Casino.

                                   DISSOLVE TO

213   CLOSE SHOT - A key is turning in a quaint latch.
       The CAMERA dollies away from the latch until
       the scene is a MED. SHOT of the inner door of
       Paul's room. The door opens and Stan and Terry
       enter. Stan hurries to a large chest in one
       corner of the room and opens it.

                         STAN (427)
              Paul kept it in here.

                         TERRY (428)
              What are you looking for?

       Stan doesn't answer but continues to search.
       Abruptly, he stops and lifts a rectangular metal
       box out of the chest. Terry steps in close
       and together they inspect the box.

                         TERRY (cont'd)
              What is it?

214   INSERT - of the metal box in Stan's hands. As
       he talks the CAMERA remains on the box and we
       see his hands operate the slide.

                         STAN'S VOICE (429)
              Using this box was Paul's idea
              and tonight I'm going to try (cont'd)

                                        (CONTINUED)

214 (CONTINUED)

> STAN'S VOICE (cont'd)
> it. Paul believes that radio-
> activity above a certain level
> causes the change in Walton
> that we saw. This box contains
> a piece of highly refined uranium.
> The box itself is made of lead
> to contain the radiation.
> When I move this slide, holes
> in the inner box are exposed
> so that a certain amount of
> radiation escapes.

> TERRY'S VOICE (430)
> Is the radiation dangerous?

215 CLOSE SHOT - of Stan as he talks with Terry.

> STAN (431)
> Radiation possible from this
> quantity of uranium is not
> dangerous for short periods
> of time but it is enough to
> blow the lid off of a geiger
> counter. Tonight, if Walton
> appears... we shall prove
> or disprove Paul's theory...
> once and for all!

DISSOLVE TO

EXT. VILLAGE - NIGHT

216 FULL SHOT - of an old dirty gray village
mission with the usual pointed steeple. A
bell begins to toll. The sound is slow and
melodious.

FADE TO

217 INSERT - of the bell in the steeple as it tolls.

218 FULL SHOT - again of the mission. The CAMERA
pans from the mission, across the dark street

(CONTINUED)

218 (CONTINUED)

        to the Casino, and dollies in on the neon lettering "Casino" above the entrance. The bell continues to toll.

                              FADE TO

INT. THE CASINO - NIGHT

219   FULL SHOT - of the table-filled interior of the Casino. The CAMERA dollies up to a single table for a TWO SHOT of Stan and Terry. The bell in the distance tolls for the last time and Stan looks at his watch.

                STAN (432)
        Just ten o'clock. If he's coming, it won't be long.

                TERRY (433)
        I have a feeling, tonight, Stan... I don't think we're going to be disappointed.

                STAN (434)
           (lays his hand over
           her's, smiles)
You have a revolting habit of being right, Terry. I've learned that in the last few days.

                TERRY (435)
And you're admitting it to me?

                STAN (436)
I am. And I'm going to admit something else. You can rough it with the best of them. I have no complaints.

                TERRY (437)
Coming from you, that's quite a compliment. I remember on the plane...

                          (CONTINUED)

219 (CONTINUED)

> STAN (438)
> Forget anything I said on the plane... please!

> TERRY (439)
> Stan, I don't understand this change that takes place in Walton... if it really does. Such a thing seems more like fantasy than a real scientific possibility.

> STAN (440)
> I don't understand it either, Terry, but Paul has made quite a study of the subject and he thinks it is possible. He says that throwbacks to other forms of life occur frequently but that this throwback is to a form of Sauros, or lizard-like reptile of the Mesozoic age, and if proven, would be the most ancient and remarkable ever discovered.

> TERRY (441)
> It all seems so weird and unreal. I guess I'm just a very ordinary person who can think only very ordinary thoughts.

> STAN (442)
> (smiling)
> ... and that's the way I like you.

> TERRY (443)
> Do you have everything ready, Stan?

> STAN (444)
> (nodding)
> If you mean the box... it's right here in my lap. You're not frightened, are you?

(CONTINUED)

219 (CONTINUED)

>TERRY (445)
>A little nervous. It's silly
>I know but I have a premonition
>that something terrible is
>going to happen tonight...
>one of those intuitive things
>women are supposed to have.

As Terry speaks the music swells, then suddenly drops as the scene changes.

220   CLOSE UP ANGLE SHOT - of Walton standing before them at the table. The CAMERA ANGLE is from below and slightly to one side of the face. For a moment Walton's expression is sinister, almost menacing; then, abruptly he smiles, bows, and seats himself.

>WALTON (446)
>I't sorry to be late. I
>drove fast but I've always
>been handicapped with an
>under developed time sense.

221   CLOSE SHOT - of Stan. He smiles, making an effort to appear perfectly natural and at ease. He rises, shaking hands.

>STAN (447)
>Don't give it a thought, Mr.
>Walton. I've enjoyed myself,
>just sitting here talking
>with Terry.

222   CLOSE SHOT - Walton smiles.

>WALTON (448)
>That is completely under-
>standable...

Walton looks around, apparently puzzled.

>WALTON (cont'd)
>Dr. Jorgeson... isn't he
>with you?

223   THREE SHOT - from the unoccupied side of the table.

(CONTINUED)

223 (CONTINUED)

>   STAN (449)
> No, he isn't. As a matter
> of fact, we don't know
> where Dr. Jorgeson is.
>
>   WALTON (450)
> I.. I'm afraid I don't
> understand.
>
>   STAN (451)
> Dr. Jorgeson disappeared
> this afternoon in the
> Quandici hills. A search
> party is looking for him
> now.
>
>   WALTON (452)
> In the Quandici hills?
>
>   STAN (453)
> Only a few hundred yards
> from your place, actually.
>
>   WALTON (454)
> Then it must have been Dr.
> Jorgeson who returned my car?
>
>   STAN (455)
> The three of us returned it.
> You see, Terry gave us a
> rather strange account of
> last night's events. We
> felt that we should invest-
> igate.
>
>   WALTON (456)
>   (shrugging)
> A hallucination... nothing
> more. Miss O'Conner was
> overtired.
>
>   STAN (457)
> Paul thought otherwise.

Walton stiffens visibly. His tone is suddenly hard.

(CONTINUED)

223 (CONTINUED)

                    WALTON (458)
          What do you mean, Paul
          thought otherwise?

A glance passes between Stan and Terry, followed by a perceptible nod from Terry.

224 INSERT - showing the lead box in Stan's hands beneath the table. As he talks, we see his fingers move the sliding lid. With the sliding lid extended, we see another metal surface, perforated with dozens of tiny holes. Continuing to talk, Stan moves the position of the box so that the perforated surface emits radiation in Walton's direction.

                    STAN'S VOICE (459)
          Paul is a peculiar fellow, Mr.
          Walton. You see, he believes
          Terry's story... that is, he
          doesn't think she had an hall-
          ucination; he thinks she saw
          exactly what she told us she
          saw.

                    WALTON'S VOICE (460)
          That's absurd, Mr. Rockwell.
          Such creatures don't exist.

                    STAN'S VOICE (461)
          True... except possibly as a
          pitiable freak of nature. Some-
          times nature plays cruel jokes,
          Mr. Walton... sometimes man
          in his half-knowledge helps
          nature play these jokes...

225   CLOSE SHOT - Terry watches Walton as Stan talks. The radiation from the uranium in the lead box has its inevitable effect. Unseen by the CAMERA, the slow metamorphis of Walton's features begins. Terry has steeled herself but she cannot suppress the horror. It builds up in her face as she stares.

226   CLOSE SHOT - of Walton. The change has only started and is very slight. He sees Terry staring at him but does not know the reason.

                                      (CONTINUED)

226 (CONTINUED)

                    WALTON (462)
     Why are you staring, Senorita?
     Is something wrong?

227   TWO SHOT - featuring Terry as she and Stan stare across the table at the changing Walton. She swallows and tries to hide her feelings. She shakes her head in response to Walton's question.

                    TERRY (463)
     No... nothing.

228   CLOSE SHOT - of Walton as the change continues in all its weird details.

229   MED. SHOT - From nearby tables people look up and stare, unable to believe their eyes at the change that is taking place in Walton. Some rise slowly to their feet with the slow-motion timing of robots, entranced. Others begin to edge their way towards the exits.

230   INSERT - again showing the lead box beneath the table. Fingers move the sliding lid to allow more radiation to escape.

231   TWO SHOT - Stan and Terry stare, without speaking and without moving, fascinated by the creature that is forming across the table from them.

232   CLOSE SHOT - of Walton. The change to monster is almost complete, yet Walton does not realize that any change has taken place. He half rises from his chair, his hands outstretched on the table before him.

                    WALTON (464)
         (shouting in a near
         hysterical voice)
     What is the matter with you
     people? Why are you all star-
     ing... Tell me!

233   REVERSE SHOT - of Walton with the CAMERA behind him and slightly to his left. His hands are still

                                  (CONTINUED)

PH   91

233 (CONTINUED)

        on the table. For a moment longer he stares at the surrounding people, completely unable to understand their horror. Suddenly, he looks down at his outstretched hands.

234   INSERT - of Walton's hands as they change from normal male hands to scaly, leather-like forepaws with sharp, reptilian claws.

235   MED. SHOT - from behind Walton. He jumps back frantically from the table. Directly before him, only ten feet away, is the full-view bar mirror. His own lizard-like reflection stares back at him. It tells its own story. The change from man to monster is now complete.

236   FULL SHOT - of the interior of the Casino. Patrons, almost paralyzed with fright, are backing away from the monster. The monster turns suddenly and bolts for the street entrance, amid screams from those he brushes as he passes. As he disappears through the door, bedlam breaks loose. Gesturing, chattering natives run in every direction.

237   TWO SHOT - as Stan and Terry jump to their feet. Stan thrusts the table out of his way, overturning it, and dashes towards the Casino entrance in pursuit. Terry follows.

238   REVERSE SHOT - from outside of the Casino entrance as Stan, followed by Terry, bursts through the door and pauses to look around for sight of the monster and then begins to run again.

239   FULL SHOT - A view of the street from the Casino entrance. The Daimler pulls over the curb and into the street with the monster visible at the wheel. The car skids and gains traction, and heads towards the distant hills.

240   CLOSE SHOT - of the front of the jeep as Stan and Terry jump into the seat without speaking. Stan grinds the starter but the jeep does not start. He tries again and again, impatiently,

(CONTINUED)

240 (CONTINUED)

    until just as it seems hopeless, the motor catches. He cuts the wheels sharply, bounces over the curb, and tears out in pursuit.

241   FULL SHOT - showing the parking area beside the Casino as natives jump into cars of all vintages and turn into the street to give chase.

EXT. MOUNTAIN ROAD - NIGHT

242   LONG SHOT - A train of auto lights moves along a winding, narrow road in the distance. Only the lights of the cars and a full moon that outlines the horizon are visible in the scene.

243   MED. SHOT - with the CAMERA positioned at the outer edge of a sharp angle in the mountain road as first the Daimler, then the pursuing cars, slide around the corner at precarious speeds. As the cars slide past the CAMERA, dirt and rocks are slung into the lower corner of the PICTURE.

244   LONG SHOT - From an adjacent peak, the train of auto lights is viewed moving slowly upward along the side of the mountain slope.

245   TWO SHOT - of Stan at the wheel of the jeep, fighting to keep the machine on the road, and of Terry sitting breathless beside him. Her hair is streaming behind her and her eyes are intent on the car ahead.

                    TERRY (465)
              (without taking her eyes
               from the road)
        It was horrible, Stan... That
        poor man! He didn't even know
        what had happened...

                    STAN (466)
        Paul was right about Walton...
        right from the first... And
        I thought Paul was crazy.

                                (CONTINUED)

245 (CONTINUED)

>   TERRY (467)
>   (pointing)
>   Walton is turning up ahead,
>   Stan. He's heading straight
>   for the cave.
>
>   STAN (468)
>   Good! He's in for a surprise
>   when he runs into Consuelo's
>   men and the fire.

246   FULL SHOT - of the narrow road as it winds in a
      steep upgrade along the side of the mountain
      peak. The approaching Daimler slides past the
      CAMERA and the pursuing cars, following closely,
      one by one disappear o.s.

247   FULL SHOT - of the huge bonfire in the middle
      of the road with Consuelo's men moving about it
      in apparent boredom. At the sound of an approach-
      ing automobile they become alert. The huge
      Daimler, traveling at high speed, pulls into
      view as it rounds a curve. It slides to a halt
      close to the fire that blocks the road. The
      monster stands up in the seat behind the wheel
      and his weird face reflects shadows in the light
      of the fire.

248   CLOSE SHOT - of the monster standing behind the
      wheel. For a moment he looks about frantically,
      then he jumps to the ground and runs towards
      the fire.

249   FULL SHOT - from behind the fire as Consuelo's
      men turn and flee in every direction. The monster
      veers off of the road and heads through the
      brush in the direction of the cave.

250   MED. SHOT - of natives crouching behind trees
      and rocks and letting go with a barrage of
      rifle fire.

251   MED. CLOSE SHOT - from behind the monster as he
      tears through the brush unscathed by the firing.

252   TWO SHOT - The jeep pulls to a sliding stop behind
      the Daimler. Stan and Terry stand up in the
      jeep and squint into the darkness.

                                        (CONTINUED)

252 (CONTINUED)

> TERRY (469)
> He's making straight for the cave entrance.

Stan follows Terry's gaze.

> STAN (470)
> I thought he would.

Stan reaches down and jerks the rifle from its mount in the jeep.

> STAN (cont'd)
> (jumping to the ground)
> You stay here, Terry.

> TERRY (471)
> No!

Terry jumps from the jeep and follows Stan into the darkness.

253 MED. SHOT - A rear view of the monster in bright moonlight as he scrambles up the side of the hill towards the cave entrance. Stan and Terry, in pursuit, cut in from the side of the PICTURE.

254 MED. SHOT - of the same action from a different CAMERA ANGLE.

255 FULL SHOT - of the front and one side of the cave entrance as the monster bursts into view. He begins to tear away a pattern of loose rock about waist high along the side of the cave entrance. As the rock is thrown to one side, an electrical mechanism is exposed consisting of a toggle switch and two multi-contact relays.

256 INSERT - of the monster's claw-like fore paws clumsily throwing the toggle switch that operates the cave entrance.

257 MED. CLOSE SHOT - of the rock entrance of the cave. It creaks and begins to move, accompanied by the whirling sound of a high-speed electric motor.

PH   95

258   MED. SHOT - A front view of Stan as he scrambles
        over the top of the rise directly behind the
        monster.

259   CLOSE SHOT - of the monster as he glances over
        his shoulder and becomes aware of Stan's approach.
        He darts a glance at the slowly rising door and
        realizes that Stan is too close and that the
        door will not open in time for him to escape
        within. In panic, he begins to scale the
        rocky side of the cave with all the agility
        of a reptile.

260   FULL SHOT - showing the monster scaling the
        side of the cave.

261   TWO SHOT - from a REVERSE ANGLE as Stan and Terry
        approach the side of the cave and stare up at
        the monster.

                        TERRY (472)
                It's almost straight up...
                like the side of a building.

                        STAN (473)
                Yes... he'll never make it.

262   FULL SHOT - of the monster, now very high on
        the side of the cave as he continues to climb.
        Progress has become difficult and his movements
        are slow and cautious.

263   CLOSE SHOT - of the monster. His claws begin to
        slip in the soft rock. He clutches desperately
        as his body slides.

264   TWO SHOT - showing Stan and Terry staring up,
        intent and motionless, lips slightly parted.

265   CLOSE SHOT - as the monster's claws loose their
        grip in the soft rock and his body slips downward,
        out of the PICTURE.

266   FULL SHOT - The falling body of the monster
        drops into an abyss to the immediate left of
        the spot where Stan and Terry stand. The creature
        screams once; an echoing, fading sound, as it
        falls into space.

267   TWO SHOT - showing a profile of Stan and Terry
       as they gaze in shocked silence into the abyss.
       The entire jungle is suddenly quiet. Stan
       looks around at Terry, and for a moment they
       stare at each other.

                         STAN (474)
                 I'm going down.

       He disappears over the side, leaving Terry
       standing alone.

268   CLOSE SHOT - from behind Terry as she stares
       into the abyss. From what seems like a great
       distance o.s. a voice, weak but distinct,
       calls out.

                         THE VOICE (475)
                 Stan! Stan!

       Terry turns about, startled, so that she faces
       the CAMERA.

                         THE VOICE (cont'd)
                 Stan!

       Terry runs towards the CAMERA and the mouth
       of the cave.

269   MED. SHOT - from inside the cave looking
       towards the entrance which is now fully open.
       The interior is dimly lighted by indirect wall
       illumination. Terry enters, walking rapidly
       yet cautiously. She moves towards the CAMERA,
       then stops and calls.

                         TERRY (476)
                 Paul!

       The call echoes like scrambled voices in an
       echo chamber.

270   LONG SHOT - showing the length of the tunnel
       and a rear view of Terry as she hurries towards
       the door at the opposite end.

271   CLOSE SHOT - from behind Terry as she approaches
       the door. She places her hand on the knob and

                                            (CONTINUED)

PH

271 (CONTINUED)

        hesitates. The voice, now very close, again calls Stan's name. Terry forces open the door and disappears.

272   FULL SHOT - of the interior of Walton's laboratory from the doorway through which Terry has just passed. In one corner of the room, bound to a chair, is Paul. Terry rushes to a long laboratory bench on which is a collection of laboratory implements. She picks up a scalpel and, turning back to Paul in the chair, she cuts the ropes that bind him.

273   TWO SHOT - Paul smiles and begins to rub the circulation back into his arms. Terry continues to clear away the ropes.

>TERRY (477)
>Are you all right, Paul?

>PAUL (478)
>Thanks, Terry... yes, I'm all right.

Terry stands behind the chair in which Paul is seated. She places both hands on his shoulders.

>TERRY (479)
>We've been scared to death, Paul. Where have you been?

>PAUL (480)
>Right here, Terry... all the time.

>TERRY (481)
>But how did you get here?

>PAUL (482)
>Not of my own free will, I'll assure you... You see, I couldn't keep up with you young folks back on the trail. I stopped to rest and Walton doubled back and forced me to go with him.

(CONTINUED)

273 (CONTINUED)

> TERRY (483)
> He didn't try to harm you?

> PAUL (484)
> He had no wish to harm me. He was impressed because I was one of the scientists who had known his father when he was conducting radiation experiments years ago. The poor fellow had a crazy idea that I could help him.

> TERRY (485)
> Then why did he tie you to this chair?

> PAUL (486)
> He felt that it was necessary to meet you and Stan at the Casino tonight and he didn't know what else to do with me.

> TERRY (487)
> The poor fellow was deathly afraid his affliction would be discovered, wasn't he?

> PAUL (488)
> Yes. It's an obsession. Yet, for some reason, he had confidence in me. He gave me all the notes and drawings of the experiments his father had conducted during the years he tried to help his son's condition. He seems to have a pitiable, almost blind faith in my ability to carry on where his father left off. I agreed to try... perhaps I can help him yet.

(CONTINUED)

273 (CONTINUED)

      STAN'S VOICE (489)
 It's too late!

274 CLOSE SHOT - of Stan framed in the doorway. He looks disheveled and physically spent, almost as though he is in a trance.

      STAN (490)
 It's strange... very strange!

      TERRY (491)
 What Stan? What is it?

275 MED. SHOT - as Stan walks slowly into the room.

      STAN (492)
    (speaking to both Terry
    and Paul)
 I climbed down into the abyss to where he had fallen. But there was no sign of a monster... only of Walton as he always looked... He was dead.

276 CLOSE SHOT - of Paul. He is disturbed by Stan's words.

      PAUL (493)
 Dead! I was afraid it would happen. It's a great pity. If circumstances could have been different... Terry, would you hand me my pipe. It's there by the beaker.

277 CLOSE SHOT - of Terry as she turns. She reaches for the pipe, but sways and partially catches herself against the laboratory bench.

278 TWO SHOT - Stan grasps Terry before she falls and holds her. His arm is around her waist and she leans limply against him. He hooks

      (CONTINUED)

278 (CONTINUED)

> his finger under her chin and raises her head

            STAN (494)
     Are you all right, Terry?

            TERRY (495)
       (smiling weakly)
     I'm all right now. Just
     for a minute I... I guess
     it was sort of a reaction
     from all the excitement.

            STAN (496)
       (still holding her)
     I'm not taking any chances
     with you, young lady.
     What you need is a couple
     days of solid sleep. You're
     going home right now.. and
     to bed.

The CAMERA ANGLE widens to include Paul as he rises stiffly from his chair. He smiles.

            PAUL (497)
     Would you two object if I
     ride along? I could use
     some sleep myself.

            TERRY (498)
       (still in the fold of
         Stan's arm. She smiles)
     We don't object.

Paul moves away from the others and the CAMERA follows. He pauses at the opposite end of the laboratory workbench.

            PAUL (499)
     You know... I've never
     stolen anything before in
     my life but this I shall
     take with me when I leave
     this room.

                       (CONTINUED)

278 (CONTINUED)

        Paul reaches down and picks up a manuscript.

                      STAN'S VOICE (500)
        What is it, Paul?

279   INSERT - of Paul's hands as he slowly thumbs the pages of the manuscript.

                      PAUL'S VOICE (501)
        Dr. Walton's notes and experiments - a complete record - of his vain efforts to return his son to normalcy. If the time should ever come when I think all of this was but a bad dream, I'll need only leaf through its pages...

                              FADE OUT

- THE END -

FINAL REVISED SHOOTING SCRIPT
October 17, 1957

THE SUN DEMON

A Screenplay by

E. S. Seeley, Jr.

Clarke-King Enterprises, Inc.
205 South Beverly Drive
Beverly Hills, California

CAST OF CHARACTERS

MALE	FEMALE
DR. GILBERT McKENNA	ANN LANSING
DR. ARTHUR BUCKELL	TRUDY
DR. JACOB HOFFMANN	MOTHER
DR. JAMES STERN	LITTLE GIRL
GEORGE WILBURFORCE	OLD NURSE
SERGEANT ALOYSIUS PETERSON	OLD WOMAN
CHIEF OF POLICE	TWO YOUNG NURSES
TWO HOSPITAL ATTENDANTS	
AMBULANCE DRIVER	
HOSPITAL INTERN	
TWO FRIENDS OF TRUDY	
ASSORTED COPS	

THE SUN DEMON

1   DAY EXT. - M.C.U. DOOR ON BACK OF AMBULANCE

    A hand enters and yanks open the door, exposing the inside
    of the ambulance. After a second, a white-coated INTERN
    jumps into the tonneau and helps to guide in a stretcher.
    On the stretcher is a limp form, heavily swathed in sheets
    so that we cannot recognize him. Two attendants (also white-
    coated) help push the stretcher the rest of the way into the
    tonneau, then slam the door and start around opposite sides
    of the vehicle.

2   DAY EXT. - M.S. AMBULANCE FROM FRONT

    Driver climbs in behind wheel and attendant climbs in beside
    him. Both slam their doors hard. Driver starts the engine
    and hits the siren. Then he jerks the ambulance into gear
    and starts it towards the Camera.

3   DAY EXT. - M.S. REVERSE ANGLE OF AMBULANCE

    Ambulance speeds towards street (away from Camera) and turns
    off screen.

4   DAY EXT. - L.S. AMBULANCE

    It careens around corner heading for Camera.

5   DAY EXT. - L.S. HIGH ANGLE OF AMBULANCE

    It is racing along a street with the siren screaming. (Milk
    the ambulance as much as necessary. More shots, etc.)

                                                DISSOLVE TO:

6   DAY EXT. - L.S. REAR OF HOSPITAL

    We can see the Emergency Entrance which is deserted. Suddenly
    the siren grows louder and the ambulance pulls up, stops and
    backs up to the Emergency Entrance.

7   DAY EXT. - M.C.U. REAR DOOR OF AMBULANCE

    Hand enters and pulls it open. Stretcher emerges with intern
    following. Camera pulls back to M.S. to reveal several white-
    coated figures crowding around to ease the stretcher out. We

                                                (CONTINUED)

7   CONTINUED:

    hear them saying such things as: "Easy now", "Watch that
    other side, Joe", etc. Camera follows them as they move the
    stretcher towards the door leading into the hospital.

8   DAY INT. - M.L.S. EMERGENCY ROOM

    A standard medical examining table is sitting in the middle
    of the room. Cabinets containing medicines and first aid
    supplies are along the walls, etc. Over in one corner, FIRST
    REGISTERED NURSE is seated behind a desk, going over some
    records.

    FIRST ATTENDANT enters.

                        FIRST ATTENDANT
        a-   They're bringing him in.

                        FIRST NURSE
        b-   The radiation case?

                        FIRST ATTENDANT
        c-   Yeah.

9   DAY INT. - M.S. DOOR TO OUTSIDE

    Two attendants enter bearing the stretcher. Camera follows
    them as they carry it over to the Examining Table, set it
    down, and proceed to lift the swathed figure carefully onto
    the table.

10 DAY INT. - M.C.U. NURSE AT DESK

    She lifts up the phone and begins talking softly but
    officiously into it.

                        FIRST NURSE
               Page Dr. Stern, please. We need
               him down here right away.

11 DAY INT. - M.S. AMBULANCE DRIVER

    He is standing next to the door leading outside holding a
    clipboard on which is fastened his trip report which he is
    now filling in with the aid of the SECOND NURSE. As she
    speaks, he writes.

                                            (CONTINUED)

11   CONTINUED:

                    SECOND NURSE
          10:42 arrival. M. Wilson, R.N.
          on duty. Dr. Harris, Intern....

Her voice trails on as the Driver continues writing.

12   DAY INT. - M.S. EXAMINING TABLE

     Swathed figure is lying on the table now and the attendants
     move away as the First Nurse moves in to question the figure.
     She speaks to him in a louder than normal voice.

                    FIRST NURSE
        a-   Sir? Sir, can you tell me your
              name? Sir?

     Figure doesn't move or reply.

                    VOICE OVER LOUDSPEAKER
                       (filter)
        b-   DR. STERN, EMERGENCY ROOM. DR.
              STERN, PLEASE.

     Nurse looks up and camera moves in to M.C.U. on her face.
     She addresses someone off-screen.

                    FIRST NURSE
        c-   Get me 4 CCs of Morphine.

     CUT TO TITLES AND RUN ALL THE WAY THROUGH. TITLES SHOULD
     BE WHITE LETTERS ON A BLACK BACKGROUND FOR THE SHOCK
     EFFECT.

13   AFTERNOON INT. - M.S. COUCH IN HOSPITAL WAITING ROOM

On the couch are seated ANN LANSING and DR. BUCKELL, looking worried and tense and as if they have been waiting for a long time.

Ann is an attractive young woman in her late twenties with dark hair cut to a "sensible" length and dressed in "sensible" clothes. All this sensibility has to do with the fact that she is trying to compete equally with men in a field of work largely dominated by men (Science) and does not dare, therefore, to push her femininity too far. Yet, under it all she is a warm-hearted, affectionate girl of the type whose greatest happiness will come from devoting her entire life to one man.

Buckell was probably just another physicist prior to WW II and never dared stray very far from whichever university claimed him. However, the war years, the arms race, the Manhattan Project, the cold war, etc. have managed to elevate him to a point where, if he is not personally famous, at least his profession is. And the result of all this was, for a while, a tendency to take himself too seriously, a Gregory Peck-like inability to recognize that there are some situations in the world that can be met with a smile, and an inner glow of accomplishment that sometimes made him act like a middle-western small businessman being honored by his fellows at their New York convention. More recently, however, he has begun to mellow and is therefore quite apt to react in different ways to the same stimulus presented at different hours of the same day. Age about 55.

The two of them sit quietly, side by side, looking anything but happy. Suddenly they see someone and their eyes brighten.

14   AFT. INT. - M.S. WAITING ROOM DOOR

A young resident physician (DR. STERN) enters rapidly. Dr. Stern is about thirty and has been toiling for his harsh and demanding mistress (Medicine) a number of years now. He doesn't get enough sleep or enough of the proper food or enough relaxation and, were he any thinner and frailer than he already is, he would no doubt have succumbed to mononucleosis years ago. But somehow he has managed to survive and, if nothing else, the years have given him the kind of assurance in dealing with people that comes from the realization that they know nothing about his field of work, an ability to live so efficiently that he scarcely ever wastes even the twitch of an eyelash, and an almost total lack of emotional awareness of anything outside the medical profession.

(CONTINUED)

14   CONTINUED:

The Camera follows Dr. Stern as he rapidly crosses the room to Ann and Buckell who are now on their feet.

      BUCKELL
a- Dr. Stern?

      STERN
b- Yes. I'm so sorry I kept you waiting.

Stern and Buckell shake hands.

      BUCKELL
c- That's all right, Doctor. We understand how busy you are. I'm Dr. Buckell and this is Miss Lansing.

      STERN
d- Oh, yes. You worked with McKenna didn't you?

      BUCKELL
e- That's right. We're all out at the Dogstar Project together.

      STERN
f- Were you there when the accident happened?

      BUCKELL
g- Yes, I'm afraid so.

      ANN
h- Doctor. Is he... going to be all right?

      STERN
i- I think so. But first I want to find out some of the details of the accident. That is, if I can steal a few moments before they start paging me again. Er, please sit down.

All three of them sit down- Ann and Buckell on the couch, Stern in a chair facing them.

      BUCKELL
j- You understand, Doctor, Security Regulations may make it impossible for me to tell you everything.

(CONTINUED)

14   CONTINUED: (2)

       STERN
k- Just tell me as much as you can.

       BUCKELL
l- Well, as you may have heard, we're doing some work with newly developed isotopes out at the Project.

Stern leans forward eagerly.

       STERN
m- Excuse me just one minute, Doctor. Are these isotopes radioactive?

       BUCKELL
n- Why, yes.

       STERN
o- Highly radioactive?

       BUCKELL
p- Yes, some of them are.

Stern leans back again.

       STERN
q- I see. All right.

       BUCKELL
r- Naturally, we take all the usual precautions in handling them- lead walls, remote controlled handling devices... You probably know what I mean.

Stern smiles and nods quickly.

       BUCKELL
s- Now one of the devices we use is a little electric train.

       STERN
t- An electric train?

       BUCKELL
u- That's right. The kind you might buy your kids for Christmas. You see, all our radioactive material is kept in a special vault.
       (MORE)

       (CONTINUED)

14   CONTINUED: (3)

                    BUCKELL (Cont'd)
              Whenever we want a particular
              isotope, we back the train into
              the vault, load the isotope into
              a lead container by means of remote
              controlled arms, put the container
              on the train, and run the train
              out of the vault.

                    STERN
                  (for a moment he is
                   entranced with this
                   novel device)
v-   That's very ingenious.
                  (then he resumes his
                   professional attitude)
              And once these isotopes are in the
              lead containers, they can be handled
              safely by laboratory personnel, is
              that it?

                    BUCKELL
w-   Yes.... Unless the container should
              break. That's what happened with
              Dr. McKenna.

                    STERN
x-   I see.

                    BUCKELL
y-   He had just transferred an isotope
              to the train and had run it out of
              the vault. And... well, Miss
              Lansing was there. Perhaps she
              can tell you better than I can.

He turns towards Ann. Ann, appearing in the spotlight for
the first time in this sequence, takes a breath and tries
to appear very calm and professional.

                    ANN
z-   The train always stops behind a
              large lead screen as an added
              precaution. Gil... Dr. McKenna
              had gone behind the screen to take
              the container off the train and...
              it must have fallen to the floor.

                    STERN
a1-   Fallen?

                                        (CONTINUED)

14   CONTINUED: (4)

Buckell hastens to speak up.

                   BUCKELL
b1- Dr. McKenna wasn't feeling any
     too well this morning. Apparently
     he had a dizzy spell and dropped
     it.

Ann knew this was coming and quickly rushes into defend Gil.

                   ANN
c1- No, I don't think he even touched
     it.
          (she turns slightly
          towards Buckell)
     Remember, Dr. Buckell? He said
     yesterday that the remote arms
     needed adjusting. They weren't
     putting the containers on the
     train properly.

Buckell knows this is just an excuse and is about to let himself be drawn into an argument when Stern, his mind always on the long-range view, interrupts.

                   STERN
d1- Well, at any rate, the container
     fell- or was dropped- to the floor.
     And it broke?

                   ANN
e1- Yes. I was working across the
     room when he went behind the
     screen. I heard a crash... and...
     and then he screamed...

                   STERN
f1- What did you do then?

Buckell breaks in again.

                   BUCKELL
g1- We have a regular procedure we
     follow when such things happen.
     There's an alarm button in the
     room and it alerts the whole
     building, including our emergency
     station.

                   STERN
h1- And then?

                                    (CONTINUED)

14   CONTINUED: (5)

>   ANN
> i1- I left the room as soon as I
>   pressed the button. That's
>   part of the procedure.
>
>   STERN
> j1- You weren't exposed to the
>   radiation yourself, were you?
>
>   ANN
> k1- No. I was on the other side of
>   the screen.
>
>   STERN
> l1- But Dr. McKenna remained behind
>   the screen.
>
>   BUCKELL
> m1- He didn't have much choice. He
>   was overcome immediately.
>
>   STERN
> n1- Hmm. And how long did he remain
>   there- exposed to the radiation?
>
>   BUCKELL
> o1- About five or six minutes, I'd
>   say. It took at least that long
>   for the men from the emergency
>   station to reach him. They had
>   to put on radiation suits so
>   that they could go behind the
>   screen safely.
>
>   STERN
> p1- Five or six minutes. Hmm. Now
>   tell me one more thing, Doctor.
>   What isotope was involved in this
>   accident?

But now Stern has trespassed onto forbidden ground and Buckell is happy to so remind him.

>   BUCKELL
> q1- I'm afraid I can't answer that.

Stern doesn't care, however. He's more concerned with the long range view.

(CONTINUED)

14   CONTINUED: (6)

                        STERN
    r1-   Well, perhaps you can tell me
           if it has any particularly special
           properties, or....

                        BUCKELL
    s1-   Frankly, we don't know. It's
           something new and Dr. McKenna
           was just beginning a series of
           tests on it this morning.

Stern purses his lips and murmurs an inward 'Hmm'. There is apparently something unusual about this case and he wants to make sure that Ann and Buckell realize it from his deep and profound attitude.

Ann, however, is more concerned with immediacies.

                        ANN
    t1-   Doctor, can't you tell us how
           he is?

Stern looks toward her.

                        STERN
    u1-   Miss Lansing, as far as we've been
           able to determine, Dr. McKenna
           seems to be suffering from nothing
           more than shock.

                        ANN
    v1-   Shock? But... the radiation
           poisoning....

                        STERN
    w1-   We've found no traces of radiation
           poisoning- none that showed up in
           our usual tests, anyway.
                (he turns back to
                  Buckell)
           That's why I wondered whether there
           was anything special about this
           particular isotope.

At that moment, a voice can be heard coming over the hospital paging system.

                        VOICE
                    (filter)
    x1-   Dr. Stern. Dr. Robert Stern. Dr.
           Stern....

                                           (CONTINUED)

14   CONTINUED: (7)

Stern pauses and holds his breath momentarily. Then he looks toward Ann and Buckell.

              STERN
y1-   I'm sorry. Will you excuse me for a moment? I'll be back just as soon as I can.

              BUCKELL
z1-   Yes, of course.

Stern gets up and leaves. Ann and Buckell remain seated.

15   AFT. INT. - M.S. ANN AND BUCKELL ON COUCH

At first they just look straight ahead, as if they intend to remain that way until Stern comes back. Then, Ann looks at Buckell and his face grows grim.

              ANN
a-   Dr. Buckell, I know what you're thinking. But you've got to realize that....

              BUCKELL
b-   I saw how he looked this morning.

              ANN
c-   He just had a headache.

              BUCKELL
d-   Headache? You mean a hangover.

Ann is hurt by this harsh word and glances away. Buckell decides to press his point.

              BUCKELL
e-   I've warned him time and time again. This constant business of going to parties and drinking so much....

Ann rushes to Gil's defense.

              ANN
f-   He's only trying to have a little fun. You know how hard he works. He's got to have some relaxation.

              (CONTINUED)

15   CONTINUED:

        BUCKELL
g- Fun's fun, but this is something
  else. Late hours and too much
  liquor are dangerous partners
  when you're handling the sort of
  stuff we handle. I was afraid
  something like this would happen.

        ANN
h- But it wasn't his fault. He didn't
  even touch the container.

        BUCKELL
i- How do you know? Did you see him?

Ann is silent. She has no real answer for this. Finally
she lowers her head and says something which she sounds as
if she can't entirely believe herself.

        ANN
j- Gil's... always careful when he
  handles isotopes.

        BUCKELL
k- How can he be careful when he's
  so hungover he can't see straight.

Now Ann is becoming annoyed at Buckell's constant harping
on Gil being hungover.

        ANN
l- He wasn't hungover. I was working
  with him all morning. Don't you
  suppose I'd know if... if...

She can't go on and, turning away from Buckell, she bows
her head and clenches her fists.

Now Buckell begins to show a little of his new mellowness.
He looks at Ann, then places his hand gently on her shoulder
and continues in a softer tone.

        BUCKELL
m- Ann, I know how you feel about him.
  You always stand up for him when
  something happens. But don't you
  see what all this is leading to?
  Gil thinks more about this... this
  night life than he does about you
  or me or his work.

        (CONTINUED)

15 CONTINUED: (2)

   Again Ann is heavily defensive.

                    ANN
      n-   That's not true. Gil's work is
           his whole life. But... he just
           wants to have a little fun. Is
           he really asking so much?

16 AFT. INT. - M.L.S. WHOLE OF WAITING ROOM

   Stern re-enters from the doorway. Ann and Buckell break
   off their face-to-face discussion and go back to presenting
   a reasonably solid front to the hospital. Stern crosses
   to his previous chair.

                    STERN
           Sorry I was so long.

17 AFT. INT. - M.S. THREE OF THEM

   Stern sits down and faces Ann and Buckell.

   Ann glances at Buckell and snatches the lead in questioning
   Stern away from him.

                    ANN
      a-   Dr. Stern. You said he was going
           to be all right.

                    STERN
      b-   Well, we haven't been able to
           find anything particularly wrong
           with him.

                    ANN
      c-   Can we see him then?

                    STERN
      d-   Oh yes. In a day or two.

                    ANN
      e-   A day or two?

                    STERN
      f-   He's asleep now. We gave him a
           pretty heavy sedative around
           noontime. Why don't you drop by
           tomorrow?

                                            (CONTINUED)

17   CONTINUED:

                    BUCKELL
     g-   When will he be discharged?

                    STERN
     h-   Well, I think we ought to keep
          him here a few more days. He's
          had quite a shock and it'll take
          him some time to get his strength
          back.

                    BUCKELL
     i-   Yes, he can use the rest.

                    STERN
     j-   I wouldn't worry about him, though.
          He'll be back to his old tricks
          inside of a week.

At this, Ann and Buckell turn and look at each other
meaningfully.

                              FADE OUT.

FADE IN:

18   AFTERNOON INT. - C.U. NEWSPAPER BEING HELD BY MAN IN
     HOSPITAL BED

     Presently it drops down and behind it we see GIL, sitting
     up in bed and looking none the worse for wear.

     Gil is a good looking man in his early thirties with a
     serious face but with eyes that twinkle. He has labored
     in science ever since his high school days but, though he
     has done well and worked hard, he has never allowed his
     work to so occupy him that he has no time for enjoyment.

     Gil looks back and forth a little restlessly, then fixes
     his gaze on the large, covered water pitcher on the table
     beside him.

19   M.C.U. WATER PITCHER ON TABLE

     Gil's hand enters and picks up a glass standing next to
     the pitcher. He holds it in frame and turns it over a few
     times as if examining it carefully. Then his other hand
     enters and removes the top of the water pitcher and lifts
     out a small flask of gin from inside.

20   M.S. GIL IN BED

He pours himself a quick one and downs it. He is just about to pour another when there is a noise outside his door. Quickly he secrets the gin flask back inside the pitcher, places the glass carefully next to it, and resumes reading his paper.

21   M.S. DOORWAY

Door opens and a NURSE enters the room. She is about fifty-five, with grey hair and a cheery smile. Obviously much of her life has been spent in hospitals and she takes things much less seriously than might younger nurses.

Camera follows as the Nurse marches over to Gil's bed. Gil pretends to be tremendously engrossed with his newspaper.

              NURSE
a-   Well now, Dr. McKenna. Are we
      feeling nice and strong this
      afternoon?

Gil looks up from his paper slowly.

              GIL
b-   Miss Wells, until a moment ago I
      felt strong enough to shake down
      the very walls of this hospital.
      But as soon as you entered the
      room, your beauty so overwhelmed
      me that now I feel as weak as a
      day-old child again.

The Nurse reacts to this in an appropriate fashion.

              NURSE
c-   Now never mind that. Doctor says
      we're to have an airing this
      afternoon.

              GIL
d-   An airing?

              NURSE
e-   On the solarium roof, where there's
      plenty of sun.

              GIL
f-   Well great. Let's go.

He starts to climb out of bed but the Nurse holds him back.

(CONTINUED)

21   CONTINUED:

                         NURSE
g-   Not so fast. Wait till I get a
      wheel chair.

                         GIL
h-   A wheel chair?

                         NURSE
i-   Doctor says we're not to overtax
      our strength unnecessarily.

Gil sits back with an amused look of resignation on his face.

                         DISSOLVE TO:

22   AFTERNOON EXT. - L.S. DOORWAY LEADING FROM ROOF INTO HOSPITAL

Nurse is wheeling Gil through the doorway and onto the roof. Camera dollies back and they come into M.L.S.

                         GIL
a-   Really, Miss Wells. This is completely
      unnecessary. I can walk without any
      trouble at all.

                         NURSE
b-   Doctor's orders. We're not to
      overtax ourself. Now let's just
      lie back and relax while I find
      us a nice sunny place.

She wheels him around some more as the Camera follows and finally places him near the edge of the roof and next to a table which is piled high with magazines.

                         NURSE
c-   There we are. How's this?

                         GIL
d-   Fine.

                         NURSE
e-   There are plenty of magazines to
      read. And perhaps some of the
      other patients will come over and
      talk to you.

                         (CONTINUED)

22   CONTINUED:

                        GIL
    f-   Dandy. We can discuss bedpan
            techniques and their applications.

Nurse hands him a couple of magazines.

                        NURSE
    g-   Now if you need anything, just
            call. There'll be somebody to
            hear you.

                        GIL
    h-   I'll keep that in mind.

Nurse walks away and Gil settles down to read.

23   M.C.U. SUSPICIOUS OLD WOMAN

She is sitting in a wheel chair and staring intently at
something. Suddenly she begins to wheel herself forward.
The Camera follows her and we see that she is headed for Gil.

24   M.S. GIL READING QUIETLY.

Old woman wheels herself into frame.

                        OLD WOMAN
    a-   Pardon me, young man.

Gil looks up and lowers his magazine.

                        GIL
    b-   Madam?

                        OLD WOMAN
    c-   You haven't by any chance seen the
            latest copy of Sickness and Health,
            have you?

                        GIL
    d-   No, I don't believe so. But it
            might be on the table.

                        OLD WOMAN
    e-   Would you see if you can find it?
            I'd look for it myself, but it's
            so hard for me to stretch. My
            arthritis, you know.

                                        (CONTINUED)

Pearl Driggs actually *was* wheelchair-bound at the time of shooting *Sun Demon,* her daughter Marilyn King told me, but she stands in this behind-the-scenes candid with son-in-law Clarke. According to Marilyn, "Mom loved it!" (loved playing the hospital roof patient).

24   CONTINUED:

Gil raises his eyebrows, then puts aside his magazine and, with some discomfort, begins to shuffle through the magazines on the table next to him.

25   M.C.U. GIL LOOKING THROUGH MAGAZINES.

                    OLD WOMAN'S VOICE
a-   But I do want to read the latest issue. The lady across the hall from me said that there's a wonderful article in it called "Making the Most of Your Hospital Vacation", or something like that. It sounds like just what I need to cheer me up. It does get awfully trying, you know- day after day, confined to a wheel chair.

Finally Gil comes across the magazine and pulls it out.

26   M.S. GIL AND OLD WOMAN

Gil hands her the magazine.

                    GIL
a-   I think this is it.

                    OLD WOMAN
b-   Oh yes. Thank you so much. Well, I hope you won't think me rude if I don't talk to you for a while. But I do want to read this article.

                    GIL
c-   Not at all.

The Old Woman wheels herself away. Gil stretches and looks around. Then he leans back and adjusts his pillow to better support his head.

27   AFTERNOON EXT. - M.C.U. GIL

He moves around to get more comfortable and finally closes his eyes. His breathing deepens until it is obvious that he is asleep. The sun is shining full on his face now.

28   L.S. SUN IN SKY

It is burning down fiercely.

                                        DISSOLVE TO:

29   L.S. SOLARIUM ROOF

Gil (back to Camera) is asleep in his chair. Old Woman (back to Gil) is seated near him, reading.

30   M.C.U. OLD WOMAN

She puts down her magazine and sighs- obviously finished with her article. Then she looks around for something else to do. Finally she decides to bother Gil again and starts to turn her chair around.

31   M.L.S. GIL AND OLD WOMAN

Gil is in foreground with his back to the Camera. Old Woman is in background and is just turning her chair around.

>   OLD WOMAN
>   Young man. I hate to bother you
>   again, but....

32   C.U. OLD WOMAN

She has caught sight of something that makes her stop short and stare with frightened fascination. Then, finding her voice, she screams loudly.

33   M.L.S. SAME SET-UP AS SCENE 31

Old Woman continues screaming. Gil is roused and sits up, though we still see only his back. Old Woman begins screaming more loudly and struggles to back her wheel chair away.

>   GIL
>   a-   What is it? What's the matter?
>
>   OLD WOMAN
>   b-   Oh, stay away. Your face.... It's
>   horrible.
>
>   GIL
>   c-   My face?

Slowly he puts his hands to his face and they freeze there as he feels something different from what he expects.

>   GIL
>   (almost a scream)
>   d-   My face!

He leaps from his chair and flees the roof.

20.

34   AFTERNOON INT. - M.S. GIL FROM REAR

He runs into the hospital corridor and the Camera dollies after him. He rushes past other patients and nurses and they are at first startled, then shocked when they see him. Finally he reaches his own room and rushes inside.

35   M.S. INSIDE GIL'S ROOM

Gil rushes in and over to the mirror above the sink. Still we cannot see enough of his face to know exactly what has happened but we get the idea that it must be something horrible. Camera dollies in quickly to a M.C.U. of his clenched fist that rests atop the sink. The lower portion of the mirror can be seen in the upper part of the frame, but we cannot see Gil's reflection. He clenches and un-clenches his fist agonizedly.

              GIL'S VOICE
            (just a whisper)
a-   Oh no, no. It' can't be.
            (yelling)
   Nurse. Nurse. Nurse.

On the last 'Nurse', Gil raises his fist and crashes it into the mirror- shattering the glass into a spider web pattern. Camera follows the fist and, in the split second before the mirror is smashed, we see just enough of Gil's reflection to know that he has changed into something horrible. Then it becomes distorted and unreal by the broken glass.

              GIL
            (still yelling)
b-   Come quickly!

He pulls his hand away from the shattered mirror and blood drips from it.

              GIL'S VOICE
            (now a whisper)
c-   Come quickly.

                            DISSOLVE TO:

"Oh noooo — it can't *beeeee!*"

STOCK SHOTS:

1. Man swathed in sheets being wheeled through hospital corridor on high stretcher.

2. Operating Room with various doctors and nurses clustered around the table.

3. Hospital Lab technician examining slides under a microscope.

4. X-rays on viewing screen being examined by doctors.

5. Another shot of man being wheeled through hospital corridor on high stretcher.

                                      DISSOLVE TO:

36   AFTERNOON INT. - M.S. AN OFFICE IN THE HOSPITAL

Stern is seated on the edge of the desk facing Ann and Buckell who are seated side by side in two chairs. Both of them look very worried.

                     STERN
a-   I hope you'll forgive my meeting you in here. But the fact is, I think we'll be able to talk a little better than in the waiting room.

                     ANN
b-   But Dr. Stern, I don't understand. You said he was going to be all right. You said there was nothing wrong with him.

                     STERN
c-   Yes, I know. And by every normal rule of Medicine.... But, that's neither here nor there.
        (he turns to Buckell)
I assume you people have read Charles Darwin.

                     BUCKELL
d-   Why yes, of course. But....

                     STERN
e-   Darwin, you know, devoted most of his life to the study of Evolution- the process by which Life has developed down through the centuries from primitive, one-celled organisms to complex organisms like Man.

                                              (CONTINUED)

36   CONTINUED:

                    ANN
f-   But I don't see what this has to do
        Gil. You said he'd had some kind
        of an attack and....

                    STERN
g-   Miss Lansing, Dr. McKenna has fallen
        victim to one of the strangest and
        most baffling medical phenomena I've
        ever seen- or even heard of.
                (he pauses a moment
                 to let this sink in)
        But let me try to explain what
        I mean.

Stern quits the desk and starts across the room to a wall
on which various rolled-up charts are hung. He glances up
and down the charts.

                    STERN
h-   Umm... I think.... Yes, here we are.

He pulls down one of the charts. On it is a series of
drawings showing the eight animal phyla- from the proto-
zoas through to Man. Stern glances over the chart, then
turns to face Ann and Buckell who are looking at him
curiously.

                    STERN
                (pointing to chart)
i-   This is a chart showing the basic
        classes of beings in the Animal
        kingdom, from the little one-celled
        Amoeba up here in the corner, through
        the intermediate classes, and right
        down to Man.
                (he turns away from the
                 chart for a second)
        All life on earth began with the
        one-celled animals and biologists
        estimate that it took several
        million years to evolve a form as
        complex as the mammals- as Man.
        But here's something very interesting.
        During the nine month period from
        conception to birth, the human being
        goes through this same evolutionary
        process in the womb.
                (he turns back to the chart)
        In other words, he first begins as a
        one-celled animal, then he becomes a
        collection of cells, then starts to
                            (MORE)

                                (CONTINUED)

36   CONTINUED: (2)

                              STERN (Cont'd)
               assume a definite form as the cells
               begin to take on specialized functions,
               then passes through a state when he's
               similar in structure to a fish, then
               similar to an amphibian, then a
               reptile, and finally he passes into
               the mammal state where he begins to
               take on more and more the appearance
               of a human being.
                        (he turns away from the
                         chart and back to Ann
                         and Buckell)
               Now. We know that each person goes
               through this evolutionary process
               before he is born. And, it's not
               inconceivable that this process
               could be reversed due to some out-
               side influence.

                              BUCKELL
       j-   What are you getting at?

                              STERN
       k-   I'm getting at something which, so
               far, has never been anything more
               than a hodge-podge of theories and
               inconclusive experiments.

Stern rolls up the chart and pulls down a movie screen.
Then he walks back to the desk.

                              STERN
       l-   I hope you don't mind if I indulge
               in a few theatrics here, but I want
               to show you some slides which may
               help you to understand what's
               happened to Dr. McKenna.

37   M.S. DESK WITH SLIDE PROJECTOR ATOP IT.

Stern is behind the desk, busying himself with the projector.
Ann and Buckell have moved their chairs so that they are
sitting directly in front of the desk, looking toward the
screen. They are facing right into the Camera, as is the
lens of the projector.

                              STERN
       a-   Er, Dr. Buckell. Could you get that
               light for me, please?

                                            (CONTINUED)

37   CONTINUED:

                    BUCKELL
       b-   Certainly.

Buckell reaches over and turns off the light. At the same time, Stern turns on the projector and flashes a picture of a particularly hideous looking insect on the screen.

(NOTE: THESE SLIDES SHOULD BE INSERTS INSERTED DURING STERN'S SPEECH AT THE DISCRETION OF THE EDITOR. THEY COULD NOT BE SEEN WITH THE CAMERA IN SCENE 37 SET-UP BECAUSE THE SCREEN WOULD BE BEHIND THE CAMERA)

                    STERN
       c-   Recently, some biochemists conducted
             a series of experiments on insects
             to see what effect radiation in
             various forms might have on actual
             living cells. They discovered that,
             in certain cases, the whole appear-
             ance of the cells- and of the insect-
             was radically changed. This is a
             red ant which had been exposed to
             intense amounts of x-rays.

Stern flashes another slide on the screen.

                    STERN
       d-   This is a common housefly after
             exposure to Gamma rays. You'll
             notice the odd attenuation of
             certain features, while others
             have almost entirely disappeared.

Stern flashes another slide on the screen.

                    STERN
       e-   These are not mutants, by the way.
             These insects were perfectly normal
             before being exposed to radiation.
             This one, incidentally, used to be
             a grasshopper.

Stern walks over and turns on the room light.

                    STERN
       f-   Well, I guess you get the idea. It's
             not very pretty, I'm afraid.

Ann and Buckell look bewildered and a little frightened.

                                          (CONTINUED)

37   CONTINUED: (2)

                    ANN
      g-   But I still don't understand. You
           said the other day that you couldn't
           find anything wrong with Gil- that
           all your tests were negative.

38   M.S. SAME AS SCENE 36

Stern is sitting on the edge of the desk again and Ann
and Buckell are facing him.

                    STERN
      a-   That's true. And you told me that
           the isotope involved in the
           accident was a new one which you
           didn't know a great deal about.
           Remember?

Ann and Buckell look at each other.

                    STERN
      b-   Well, now we know something. We
           know that the radiation from that
           isotope caused a peculiar and
           subtle change in the cells of Dr.
           McKenna's body- just as other
           radiation had done to the cells
           in the bodies of those insects.
           It was a change that made him
           unusually sensitive to the normal
           radiation from the very source of
           all life itself- from the sun.

                    BUCKELL
      c-   The sun?

                    STERN
      d-   That's what happened the other
           afternoon. He was sitting out in
           the sun and suddenly... the cells
           of his body reacted. His... whole
           appearance changed into something...
           scaly... almost lizardlike.

                    ANN
      e-   Oh, no.

                    STERN
      f-   The sun was the catalyst. But only
           because his cells have been already
           changed by exposure to whatever
           radiation was emitted by that isotope.

                                        (CONTINUED)

38   CONTINUED:

         ANN
g- But... can't anything be done?
  Surely....

         STERN
h- Not as far as we know.

         ANN
i- Then what's going to... to happen
  to him?

         STERN
j- That's hard to say. He'll have to
  stay out of the sun of course- that
  much is certain. We were able to
  get him over his first attack by
  simply putting him in a dark room.
  Whether or not that would work
  again is a question. Presumably
  these attacks could increase in
  severity and duration until the
  transformation became permanent.

         BUCKELL
k- And, artificial light...?

         STERN
l- No problem with that. As you know,
  the radiation spectrum of tungsten
  and illuminated gas light is quite
  different from that of sunlight.

         BUCKELL
m- Have you told him?

         STERN
n- Yes.

         BUCKELL
o- How's he taking it?

         STERN
p- Not too well, I'm afraid. At first
  he was very bewildered and upset.
  But then, once he understood what
  was wrong with him, he... well, sort
  of retreated into himself like a
  wounded animal.

         (CONTINUED)

38 CONTINUED: (2)

                    BUCKELL
    q-   I received a letter from him this
         morning. He's resigned from the
         Project.

                    STERN
    r-   Yes, he told me. It seems he's
         planning to leave this area en-
         tirely and go off somewhere all
         by himself.

                    BUCKELL
    s-   Is he able to leave? I mean, is
         he well enough?

                    STERN
    t-   Well, that's a question. Physically,
         he's all right- except for this
         terrible sensitivity to sunlight.
         However, this goes beyond just the
         physical.

                    ANN
    u-   Dr. Stern, you don't mean that...
         that something's happened to his
         mind....

                    STERN
    v-   Miss Lansing, he's a very sick man.
         A terrible thing's happened to him
         and he must learn to live with it. To
         To do that, he'll need the help of
         good doctors and the help of his
         friends. If he goes off by himself
         where he'll have neither friends
         nor doctors... well, there's no
         telling what could happen.

                    ANN
    w-   But can't you make him stay in the
         hospital?

                    STERN
    x-   No, I'm afraid we can't do that. All
         we can do is recommend that he stay.
         If he still insists on leaving...
         then we have to discharge him.

39 AFTERNOON INT. - M.S. STERN, ANN AND BUCKELL

    New angle favoring Ann and Buckell. Ann turns to
    Buckell.

                                            (CONTINUED)

39   CONTINUED:

                    ANN
    a-   Dr. Buckell, perhaps if you talked
         to him....

                    BUCKELL
    b-   No, I'm afraid not.

                    ANN
    c-   But he's always looked up to you
         and....

                    BUCKELL
    d-   Ann, nothing I could say would make
         any difference.
                  (he looks at her
                    more directly)
    B   But he might listen to you.

                    ANN
    e-   Me?

                    BUCKELL
    f-   You love him, Ann. You've loved
         him for a long time.

                    ANN
                  (she looks away)
    g-   But... he doesn't love me.

                    BUCKELL
    h-   We can't be sure about that. You
         know how shy he is about expressing
         his feelings. In any case he knows
         how you feel about him. It might
         make a difference.

Ann looks into Buckell's eyes, then she draws herself up
and turns to Stern.

                    ANN
    i-   Dr. Stern, when may I see him?

                    STERN
    j-   Now, if you wish. He's in his room.

                    ANN
    k-   Thank you.
                  (she turns back to Buckell)
         Dr. Buckell, will you wait for me?

                                          (CONTINUED)

39   CONTINUED: (2)

>   BUCKELL
> 1-   Yes, of course, Ann. And good luck.

Ann walks slowly to the door, looking very serious and very lovely. Buckell and Stern stare after her.

                                        DISSOLVE TO:

40   AFTERNOON INT. - M.L.S. HOSPITAL CORRIDOR

Ann is walking along the corridor. She comes to Gil's door.

41   M.S. ANN AT DOOR

She knocks and waits for an answer.

>   GIL'S VOICE
>   (within)
>   Come in.

She opens the door and we see Gil standing by the bed, fully dressed, throwing things into a small suitcase. The windows are covered and the room is illuminated only by a few weak artificial lights. Gil starts to turn toward the door as it opens.

42   C.U. ANN

Her face lights up with happiness at seeing Gil again.

>   ANN
>   Gil.

43   M.C.U. GIL

His face lights up momentarily.

>   GIL
> a-   Ann.

But then the light dies and he turns back to his packing.

> b-   What are you doing here?

44   C.U. ANN

>   ANN
> a-   I came to see you. May I come in?

                                        (CONTINUED)

44   CONTINUED:

                    GIL'S VOICE
     b-   Sure. Why not?

Ann starts into the room.

45   M.S. GIL AND ANN INSIDE ROOM.

Camera is shooting from the other side of the bed. Ann approaches and places her hand on his shoulder.

                    ANN
     a-   Gil....

Gil doesn't look at her but goes on packing.

                    GIL
     b-   So you came to see me, eh? Are you
           sure you didn't just come to see the
           monster? Because if you did, let me
           warn you, I have to be exposed to the
           sunlight for the miraculous trans-
           formation to take place.

                    ANN
     c-   Don't be ridiculous. I came to see
           you. I came to ask you....

                    GIL
     d-   To ask me if I'd stay here and play
           guinea pig for a bunch of idiot
           doctors? No thank you.

                    ANN
     e-   Gil, the doctors might be able to
           help you.

                    GIL
     f-   Huh.

                    ANN
     g-   And it isn't just the doctors. It's
           your friends. We want you to stay.
           We want to be able to help you, too.

                    GIL
     h-   I don't want anybody's help. I just
           want to be left alone.

                    ANN
     i-   But....

                                        (CONTINUED)

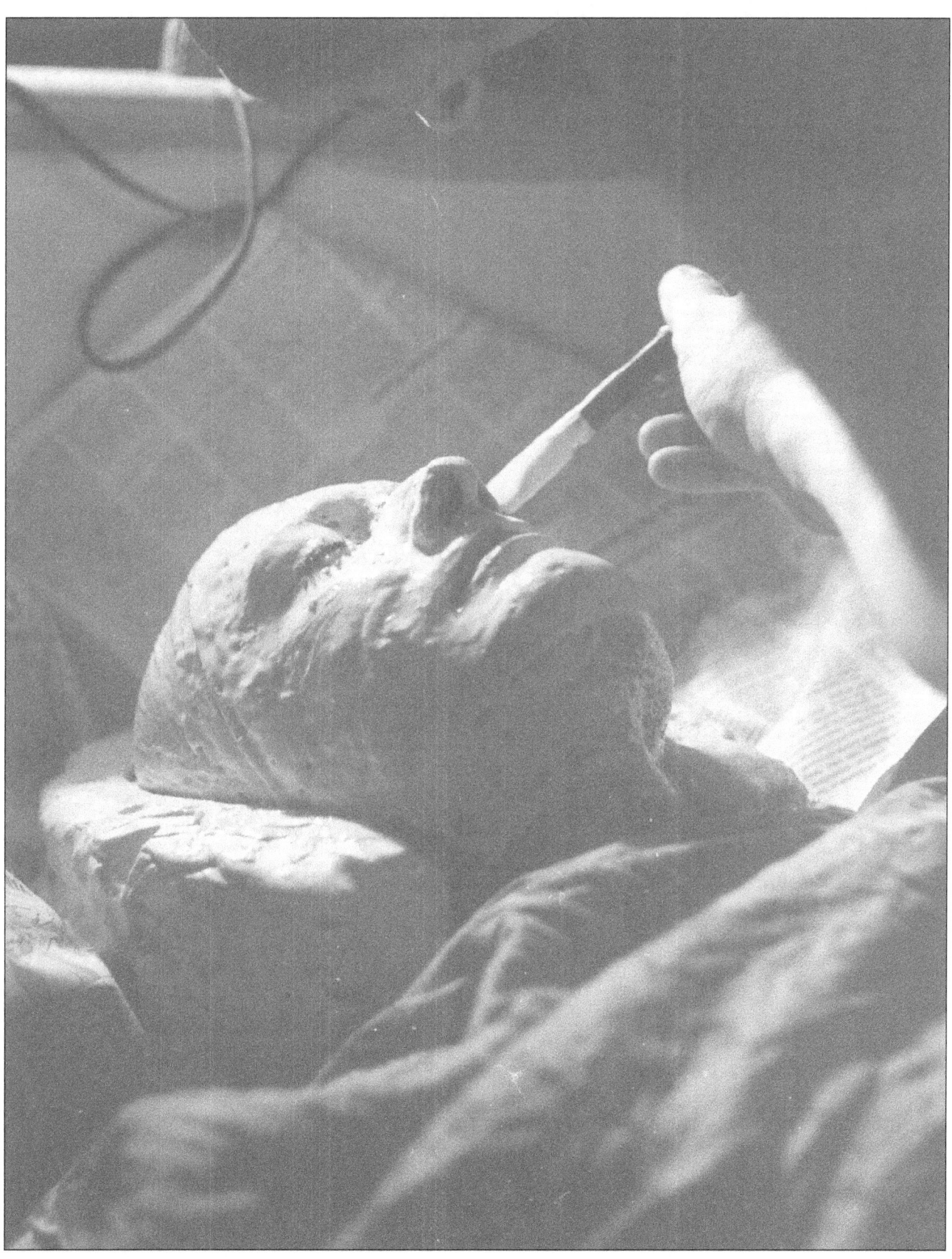

How to Make a Monster: Clarke holds still as Richard Cassarino paints his face with alginate in preparation for making a negative mold of his head. Cassarino would later fill that negative mold with plaster, thus producing a positive head of Clarke. On that plaster head, he would then sculpt in clay the Sun Demon head.

45   CONTINUED:

       GIL
j- Alone, completely alone. That's
  why I'm leaving here tonight.

       ANN
k- Where will you go?

       GIL
l- Does it matter? Just so long as
  I stay out of the sun and don't
  frighten little children.

       ANN
m- Please, Gil....

       GIL
n- Well, if you must know, I'm going
  out to my father's old place.

       ANN
o- Your father's place?

       GIL
p- Yes. It hasn't been occupied since
  he died. But it's far away from
  everything and... and has a lot of
  dark rooms.

       ANN
q- Oh Gil....

       GIL
    (he turns to her and places
    his hands on her shoulders)
r- I've got to go, Ann. This... this
  thing that's happened to me... it's
  changed so much. I'm not the same
  guy any more. I've become something
  horrible. And I don't want people
  to think of me that way. I'd rather
  have them remember me as I was.
  I'd rather have you remember me that
  way.

       ANN
s- Gil....

       GIL
t- No Ann. Don't say anything more.

       (MORE)

       (CONTINUED)

45   CONTINUED: (2)

>   GIL (Cont'd)
>   You'll make me regret too many
>   things, and there's enough to
>   regret as it is. Goodbye. I
>   won't forget all the fine times
>   we had together.

He turns back and resumes his packing.

>   ANN
> u-   Gil, listen to me.

He stops and stares straight ahead, obviously fighting for control of himself.

>   GIL
>   (in a harsher voice)
> v-   Goodbye Ann.

She stops and looks at him.

>   ANN
>   (softly)
> w-   Goodbye.

She steps back out of frame and presently there is the sound of a door closing. Gil bows his head, closes his eyes, and clenches his fists as if he is fighting with himself to keep from running after her. Suddenly he bangs his fists together, rummages in his bag, pulls out a flask of gin, and takes a long drink.

>   DISSOLVE TO:

46   AFTERNOON INT. - M.C.U. BUCKELL

He looks very disturbed. The Camera pulls back to M.S. and we see that he is comforting a broken-hearted Ann in the Waiting Room.

>   ANN
> a-   ... and... and he thinks he's
>   become something... something
>   horrible.

Buckell pats her on the shoulder consolingly.

>   (CONTINUED)

46   CONTINUED:

                    ANN
b-   Oh, Dr. Buckell. We've got to do
       something to help him get well. He's
       going to lock himself away from the
       world, and....

                    BUCKELL
c-   I wonder....

Ann catches a gleam in his eye and she immediately catches hold.

                    ANN
d-   What?

                    BUCKELL
e-   May not mean anything, but I was
       just thinking about Jacob Hoffmann.

                    ANN
f-   You mean Dr. Hoffmann?

                    BUCKELL
g-   He and Gil's father and I went to
       school together, you know. He's
       been working on this problem of
       radiation poisoning for a long
       time. I don't know whether he'd
       be able to do anything, of course....

                    ANN
h-   But if you think.... We've got to
       try something.

                    BUCKELL
i-   He's in Europe right now, though
       perhaps if we wrote him....

                    ANN
j-   Yes, yes. Anything. As long as
       there's even a chance.

She calms down a bit and looks away.

                    ANN
k-   Gil's leaving tonight for his
       father's place. Once he locks
       himself up there, it won't be
       easy to get to him.

                                    (CONTINUED)

46   CONTINUED: (2)

> BUCKELL
> 1- I know. Well, we'll give it a try. Jacob should find this case an interesting one, if nothing else.

FADE OUT.

47   NIGHT EXT. - L.S. SPORTS CAR

It pulls into a gas station in a small beach town and stops near the pumps.

48   NIGHT EXT. - M.S. GIL IN SPORTS CAR

He gets out as the attendant comes over.

> GIL
> a- Fill it, please.

> ATTENDANT
> b- Yes, sir. Check the oil and water, too?

> GIL
> c- May as well.

49   NIGHT EXT. - M.C.U. GIL

He is standing there, near the car, as the attendant takes care of things. He stretches a bit, as if he has been seated in the sports car for a long time. Then he lights a cigarette and looks idly around. Suddenly he sees something.

50   NIGHT EXT. - L.S. LITTLE NIGHT CLUB ACROSS STREET (GIL'S ANGLE)

It is not a particularly high class looking place, but the big neon sign over the door promises liquor and "entertainment".

51   NIGHT EXT. - M.C.U. GIL

He is looking at the bar. Then he comes to a decision and turns his head to address the attendant.

(CONTINUED)

51   CONTINUED:

                          GIL
      a-   I'll be back in a minute. Just...
            going across the street for some
            cigarettes.

                          ATTENDANT'S VOICE
      b-   Right, sir.

Gil steps forward.

52   NIGHT EXT. - L.S. GIL AT CURB

He pauses, checks the traffic, then crosses the street
towards the club on the other side. He disappears inside
the door.

53   NIGHT INT. - M.L.S. INSIDE CLUB

There are a fair number of people about and in the background is the sound of a young woman singing to the
accompaniment of a piano.

Gil enters, pushes his way past several people, and reaches
the bar.

54   NIGHT INT. - M.S. GIL AT BAR

Bartender walks into frame and looks at Gil.

                          BARTENDER
      a-   What'll it be?
                          GIL
      b-   Double gin.

Bartender puts a glass on the bar and fills it. Gil takes
a sip from the glass, then turns sideways (so that one arm
is leaning on the bar) and looks across the club toward
the singer.

55   NIGHT INT. - M.S. SINGER

It is TRUDY and she looks rather interesting. She is
singing some sort of song about being lonely at night.
Camera holds on her long enough to establish something
of her personality from the way she is singing.

56   NIGHT INT. - M.S. GIL

He is watching Trudy, but only because there's not much else in the club worth watching. It is obvious that he doesn't regard her with any particular interest.

57   NIGHT INT. - M.C.U. TRUDY

She continues to sing and, though this is probably not so, it almost appears as if she has noticed Gil, has found something intriguing about him, and is singing her song just to him.

58   NIGHT INT. - M.S. GIL AT BAR

He finishes his drink, puts some coins next to the glass on the bar, and turns to leave.

59   NIGHT INT. - M.C.U. TRUDY

She is still singing. We can see her eyes move as if they're following Gil to the door. And on her face is a smile that almost seems to say: "He'll be back. I know men."

The sound of the music grows louder and continues over a

DISSOLVE TO:

60   NIGHT EXT. - M.S. GIL AT WHEEL OF SPORTS CAR

Camera is shooting through the windshield and catching Gil in full face. He is driving along a dark country road and the light on his face comes largely from the instruments. The music is coming from the radio now (no singing- just an orchestra). The car swings around a corner and Gil catches sight of something. He slows the car to a stop.

61   NIGHT EXT. - L.S. LARGE OLD HOUSE (FROM GIL'S ANGLE)

It is dark and closed up and looks quite lonely in the moonlight. As it flashes on the screen, the music stops and there is a long second or two of just silence- lonely silence. Suddenly the voice of the radio announcer breaks in.

(CONTINUED)

61   CONTINUED:

                    ANNOUNCER'S VOICE
                       (filter)
            That was Tony Trumbull and his
            orchestra playing, "I'm All Alone
            Each Night".
                       (pause)
            And now, I'd like to say a few words
            to you fellas and gals who are "all
            alone each night."

62   NIGHT EXT. - M.C.U. GIL

       He is looking at the house and doesn't hear the radio at all.

                    ANNOUNCER'S VOICE
                       (filter)
            The Stanton Institute's personality
            course has helped many people with
            just such a problem. Psychologists
            tell us that a person's usually
            lonely because he or she shuts him-
            self away from other people. And
            he shuts himself away because of
            fear or shyness. But the Stanton
            Institute has enabled these people
            to overcome....

       Gil reaches down (keeping his eyes on the house) and shuts
       off the radio. Then he shoves the car into gear and starts
       off again.

63   NIGHT EXT. - L.S. SPORTS CAR

       It moves slowly along the road leading to the house, passing
       the Camera which follows it until the house comes into
       frame. Then it holds on the house as the car continues
       along the road. Everything is absolutely still except
       for the muffled sound of the sport car's engine which grows
       fainter and fainter as the car gets farther away from the
       Camera.

                                                  FADE OUT.

       FADE IN:

64   AFTERNOON INT. - M.S. DESK IN CORNER OF LABORATORY

       Ann is seated behind the desk going over some reports.

                                                  (CONTINUED)

64   CONTINUED:

Suddenly Buckell enters, bearing an open letter. Ann looks up.

                  BUCKELL
a-   I thought you might find this interesting.

He hands her the letter. She reads it over rapidly; then, as its full import strikes her, her face takes on an expression of happiness and relief.

                  ANN
b-   Why, it's from Dr. Hoffmann.

                  BUCKELL
c-   That's right.

Ann reads on a little farther.

                  ANN
d-   And... and he wants to help Gil. Oh, this is wonderful.

                  BUCKELL
e-   I thought he'd come through.

                  ANN
f-   It's been nearly two weeks since we wrote him. I... I'd almost given up hope.

                  BUCKELL
g-   I guess our letter didn't reach him until he got back from Europe.

                  ANN
h-   But he must have answered it right away. Look. He says that he's already on his way here from New York. We'll have to let Gil know right away.

                  BUCKELL
i-   You... haven't heard from him, have you?

Ann looks away, her enthusiasm momentarily dampened.

                  ANN
j-   No.
               (then her enthusiasm
                picks up again)
                        (MORE)
                              (CONTINUED)

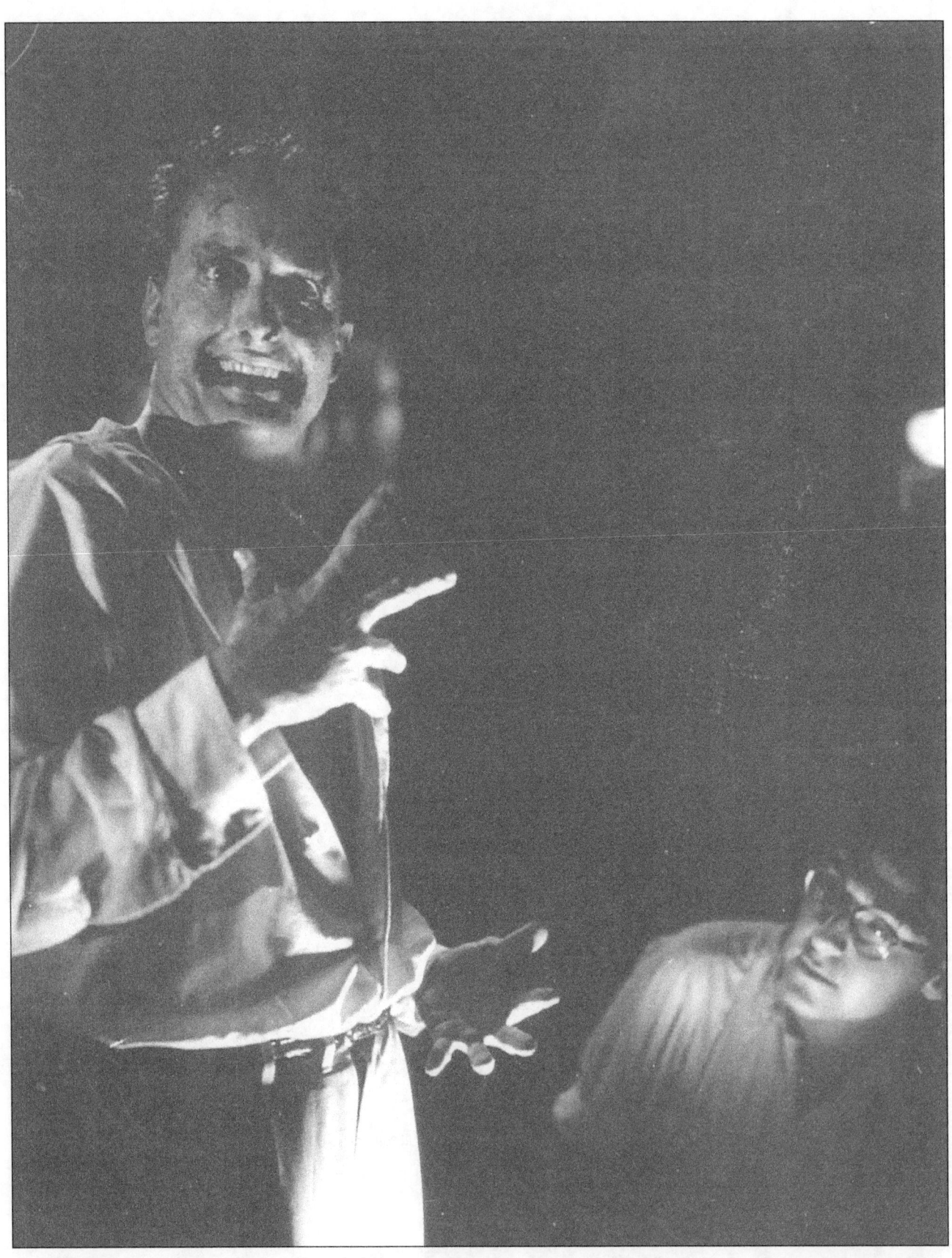

Clarke strikes a wild pose. Lurking below is USC student Marvin Walowitz, who must have been helping out that day. Walowitz later became a sound editor (*Night Tide, Wolfen, TRON, Basic Instinct, Twister,* the 2001 *Planet of the Apes,* dozens more).

64   CONTINUED: (2)

                    ANN (Cont'd)
               But that doesn't matter.. Things
               will be different now. Once we
               let Gil know.... I wonder if we
               can reach him by phone.

                    BUCKELL
k-   Umm, I doubt it. But why don't
               you drive out there and see him.

                    ANN
l-   Do... do you think I should?

                    BUCKELL
m-   I think you want to.
                    (he pauses while she
                     reacts to this)
               And, I think he should be told
               personally, rather than by phone
               or letter. It's probably been a
               long time since he's talked to
               anyone.

                    ANN
n-   You're right. I'll drive out to
               see him in the morning.

                                        DISSOLVE TO:

65   EVENING EXT. - L.S. GIL'S LARGE OLD HOUSE

     It is night and the moon is shining down from overhead.

                                        DISSOLVE TO:

66   M.S. ONE WING OF THE HOUSE

     We can see that all the windows are tightly shuttered.
     Camera pans slowly along the wall, taking in whatever
     items of interest are to be found there, then pans down
     to rest upon a particularly heavily shuttered cellar
     window.

                                        DISSOLVE TO:

67   EVENING INT. - M.L.S. INSIDE CELLAR STUDY

     This study is a room that Gil has fixed up to live in down

                                        (CONTINUED)

67 CONTINUED:

in the cellar. Over in one corner is a small bed that looks as if it has been slept in recently. In the center of the room is a large table piled high with books, papers, and a large gin bottle. Gil is seated behind this table concentrating on a book. His eyes seem more sunken and nervous, there is a look of strain on his face, and he is considerably paler. The room is dimly lit by just a lamp on the table.

68 M.S. OVER GIL'S SHOULDER

We can see that he is reading from a large medical book. On the top of the page is the heading "Diseases of the Skin". Finally Gil pauses, closes the book, and pushes it aside with a sigh.

69 M.C.U. GIL

He sits with his head in his hands for a moment. Then, he reaches for a sheet of paper and a pen. He starts writing furiously but quickly reaches an impasse. His head droops again.

70 M.S. OVER GIL'S SHOULDER

We can see that he has written, 'Dear Ann, I...' It's apparent that he would like to write more, but finds himself unable to.

71 M.C.U. GIL

He looks very unhappy. Finally he crumples up the unwritten letter, tosses it onto the floor, and stands up.

72 M.L.S. INSIDE STUDY

Gil walks to the door, opens it, and exits.

73 M.S. CELLAR

Gil emerges from the study, closes the door behind him, walks across the cellar, and starts to mount the stairs.

74. M.S. INSIDE KITCHEN

Gil emerges from the door leading to the cellar and stands for a moment in the kitchen. The kitchen is large and old fashioned and has not exactly been maintained in too good a state of cleanliness. Dirty dishes from many meals are piled in the sink and other items are strewn around. Gil walks over to the cupboard and, after searching through it, comes up with a can of food. Carefully reading the instructions, he walks over to the stove, then back to the sink where he picks up one of the pots and washes it. Then he empties the contents of the can into the pot and places it on the stove.

DISSOLVE TO:

75. M.S. GIL SITTING AT TABLE

There is an uninspiring plate of hash before him but he has not been looking at it, so preoccupied is he in his thoughts. Finally, he pushes the untouched plate away, stands up, and wanders slowly from the kitchen.

76. M.S. GIL

He walks slowly through the long entry hall on the first floor. Then he stops and looks at something.

77. M.C.U. FRONT DOOR

It is securely locked and bolted.

78. EVENING INT. - M.C.U. OF GIL

The locked and bolted door has obviously served to remind him of his plight.

79. M.S. HALLWAY

Gil turns and starts toward the living room.

80. M.S. LIVING ROOM

Most of the furniture is covered with white dust cloths and thus looks quite eerie. Gil enters and stands for a moment near the gigantic, unused fireplace. Then he crosses

(CONTINUED)

80   CONTINUED:

   to one of the great windows at one end of the room. Almost hesitantly, he pulls back the drapes and opens the casement.

81   M.C.U. WINDOW

   Gil's hands can be seen opening the casement. Beyond is a flat, dark shutter. Gil's hands reach in, unfasten the shutter, and push it open.

82   EVENING EXT. - M.C.U. GIL (FROM OUTSIDE WINDOW)

   The moonlight falls across his face and, for a moment, he almost shrinks back from it. But he blinks his eyes and recovers and gazes out at something.

83   L.S. OCEAN (AS MIGHT BE SEEN FROM GIL'S WINDOW)

   It is shimmering softly in the moonlight.

84   M.C.U. GIL - SAME AS SCENE 82

   He continues to gaze, then a look of bitterness comes over his face and, with a sigh, he withdraws from the window.

85   EVENING INT. - M.S. INSIDE LIVING ROOM

   Gil closes up the window, redraws the drapes, and starts slowly back across the room. Suddenly something on a small table catches his attention.

86   M.C.U. TABLE - GIN BOTTLE AND GLASSES ON TOP

87   EVENING INT. - M.S. GIL

   He pours himself a drink and downs it quickly. He pours another and downs that quickly. But liquor cannot assuage the loneliness inside him and, in a burst of agony, he flings the glasses to the floor and stalks out of the room. Camera follows him until he disappears into the hallway, then holds there. After a moment we hear the front door open and shut.

                                                  DISSOLVE TO:

88   EVENING EXT. - V.L.S GIL

He is walking, all alone, near the edge of a cliff overlooking the ocean. Finally he stops and stares out at the water.

89   M.C.U. GIL

He is looking down at the water and appears dreadfully unhappy.

90   L.S. WATER (HIGH ANGLE FROM TOP OF CLIFF)

It surges back and forth around some wicked looking rocks directly below.

91   M.C.U. GIL

He is looking down at the water with a gleam of fascination in his eyes. Perhaps he might even be wondering if he shouldn't simply end it all then and there. Suddenly there is the sound of a girl's voice far off in the distance.

                GIRL'S VOICE
Tom. Stop it.

Gil is distracted by this and looks towards the sound.

92   L.S. BEACH (FROM TOP OF CLIFF WHERE GIL IS STANDING)

It is very dim down there but the darting figures of several young people can be made out having some sort of midnight beach party.

                BOY'S VOICE
a-   What's the matter? I didn't do anything.

                GIRL'S VOICE
b-   I don't want sand inside my bathing suit.

                2ND BOY'S VOICE
c-   Hey Tom. Did you put the beer in the surf to get cold?

                BOY'S VOICE
d-   Yeah. Long ago.

93 M.C.U. GIL

He almost smiles as he hears these voices. Perhaps they have made him realize that the world is not as dead and as dormant as he has come to believe in recent weeks. Now he turns and looks further down the beach.

94 L.S. LOOKING FAR DOWN THE COAST

Several miles away, the lights of a beach town can be seen.

95 M.C.U. GIL

He is looking at the lights.

96 M.S. GIL

He turns away from the edge of the cliff and starts back along the path leading up to his house.

DISSOLVE TO:

97 M.L.S. SPORTS CAR DRIVING ALONG THROUGH NIGHT

DISSOLVE TO:

98 M.L.S. SPORTS CAR

It pulls up in front of the little club we saw back in scene 50.

99 M.C.U. GIL

He looks towards club.

100 EVENING EXT. - M.L.S. FRONT OF CLUB

Neon sign is flashing off and on, etc.

DISSOLVE TO:

101 NIGHT INT. - M.C.U. TRUDY

She is sitting at a piano and singing a blues song.

(CONTINUED)

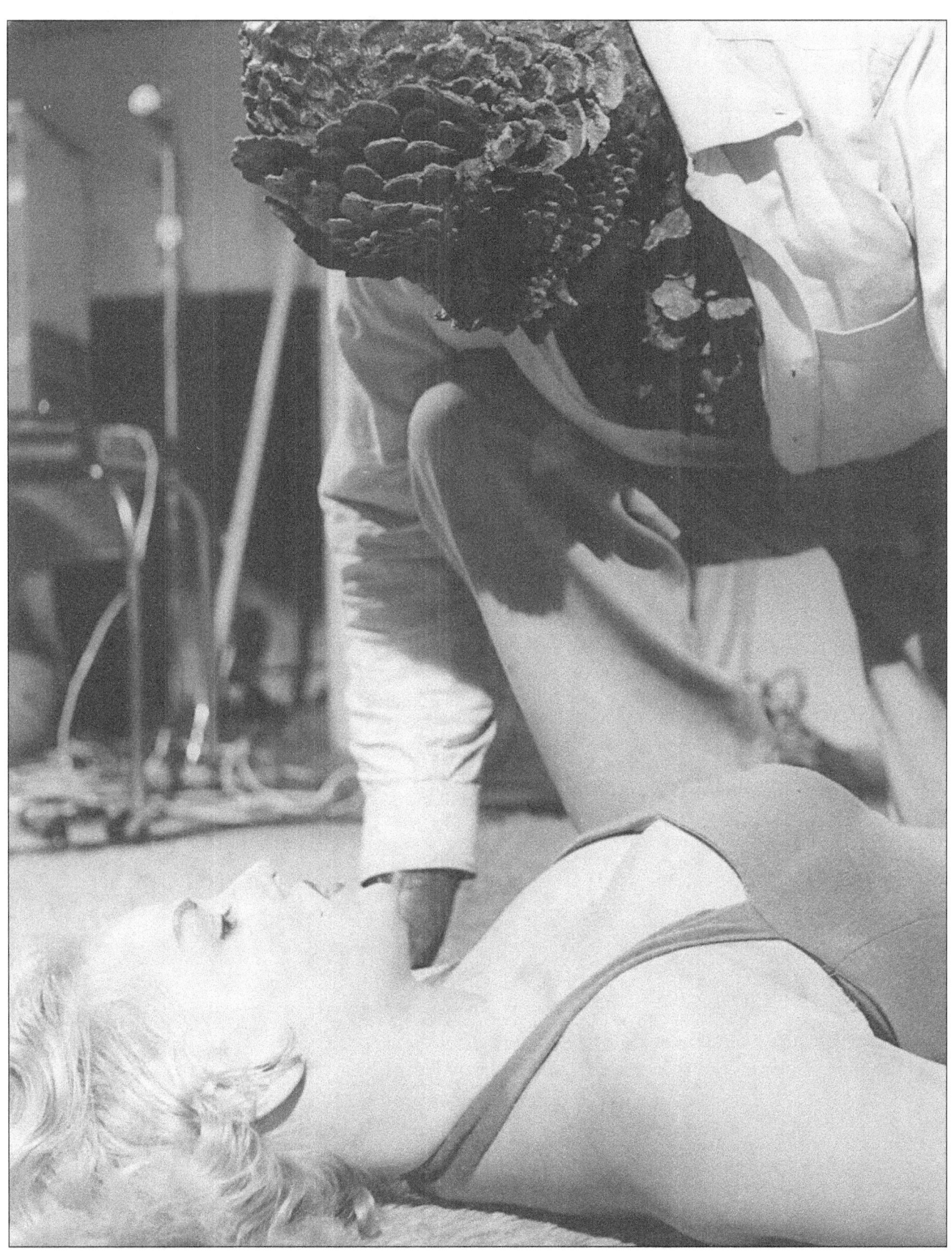

One of the many "Sun Demon menaces Trudy" photos shot for publicity purposes. In the movie, Trudy only sees the Sun Demon once, at a distance, as he strangles George.

101   CONTINUED:

Camera pulls back to M.S. so that we can see a bit more of the club.

102   M.S. GIL AT TABLE

He has a bottle of gin in front of him and is staring dejectedly into his half-empty glass. He doesn't even seem to notice that Trudy is singing.

103   C.U. TRUDY

She continues to sing and, by the angle and the direction of her eyes, it is apparent that she has seen Gil and has recognized him. She smiles knowingly as she sings.

Camera pulls back to M.S. as Trudy finishes her song. There is a scattering of applause which Trudy acknowledges only vaguely. She gets up from behind the piano and starts across the club to Gil's table.

104   M.S. GIL'S TABLE

Gil is sitting there, oblivious to everything. Trudy approaches with a smile on her face. Gil doesn't even notice her.

                      TRUDY
a-   Hello.

Gil doesn't look up.

                      GIL
b-   'Lo.

                      TRUDY
c-   Mind if I sit down?

                      GIL
d-   No, go ahead.

                      TRUDY
               (almost sarcastically)
e-   Thanks.

She sits down, crosses her legs carefully, and leans forward on her elbows.

105   M.S. GIL AND TRUDY

Trudy is leaning forward in such a fashion that the Camera is able to shoot rather far down her cleavage, producing a rather interesting shot. She is smiling at Gil as sweetly as she can.

      TRUDY
a- How about buying me a drink?

      GIL
b- Huh? Oh.
    (he looks at his bottle,
    then pushes it towards
    her)
 You can have some of this, if you like.

      TRUDY
c- I'll need a glass.

      GIL
d- Oh. Yeah.
    (he turns to hail
    a waiter)
 Waiter? Could you bring another glass over here please?

Then he turns back and continues staring into his own glass- his mind far away. Trudy looks at him and appears ready to admit defeat. The waiter enters with the glass. Trudy turns to him.

      TRUDY
e- Never mind, Jack. I'll just have a Creme de Menthe.

These last words get through to Gil and, for the first time, he raises his head and looks at Trudy. Trudy has stopped smiling now, but the certain hardness and look of annoyance that have replaced the smile make her seem even more interesting. Gil stares at her and is evidently taken by what he sees.

      GIL
f- Oh... er, I'm sorry. I'm afraid I haven't been very cordial.

Trudy is ready to get up and leave.

      TRUDY
g- Forget it, Mister. I get the idea.

      (CONTINUED)

105   CONTINUED:

                    GIL
    h-   No, please.

Trudy pauses and looks at him.

                    GIL
    i-   Have a drink with me. How about
         it?

Trudy hesitates, then smiles and sits down again.

                    TRUDY
    j-   Okay, honey.
              (she looks up at
               the waiter)
         Guess you can leave that glass
         after all, Jack.

The waiter leaves the glass and moves off. Trudy leans
forward on her elbows again, smiling, and Gil manages to
smile back as he pours her a drink from his bottle. Both
appear quite ready to become chummy now.

106   C.U. GIN BOTTLE

As Gil sets it back on the table. Gin level can be seen.

                                        DISSOLVE TO:

107   C.U. GIN BOTTLE (SAME AS SCENE 106)

Gin level is much lower now and apparently some time has
passed. We can hear the voices of Trudy and Gil laughing
and enjoying themselves. Camera pulls back to M.S. (same
as Scene 105) and we see Gil and Trudy still seated in the
same position at the table. They've had rather a bit to
drink and this has helped to loosen up Gil considerably.
When the Camera picks them up, they are laughing.
Presently Gil pauses and glances around the club.

                    GIL
    a-   Say, this place is closing up.
         Must be getting late.

                 TRUDY TRUDY
    b-   Don't be silly. It's never late
         until the sun comes up.

                                        (CONTINUED)

107   CONTINUED:

Gil freezes at the mention of "sun" and his problems, temporarily forgotten while he's been talking with Trudy, come back into sharp focus again. Trudy notices Gil's odd reaction and looks concerned.

      TRUDY
c- What's the matter?

      GIL
     (distantly)
d- Nothing.
    (he looks wildly around,
     as if he feels the walls
     closing in on him.)
 Let's get out of here.

      TRUDY
e- Leave? You mean now?

      GIL
f- Sure. Let's... let's take a
 drive. My car's outside.

      TRUDY
g- I'm afraid not tonight.

      GIL
h- Why not? We'll enjoy ourselves.
 We can sit on the beach and...

But Trudy just looks back at him with a disapproving look on her face. Gil calms down.

      GIL
i- Oh. Somebody else, eh?

As if in answer, a large figure suddenly appears next to the table, visible only from the waist down. Trudy's eyes dart over to the figure, then up to his face. Gil's eyes follow hers.

108   NIGHT INT. - M.C.U. GEORGE (GIL'S ANGLE)

George is a large, monolithic sort with enormous shoulders and a rather small head. He is staring at Trudy with something of a lascivious gleam in his eyes.

109   M.S. THREE OF THEM.

George concentrates his attention solely on Trudy.

(CONTINUED)

109   CONTINUED:

                        GEORGE
a-   You ready, Trudy?

                        TRUDY
b-   Oh. George. I... I told you I'd let you know about tonight.

                        GEORGE
c-   Well, I thought I'd make it easy for you and come right on down anyway.

                        TRUDY
d-   Oh...
        (then she remembers Gil)
   Er, George. This is Gil.

                        GEORGE
       (looking quickly over his
        shoulder at Gil)
e-   Hi.
       (looks back at Trudy while Gil,
        who has made a move to shake
        hands, returns to his former
        position)
   Well? Are you ready?

                        TRUDY
f-   I... I haven't finished my drink yet.

                        GEORGE
g-   Okay. Finish it.

                        GIL
h-   Won't you sit down and have one with us?

                        GEORGE
       (looking back over his
        shoulder again)
i-   No.
       (then he turns to face
        Gil more fully)
   And if you don't mind, she's going with me.

                        GIL
j-   Well, it isn't that I mind.... I'm just not sure that she is.

                                    (CONTINUED)

109 CONTINUED: (2)

                    GEORGE
k-   Oh yeah?
              (he turns back to
               Trudy)
     How about it, Trudy?

                    TRUDY
l-   Well George, I don't want to
     leave just yet. Why don't you...

                    GIL
m-   Why don't you leave- that is, if
     you want to, of course.

                    GEORGE
              (turns back to Gil)
n-   Now look, Mister.

                    GIL
o-   Yes?

                    GEORGE
p-   I had a date to take Trudy home,
     and that's exactly what I'md
     going to do.

                    GIL
q-   Not if she doesn't want to go,
     you're not.

George reaches over and takes Trudy's arm, pulling her
to her feet.

                    GEORGE
r-   Come on, Trudy.

                    TRUDY
s-   George. What do you think you're
     doing?

Gil leaps to his feet and catches George by the shoulder.

                    GIL
t-   I guess you didn't hear me. I
     said it's up to her.

George whirls around, tremendously angry now.

                    GEORGE
u-   I don't care what you said.

He smashes Gil in the face.

110   M.L.S. - AREA AROUND GIL'S TABLE

Gil and George begin to fight, violently and spectacularly. After the normal series of ups and downs, Gil finally manages to land a blow that sends George sprawling into the corner and leaves him stunned.

111   M.S. GIL AND TRUDY

Gil wipes his hands and turns to Trudy.

> GIL
> I guess that'll cool him off. Come on. Let's take that drive now.

He takes her by the arm and, before she can say anything, leads her from the club.

                                          DISSOLVE TO:

112   NIGHT EXT. - L.S. SPORTS CAR

It is racing along a deserted road near the ocean. Various shots of this should be interspersed with:

113   M.S. GIL AND TRUDY

They are seated in the front seat of the sports car and the Camera is shooting through the windshield at them.

                                          DISSOLVE TO:

114   M.L.S. ROAD NEXT TO BEACH

Sports car pulls up, stops, and engine shuts off. Gil switches off the lights and leans back.

115   M.S. GIL AND TRUDY

They are seated quietly in the front seat of the car. Trudy's hair is somewhat windblown, making her look even more high grade.

> TRUDY
> a-   Well, that was quite a drive.

                                          (CONTINUED)

115   CONTINUED:

                            GIL
b-   I like to drive fast. Makes it
      easy to forget unpleasant things.

                        TRUDY
c-   That's as good an excuse as any,
      I guess.

                            GIL
d-   How about another drink?

                        TRUDY
e-   Don't tell me you've got a bottle
      in the glove compartment.

                            GIL
f-   Better than that. See that little
      button next to the cigarette lighter?

                        TRUDY
g-   You mean this one?
         (she indicates a button
          on the facia)

                            GIL
h-   Yes. Push it.

116   C.U. TRUDY'S HAND AND BUTTON

Her hand enters and pushes the button. There is a click and a whirring sound and a portion of the facia drops down to reveal a small, well-equipped bar.

                    TRUDY'S VOICE
    A bar.

117   M.S. TWO OF THEM (SAME AS SCENE 115)

Trudy is looking surprised and Gil is smiling.

                            GIL
a-   All the comforts of home. I had
      it put in when I bought the car.

He reaches over, picks up one of the decanters, and pours some gin into two small glasses. He hands one of the glasses to Trudy and keeps one himself.

                                      (CONTINUED)

117   CONTINUED:

                    GIL
    b-   Well....

                    TRUDY
    c-   To the comforts of home.

                    GIL
    d-   Be they ever so humble.

They raise their glasses and drink, then lean back and
stare at the ocean.

                    TRUDY
    e-   You're a strange guy.

                    GIL
    f-   Am I?

                    TRUDY
    g-   When I first came over to your
          table, you didn't even bother
          to look at me. And now look
          where we are.

                    GIL
                (he laughs)
    h-   Well, where are we?

                    TRUDY
    i-   I know where I am, anyway. And
          it's a lot different from what
          I expected.
                (she purses her lips
                 and stares at the ocean)
          You know, George isn't really so
          bad.

                    GIL
    j-   No?

                    TRUDY
    k-   He just gets so... possessive
          sometimes.
                (she turns to him)
          But I like you better.

                    GIL
    l-   I'm glad somebody does.

                              (CONTINUED)

117   CONTINUED: (2)

>   TRUDY
> m-   What? Like you? Oh... Sure I
>   like you. Do you think I would
>   have come out here with you if I
>   didn't?

They are gazing into each other's eyes now, and Gil is beginning to think in terms of something that has not been a part of his life since his accident. Finally he sighs and looks away.

>   GIL
> n-   Trudy, let's take a walk.

>   TRUDY
> o-   A walk?

>   GIL
> p-   Sure. Down by the water. It's
>   a beautiful night.

>   TRUDY
>   (she demures for a
>   moment then gives in)
> q-   Well.... All right.

They set their glasses back in the bar and get out of the car.

>   GIL
> r-   Come on. I'll race you to the
>   water.

>   TRUDY
> s-   Oh wait. I can't run in these
>   heels.

118   M.C.U. TRUDY

She takes off her shoes and carries them in her hand.

119   M.S. GIL AND TRUDY

Gil takes her by the hand and they start running toward the water.

120   V.L.S. HIGH ANGLE OF GIL AND TRUDY RUNNING ACROSS THE
        SAND

        They reach the edge, then leap back to avoid an incoming
        wave. We can hear their squeals of enjoyment.

                                                DISSOLVE TO:

121   L.S. LOW ANGLE OF GIL AND TRUDY WALKING ALONG BEACH

        They are walking slowly and arm in arm down next to the
        water. Presently they stop.

122   M.S. GIL AND TRUDY

        Gil looks straight at Trudy, while Trudy looks off at
        the ocean.

                          TRUDY
        a-   I've always liked the ocean-
                particularly at night with the
                moon on the water. It's so
                lovely.

        Gil slips one arm around her and pulls her a little
        closer.

                          GIL
        b-   In the right company, anyway.

                          TRUDY
                    (not appearing to notice his
                     arm, but still gazing at the
                     ocean)
        c-   Or even when you're alone. The
                ocean doesn't seem to care who
                you're with.

                          GIL
        d-   I do, though.

        He starts to embrace her.

                          TRUDY
        e-   Hey. This is a pretty public
                place.

        Gil pulls her closer and she starts to relent.

                          TRUDY
                    (weakly)
        f-   Take it easy, honey.

                                                (CONTINUED)

122   CONTINUED:

Gil kisses her wetly. She holds on for a moment, then struggles to get loose. Gil continues to hold her and she struggles harder. She tries to push him away, and in doing so, pushes herself back into the water where she slips and falls, getting quite wet. Gil rushes in to help her, once he sees what has happened, and gets his feet soaked in the process. Trudy makes the usual noises of a female who has received an unexpected dousing.

DISSOLVE TO:

123   M.C.U. SMALL DRIFTWOOD FIRE

Gil's hand enters and piles some more wood on the blaze.

124   NIGHT EXT. - M.S. GIL AT FIRE

He is putting more wood on the blaze. His shoes and socks are off and his trousers are rolled up to his knees. In the background are some good sized rocks. Gil turns toward them.

                    GIL
a-   How are you doing?

                    TRUDY'S VOICE
b-   I'll be out in a minute.

                    GIL
c-   I hope that blanket's big enough.
      It's the only one I had in the car.

                    TRUDY'S VOICE
d-   It's fine.

Gil goes back to the fire and pokes it busily. Suddenly there is a slight noise from the direction of the rocks and Gil turns.

125   M.S. TRUDY MAKING ENTRANCE FROM BEHIND ROCKS

She is clad only in a blanket that has been arranged with more of an eye for flattering exposure of the female form than for adequate protection against the night air. She walks slowly toward Gil and the Camera follows her until it includes him.

(CONTINUED)

125   CONTINUED:

                        GIL
a-   Well. You don't look too bad at
        all.

                        TRUDY
b-   I'm just glad this isn't a wool
        blanket.

She sits down next to the fire.

                        GIL
c-   Why?

                        TRUDY
d-   Are you serious? Remember, honey.
        I've got nothing on under this.
        And you know how wool is against
        the skin.

                        GIL
e-   Oh.
            (he reaches for one of
             the decanters which he
             has brought down from
             the car)
        Here. You'd better have some of
        this.

                        TRUDY
f-   Don't you think we've had enough?
        We've already fallen in the water
        once tonight.

                        GIL
g-   Just a sip. So you won't catch
        cold.

                        TRUDY
h-   All right.

Gil pours a small amount into a glass and hands it to
Trudy. She downs it quickly and hands the glass back
to him.

                        GIL
                    (flippantly)
i-   I'm sorry about what happened.

                        TRUDY
j-   Forget it. I think it's kind of
        fun.

                                    (CONTINUED)

125   CONTINUED: (2)

                    GIL
              (with a tantalizing
               gleam in his eye)
  k-   If you like, I could take you
       home.

                    TRUDY
  l-   Don't be silly. I can't go home
       like this. We'll have to stay
       here until my clothes dry out.

Gil smiles, having expected this reply. They are seated side by side now and Gil moves a little closer to her. Trudy looks particularly interesting, sitting there on the sand with the firelight flickering on her face and only a thin blanket clothing her. Gil bends down slowly and places a gentle kiss on her partially open lips. At first she doesn't respond, then her one hand slowly reaches up, wraps itself around his neck, and pulls him down upon her. He grabs her more passionately and their hoarse excited breathing rises above the distant accompaniment of the surf. Camera holds on them, then pans slowly down their interlocked bodies until their faces are out of frame.

                    GIL'S VOICE
              (whisper)
  m-   Oh Trudy....

                    TRUDY'S VOICE
  n-   Okay, honey....

Camera continues panning down their bodies until it reaches their feet which are seen intertwining and caressing each other.

126   M.S. OCEAN WAVE

It crashes explosively against a pointed rock. The spray dashes high into the air as an obvious symbol of what has just occured between Gil and Trudy, then the spent water ebbs slowly back into the surging ocean.

                                        FADE OUT.

FADE IN:

127 MORNING EXT. - M.S. STRETCH OF SAND

It is early morning and the sun is casting long shadows of rocks, etc. over the sand. The Camera pans over and we see Gil and Trudy lying side by side on the sand, fast asleep. Their hands are clasped together and it is easy to tell, from the depth of their slumber, that they are rather exhausted from an eventful night.

128 L.S. CLIFF BEHIND BEACH (SHOT FROM BEACH)

The great, round, red ball of the sun is halfway above the ledge.

129 M.C.U. GIL

He is still lying on the sand, fast asleep. The last of the shadows passes from his face and it becomes fully illumined by sunlight. Suddenly his eyes snap open and he looks straight up at the sky- horrified by the fact that it is daylight.

130 M.S. GIL AND TRUDY

Gil sits bolt upright and looks wildly around. He glances once at Trudy, then leaps to his feet and races for his car. The Camera follows him.

131 M.S. SPORTS CAR

It is sitting at the edge of the road where Gil had parked it the previous evening. Gil rushes up to it, climbs behind the wheel, and presses the starter button. The engine refuses to respond and, panic-stricken, he presses the button again and again.

132 M.S. TRUDY

She is still sleeping peacefully on the beach. In the background we can hear Gil trying to start his car. Trudy turns over lazily and prepares to go on sleeping, but suddenly she hears the car trying to start and this rouses her. She sits up and looks toward the car.

60.

133 MORNING EXT. - L.S. SPORTS CAR (FROM TRUDY'S ANGLE)

Gil is still pushing the starter button frantically. Suddenly the car roars into life.

134 M.S. TRUDY

She leaps to her feet and runs toward the car, shouting. Camera follows her. In the background we see the car pulling away.

135 M.S. TRUDY (FROM ROAD)

She runs toward the Camera until her face is in C.U. She calls loudly and angrily, but to no avail. Then, looking anything but happy, she turns back to the beach.

136 M.S. SPORTS CAR (FROM SIDE-TRUCKING)

Gil is hunched over the wheel and racing along, trying desperately to get back to the darkness of his house before another transformation sets in. The sun is farther up now and things are much brighter. There is no top to the car and Gil can find nothing with which to shield himself.

137 M.L.S. SPORTS CAR (CAMERA STATIONARY)

It races past the Camera in a cloud of dust. After it passes, the Camera swings around to reveal a motorcycle cop hiding behind a bush.

138 M.S. MOTORCYCLE COP

He looks after the Sports Car, then starts up his vehicle and roars off in pursuit.

139 VARIOUS SHOTS OF COP CHASING SPORTS CAR

140 M.S. GIL (THROUGH WINDSHIELD)

He looks desperately on either side of the road for some way to escape the cop. Suddenly he sees something.

141 MORNING EXT. - L.S. SPORTS CAR

It roars up to a tiny side road, largely hidden by overgrowth, and slides into it.

142   M.S. GIL (THROUGH WINDSHIELD)

He is fighting with the wheel as the car slides through the abrupt turn and into the road.

143   M.L.S. SPORTS CAR

Gil pulls it behind a tree and looks anxiously out at the main road.

144   M.C.U. GIL

He is looking anxiously out at the main road. The sound of the cop's motorcycle grows closer and closer.

145   M.L.S. MAIN ROAD (FROM SIDE)

The cop on the motorcycle grows closer and zips past Gil's hiding place without seeing him.

146   M.C.U. GIL

He breathes a sigh of relief, then starts the car again and prepares to pull away.

DISSOLVE TO:

147   M.S. GIL (SIDE-TRUCKING)

He is still driving furiously. Then, he abruptly turns into a side road.

148   M.S. GIL (THROUGH WINDSHIELD)

He roars along. Suddenly he sees something and pulls to a stop.

149   MORNING EXT. - L.S. FRONT OF GIL'S HOUSE (FROM GIL'S ANGLE)

A sedan has just pulled up and the figure of a woman can be seen getting out.

150   M.S. CAR, HOUSE, AND WOMAN

The woman is Ann. She goes over to the front door and stands there hesitantly.

151   M.C.U. GIL

He is staring at Ann from front seat of the Sports Car and it is obvious that he is not happy to see her under the present circumstances. For the moment, the fact that she is there, blocking his way (as it were) to the house, makes him forget about the blazing sun overhead. He absently puts his hand to his brow as if he has a headache. Suddenly, the spell comes on and he flings both hands over his face.

152   L.S. SUN

It seems to come closer and closer until it fills the entire screen.

153   M.S. ANN AT FRONT DOOR

She has been ringing the bell but has gotten no answer. This surprises her because she knows that Gil cannot be out in the daytime and she wonders, therefore, if he is sick or hurt somewhere within the walls of that gigantic old place. She is just about to look for another way to gain entrance when she hears the sound of the Sports Car engine growing closer and closer. She turns quickly (into Camera and M.C.U.) and looks. An expression of recognition comes over her face.

154   L.S. SPORTS CAR (ANN'S ANGLE)

It is roaring up the hill towards the house.

155   M.C.U. ANN

She is looking at the Sports Car.

                    ANN
        Gil....

156   MORNING EXT. - L.S. ANN

She walks down from the front porch and out onto the driveway, as if to meet the car. The car roars towards her without slackening its speed. The question almost arises as to whether Gil might actually be intending to run her down. Ann just stands there innocently.

157 M.C.U. ANN

She is looking towards the car with a smile on her face. The sound of the car grows louder and louder.

158 M.S. ANN IN DRIVEWAY

The sports car races towards her, swerves at the last minute, and, in a cloud of dust, tears past her -- barely avoiding hitting her. We can just catch a glimpse of Gil hunched over the wheel as the car passes the Camera, but not enough of a glimpse to see what is exactly wrong with him. The car speeds on and disappears around the corner of the house.

159 M.C.U. ANN

She is surprised and bewildered. She gazes after the car and calls.

              ANN
    Gil....

Then she starts walking after it towards the corner of the house.

160 M.S. ANN

She is walking around the corner of the house from the front and is heading along the side. We hear the sports car engine (distant) stop.

161 M.C.U. ANN

She starts walking faster and calls out.

              ANN
    Gil....

There is the sound of a door slamming somewhere in the back of the house. Ann reaches the corner.

162 MORNING EXT. - M.S. ANN

She comes around the corner from the side and pauses in the back yard. The sports car is sitting there, deserted. There is no sign of life anywhere. Ann looks around, puzzled. Then her gaze fastens on the back door.

Gil (Clarke) arrives home from the beach after fully transforming behind the wheel of his MG. When Clarke had trouble scaling the side of the house, Tom Boutross parked his Dodge so that Clarke could start his climb from its roof.

163   M.C.U. BACK DOOR

It is not quite closed and it is obvious that Gil must have just passed through it.

164   M.S. ANN

She walks over to the back door and knocks cautiously.

                ANN
     Gil...? Gil...?

There is no answer and, after a moment's hesitation, she pushes the door open and steps inside.

165   MORNING INT. - M.S. FIRST FLOOR HALLWAY

Ann has entered hallway from back door and walks cautiously around. She stops at the foot of the stairway leading to the second floor and calls.

                ANN
     Gil? Please answer me. It's Ann.

Her voice rings hollowly, but there is no reply.

166   M.S. GIL

He is crouching in the murk of his cellar room, his face veiled in shadows so that we just see the slight, nervous glow of his eyes. He is breathing hard and listening to Ann's footsteps which can be heard coming from above.

              ANN'S VOICE
     Gil? I know you're here somewhere.

167   M.S. ANN

She is walking down the hall towards the kitchen. She tries several doors on the way but they are all locked. Finally she heads into the kitchen.

168   M.S. GIL (SAME AS SCENE 166)

He is still crouching in his cellar room. Ann's footsteps have come closer now that she has entered the kitchen.

169 M.S. ANN IN KITCHEN

She looks around as if undecided what to do next. Suddenly something catches her eye.

170 M.C.U. CELLAR DOOR

It is not quite closed.

171 M.S. ANN IN KITCHEN (SAME AS SCENE 169)

She is looking at the door and pauses for a second. Then she walks over and pulls it open. She peers into the darkness below and, after a second, calls.

                    ANN
        Gil? Are you down there?

172 M.S. GIL (SAME AS SCENE 166)

He is becoming more and more disturbed for he realizes that he is trapped if Ann comes down.

173 M.S. CELLAR

Door at top of stairs is open and Ann is silhouetted against the light from the kitchen.

                    ANN
        Gil? I'm coming down.

She starts down the stairs, each footstep echoing clearly through the murky dimness of the cellar. She reaches the bottom and starts walking in the general direction of Gil's room.

174 MORNING INT. - M.S. GIL IN ROOM (SAME AS SCENE 166)

He can hear Ann's footsteps getting closer and closer and he grows more and more upset. Suddenly the footsteps stop. He listens, scarcely daring to breath.

175 M.S. ANN

She is standing outside the door to Gil's room. She feels certain that he is in there but she is now a little hesitant about invading his privacy. Finally, she screws

(CONTINUED)

175   CONTINUED:

up her courage and reaches for the door. She pushes it open slowly and stands there in the doorway, trying to pierce the gloom inside.

           ANN
a-   Gil?

           GIL'S VOICE
b-   Go away.

           ANN
c-   No, Gil. I must talk to you.

           GIL'S VOICE
d-   I don't want to talk to anyone.

           ANN
e-   But it's important. Please come out.

           GIL'S VOICE
f-   I... I can't

           ANN
g-   Then I'll come in. Where's the light switch?

           GIL'S VOICE
h-   No, no. Don't turn on the light. Please....

Ann fumbles along the wall next to the door and finds the light switch. There is a click as she flips it on.

176   M.C.U. ANN

She sees Gil and there is something like a look of surprise on her face.

177   MORNING INT. - M.S. GIL SITTING ON EDGE OF BED

His head is buried in his hands so that she cannot see his face. Finally he raises his head slowly and the dimish light falls across his face -- and we see that it has changed back to normal. There is a mixture of emotions in his eyes. He is glad to see Ann, yet he is also ashamed to face her. Ann enters the frame and sits down on the bed next to him. He doesn't look at her but continues to stare at the floor in front of him, an utterly dejected figure.

(CONTINUED)

177   CONTINUED:

                    ANN
a-   Oh, Gil....

                    GIL
b-   You shouldn't have come.

                    ANN
c-   But I had to. I've got some
        good news.

Gil doesn't react to this and there is a pause.

                    ANN
d-   How have you been?

                    GIL
e-   All right.

                    ANN
f-   We've missed you, back at the
        Project.

He says something but continues to stare at the floor.

                    ANN
g-   Things... don't seem the same
         anymore. We're hoping you'll
        come back to us some day.

                    GIL
h-   Come back? How can I ever come
        back with this... this....

                    ANN
i-   But that's what I wanted to talk
        to you about. Do you remember
        Dr. Jacob Hoffmann?

                    GIL
j-   Hoffmann? No.

                    ANN
k-   Yes you do. He and your father
        went to school together.
        Dr. Buckell knows him too.

                    GIL
l-   Yeah. So what?

                                    (CONTINUED)

177   CONTINUED:

                        ANN
        m-   Well, Dr. Hoffmann's been
                studying radiation poisoning
                for a long time. He's been
                able to cure a lot of people.
                And after you left, Dr. Buckell
                and I wrote him about you.
                Yesterday, we got a letter back.
                He's offered to help you.

Gil says nothing.

                        ANN
        n-   Gil, don't you realize what
                this means? Maybe he can cure
                you.

178   M.S. ANN AND GIL (ANOTHER ANGLE)

Gil leaps to his feet impatiently and begins pacing up
and down.

                        GIL
        a-   I don't want anybody's help.
                I just want to be left alone.

                        ANN
        b-   But....

                        GIL
        c-   Ann, can't you understand? I'm
                beyond anybody's help. This...
                this thing I've got is different
                from normal radiation poisoning.
                What do you think all these
                medical books are doing here?
                For days I've been reading every-
                thing I could find about radiation
                poisoning. My case is different.
                It's not in any of the books. I
                can't be cured.

                        ANN
        d-   But you can't stay locked up
                here for the rest of your life.

                                        (CONTINUED)

178   CONTINUED:

                    GIL
    e-   What else can I do? I can't run
         the risk of being exposed to the
         sun. You don't realize how
         horrible it is. I turn into...
         into something hideous. My face
         gets.... Oh, what's the difference?

He sits down on the bed again, looking utterly discouraged.

179   M.S. GIL AND ANN (SAME AS SCENE 177)

Ann leans towards him, sympathetically.

                    ANN
    a-   Gil, why don't you try? Dr.
         Hoffmann's a very brilliant man.
         I'm sure he can help you.

                    GIL
    b-   How can he?

                    ANN
    c-   At least let him try. He's
         offered to come here and examine
         you. You won't even have to
         leave the house.

Gil says nothing.

                    ANN
    d-   He'll be here this afternoon. I
         can drive him up here to see
         you. Please Gil.

                    GIL
    e-   No, no. It won't do any good.

                    ANN
    f-   Please Gil. You can't just give
         up. You've got to at least see
         him. He's come all this distance....

                    GIL
    g-   No.

Now, in her earnestness and desperation, Ann takes Gil
by the arm and tries to make him face her. Her voice
becomes filled with more and more emotion.

                                            (CONTINUED)

179   CONTINUED:

                    ANN
    h-   Why not? Why can't you let
         us help you? Don't you want
         to get well and... and live
         in the world again?

These words have caught Gil and he looks at her. She has
lost nearly all her reserve now and in her eyes is an
open confession of the love she bears for this afflicted
man before her.

                    ANN
    i-   I.... You don't know how awful
         it's been, wondering about you,
         worrying, hoping. In the
         name of Heaven, if you don't
         care about yourself, at least
         consider the people who...who
         do.

He realizes what she has been saying between the lines
and with her eyes and, as he gazes at this lovely woman
who is pleading with him about something that has larger
ramifications than just the destiny of one man, his heart
melts.

                    GIL
    j-   Ann.

It is a cry of agony and, at the same time, a sigh of
relief. Ann buries her head against his chest and he
flings his arms around her and closes his eyes, as if to
shut out everything save the wonderful feeling of Ann
cradled in his arms.

                    GIL
                 (a whisper)
    k-   I'll see him.

                    ANN
    l-   Oh, Gil.... Th...thank you.

                                        FADE OUT.

180   AFTERNOON INT. - C.U. GIL'S BARE CHEST

A hand is holding a stethoscope on it. The Camera pulls back to M.S. to reveal Gil seated on the edge of the couch in the living room. DR. HOFFMANN is bending over him. Dr. Hoffmann is a sort of modern Van Selsing -- that is, he wears neither pince-nez nor standing collar but is nonetheless a fine symbol of the dedicated, wise, Man of Science. Gil has recovered from his display of emotion at the end of the last scene and his wall of cynical reserve has returned.

                    GIL
a-   You're not going to find out anything that way. My heart's all right.

Hoffmann straightens up and smiles.

                    HOFFMANN
                (German accent)
b-   Now, my boy. You must let us doctors play our games in our own way. We are like actors, you know. We love to show off.

Hoffmann pulls up a chair and sits down.

                    GIL
c-   It's all very well for you to joke. But it's not very funny to me. I thought you were going to help me.

                    HOFFMANN
d-   I hope to, my boy. I hope to. Yours is not such a difficult case as you might think.

                    GIL
e-   No? What are you going to do, cure me by waving a magic wand?

                    HOFFMANN
f-   Not exactly. But from what I know of your case, I believe things are not as bad as you have feared. Fortunately, Buckell was able to send me a sample of the isotope you were working on. I had it analyzed by a good friend of mine in New York. Yes, I think there is hope for you.

                    GIL
g-   Do you really mean it?

(CONTINUED)

180 CONTINUED:

                    HOFFMANN
h-   Gil, I would not mislead you
      about such a thing. It is true,
      you are a very sick man. But you
      can be cured. Of that I am sure.

At last, Gil drops his protective mask of antagonism and
his eyes light up with hope.

                    GIL
i-   Doctor, you don't know how much
      it means to me to get well. For
      weeks I've been locked up in
      this...this mausoleum, only able
      to go out at night, afraid of the
      sunlight. And those horrible
      attacks.... I'll do anything to
      get well.

                    HOFFMANN
j-   Anything?

                    GIL
k-   Yes, yes.

                    HOFFMANN
l-   Because you must be willing to do
      a great deal. I am going to take
      you to a hospital back East.

                    GIL
m-   But... how? I can't be exposed
      to the sunlight. Not even for a
      little while.

                    HOFFMANN
n-   I know that, my boy. And we will
      have to make special arrangements.
      In the meantime, you must not
      leave the house. Not under any
      circumstances.

                    GIL
o-   Not even at night?

                    HOFFMANN
p-   Not even at night. After what
      happened last evening, there is
      too much risk. No doubt you have
      noticed that the transformation
      this time came after less exposure
      to the sun than it did the first
      time.

                                        (CONTINUED)

180 CONTINUED: (2)

                    GIL
    q-   Yes, I did notice.

                    HOFFMANN
    r-   That is because the skin becomes
         more sensitive as time goes on.
         If there should be a next time,
         you might find that it took only
         a very brief exposure to the
         sun for you to change. And you
         might also find that it took a
         very long time to change back.

Gil is visibly shaken by this.

                    HOFFMANN
    s-   So, there must be no more
         wanderings at night. And no
         more drinking. You must rest as
         much as possible while we prepare
         to move you to the hospital.

At this point, Ann enters from kitchen.

                    ANN
    t-   Dinner's ready.

                    GIL
    u-   Ann. You mean you actually got
         that old stove to work?

                    ANN
    v-   Oh, it wasn't so bad. But our
         dinner will be mostly out of cans.
         Really, Gil, you certainly don't
         have much talent for shopping.

They all laugh at this and exit towards the dining room.

                                        FADE OUT.

FADE IN:

181 NIGHT EXT. - L.S. GIL'S HOUSE

It is very late at night and the house looks lonely and
quiet.

182 M.S. WING OF HOUSE

Camera pans along the dark and silent walls and finally
comes to rest on that heavily shuttered cellar window.

                                        DISSOLVE TO:

74.

183 NIGHT INT. - M.S. CELLAR STUDY

Gil has retired for the night and is lying on the bed.

184 M.C.U. GIL'S FACE

His eyes are shut and he is sleeping. Then, very faintly we begin to hear the disembodied sound of happy voices and clinking glasses -- such sounds as we might hear in a bar -- and the Camera begins to dolly in on Gil's face. The sound grows louder as the Camera gets closer. Suddenly Gil's eyes jerk open and the sound halts abruptly. His eyes dart back and forth for a moment, then he relaxes, scrunches around, pulls the covers up, and closes his eyes again.

185 M.C.U. GIL'S FACE

His eyes are shut and he is going back to sleep. But very faintly, we hear Trudy's voice singing that blues song she sang the previous evening. Camera begins to dolly in on Gil's eyes and the sound grows louder. Then, as we are on an E.C.U. of Gil's eyes, they fly open again and the sound stops. His eyes look back and forth more anxiously this time. Then, very faintly, we hear the sound of waves breaking on a beach. A look of alarm comes into Gil's eyes. Then we hear Trudy singing again and the sound of waves segues into the sound of voices laughing and glasses clinking. Suddenly Gil's eyes move violently.

186 M.S. GIL

He sits bolt upright and the sound stops. He waits and listens to see if it will begin again, but there is only silence. Then he untenses himself, swings his legs out from under the covers, and sits dejectedly on the edge of the bed. The Camera moves back a bit until the liquor bottle and glass on the table are on one edge of the frame, of gigantic size in comparison with Gil. He sits there with his head in his hands, then slowly looks up and fastens his gaze on the liquor bottle. The sound of laughing voices and clinking glasses begins again. Gil shakes his head and it stops. He looks at the liquor bottle again. This time the sound of Trudy singing can be heard. Slowly Gil gets to his feet and walks over to the table. He grows larger and larger in the frame as he comes closer until, at the table, only his hands are actually in frame. His hands reach out for the bottle and glass. The sound of laughing voices and clinking glasses fades up behind Trudy's voice and both grow louder as he pours himself a drink. His hand carries the glass up out of frame and the sound grows louder and louder until he swallows the drink, which causes the sound to cease abruptly.

75.

187   M.S. GIL (ANOTHER ANGLE)

He is standing by the table. He puts down the bottle and glass and listens. There is no sound now. Looking somewhat easier at this, he starts back to bed. He reaches the bed and sits down on the edge of it for a moment, rubbing his face with his hands. Suddenly he pauses and his eyes fix on something.

188   M.C.U. DOOR OF HIS ROOM

There is silence at first, then the sound of laughing voices, the sound of Trudy singing, and the sound of the waves begin again. The Camera (subjective now) holds on the door for a moment as the sound grows louder, then it rises slightly and moves slowly towards the door. The sound grows louder and louder and finally, just as the Camera (i.e. Gil) is at the door and about to open it, the laughing voices become dominant and carry across the dissolve.

                                                DISSOLVE TO:

189   M.C.U. TRUDY

She looks very annoyed.

                        TRUDY
a-   ... and without even so much as
        a goodbye, he jumped in his car
        and drove off.

The Camera pulls back to M.S. and we see that she is standing at the bar in the club, surrounded by George and several other male friends. They are listening intently to her story.

                        TRUDY
b-   I've been out with some odd ones
        in my time, but he sure takes the
        cake. He didn't even bother to
        wake me up. Just snuck off like
        a snake.

                        FIRST EXTRA
c-   How did you finally get back
        to town?

                                                (CONTINUED)

189   CONTINUED:

                    TRUDY
    d-   I hitch-hiked. And let me tell
          you, that was no fun either.
          I must have stood there for nearly
          half an hour -- watching car
          after car go by. Most of them
          didn't even bother to look at me.
          Why, I could have been standing
          there with my clothes off and
          they wouldn't even have slowed
          down.

The listeners all smile at this obvious exaggeration.

                    TRUDY
    e-   Finally, I managed to flag down
          an old guy in a truck. And it
          was easy to see what was on his
          mind. But after last night, I'm
          cured. I'm going to stick with
          guys I know.

She slips one arm across George's shoulders.

                    TRUDY
    f-   George honey, I'm sorry about
          what happened last night. He
          must have slipped me one too many
          from that bottle of his.

                    GEORGE
    g-   Forget it, baby. But I'd just
          like to get my hands on that guy.
          Leaving you out there on the beach...

                    TRUDY
    h-   Don't worry. I'm not going to
          let him get away with it. If I
          ever see him again....

Suddenly one of the extras spots something beyond the frame
line and taps George on the shoulder.

                    SECOND EXTRA
    i-   Hey, George.

                    GEORGE
    j-   What?

                    SECOND EXTRA
    k-   Look who just came in.

They all look in the direction indicated by the Extra.

190   M.S. GIL

He walks up to the bar and, without bothering to look around, leans on the rail and beckons to the bartender.

                      GIL
a-   A double gin.

He drums nervously on the bar with his fingers while the drink is being poured and set before him. As soon as it is ready, he seizes it and downs it in two gulps. Then, with the glass still to his mouth, he notices people drawing up on either side of him and his eyes dart back and forth at them. They are Trudy's friends and they press in close, completely surrounding him. He would like to ignore them but he cannot, for they are too many and too close.

                      GEORGE
b-   You've got your nerve, coming
       in here.

Gil lowers the glass slowly.

                      GIL
c-   I beg your pardon?

                      GOERGE
d-   Beg it all you want. After what
       you did last night....

Gil looks down at the bar, trying to ignore them. Trudy pushes her face into the center of the group and forces Gil to face her.

                      TRUDY
e-   Remember me, Honey?

Gil looks at her, embarressed.

                      GIL
f-   Believe me, Trudy, I....

                      TRUDY
g-   Believe you? Not on your life.
       Not if you told me the grass
       was green and the ocean salty.

                      GIL
h-   Look, I know you're mad at me,
       but....

(CONTINUED)

190   CONTINUED:

                        TRUDY
    i-   Mad? Whatever gave you the idea
         I was mad. Why honey, I'm not
         mad. I'm... livid.

    She flings her drink in his face as the others grab him
    and drag him towards the door. He tries to battle, but
    the alcohol in his eyes has temporarily blinded him.

191   NIGHT EXT. - M.L.S. OUTSIDE CLUB

    Trudy's friends drag Gil outside, followed by Trudy, and
    haul him into the alley next to the building.

192   MS. ALL OF THEM IN ALLEY

    They release Gil and back him against the wall.

                        GEORGE
    a-   Now. Anything to say before
         we start in on you?

                        GIL
    b-   I don't suppose you'd let me take
         you on one at a time.

                        GEORGE
    c-   Right.

    He smacks Gil in the stomach. Gil bends double and George
    follows up with a tremendous crack on Gil's chin. Then the
    others leap in and the beating is on.

193   M.C.U. TRUDY

    The shadows of the beating are flickering over her face.
    In the background is the noise of blows landing and
    various moans from Gil. At first, Trudy's expression is
    one of grim satisfaction that Gil is getting paid back for
    the way he humiliated her, but presently it changes to an
    expression of fear and concern. Suddenly, she can stand
    it no longer.

194   M.S. ALL OF THEM

    Trudy leaps at her friends (who now have Gil on the ground)
    and starts pulling them off.

         a-   No, no. Stop. That's enough.

                                              (CONTINUED)

A posed publicity shot with Clarke as Gil and Peter Similuk as tough-guy George, who goes through the movie like Murder looking for a place to happen. The Canadian-born Similuk, a real estate broker and (very) occasional movie actor, died in 2003.

194 CONTINUED:

The friends pause and look at her oddly. Ignoring them, she kneels down next to Gil and cradles his head on her lap.

          GEORGE
b- Hey. What's the big idea?

          TRUDY
c- Oh shut up. Did you have to kill him?

          GEORGE
d- Who's killing him? We're just roughing him up a little.

          TRUDY
e- Roughing him up? Look at his face.

Gil's face is badly cut and bruised and he is only semi-conscious. Trudy struggles to get one arm under his shoulders and raise him up.

          TRUDY
f- Come on. Give me a hand.

          FIRST EXTRA
g- What are you going to do?

          TRUDY
h- I'm going to take him over to my place. That's what I'm going to do.

          GEORGE
i- What?

          TRUDY
j- Well, we can't leave him here. And you guys have done such a job on him that we can't send him home. Come on. Help me.

The friends look at each other doubtfully, then help Trudy pull Gil to his feet.

          TRUDY
k- Okay, honey. Just hold on now and we'll have you all fixed up.

She drapes his arm over her shoulder and indicates for George to get on the other side of him.

(CONTINUED)

194 CONTINUED: (2)

                          TRUDY
1-   Now. Let's see if we can get
       him to my car.

They start walking Gil out of frame.

                                          FADE OUT.

FADE IN:

195 MORNING INT. - C.U. WRISTWATCH ON ARM

It is so placed that we can read the dial. The time is
nine twenty-five. The Camera pans up the arm to the owner's
face. It is Gil and he is fast asleep on a couch somewhere.
Suddenly his eyes open and stare at the wristwatch dial
in panic.

196 M.S. GIL ON COUCH

He is in the living room of Trudy's flat. He rolls over
and sits up. Sunlight, in not overly abundant quantities,
is coming into the room via the windows. Gil rushes over
and pulls down all the shades. Then he looks around and
tries to figure out where he is, and at that moment Trudy
enters from the kitchen bearing a cup of coffee. Trudy is
garbed in tight-fitting slacks and one of those colored
bras that women have taken to wearing in public. Gil
regards her with surpirse.

                          GIL
a-   You.

                        TRUDY
b-   Yes.

                          GIL
c-   But I thought....

                        TRUDY
d-   Honey, I have a soft heart,
       underneath it all. And after
       the boys worked you over, I
       couldn't see leaving you in that
       alley. So we brought you here
       to my place.

                          GIL
e-   Where...?

                                                (CONTINUED)

196 CONTINUED:

                    TRUDY
f-   Don't worry. They're not here.
    You're all alone with me.
         (she hands him the
          cup of coffee)
    Here. Drink some of this.

Gil takes the cup and Trudy starts over to the windows to raise the shades. Gil sees what she is doing and calls to her.

                    GIL
g-   No. Don't.

                    TRUDY
        (she pauses and
         turns to him)
h-   What's the matter?

                    GIL
i-   Don't... pull up the shades.
    You'll let the sun in.

                    TRUDY
j-   So what?

                    GIL
k-   The... er, the sunlight's bad
    for my eyes.

                    TRUDY
l-   Oh. I'm sorry.

She leaves the windows and returns to Gil.

197   M.S. GIL AND TRUDY (ANOTHER ANGLE)

                    TRUDY
a-   How are you feeling?

                    GIL
b-   Awful. My face feels as if a
    bulldozer ran over it.

                    TRUDY
c-   Well, you just lie down and get
    some more rest. I don't mind
    if you stay here.

                    GIL
d-   Stay here? Oh no. I can't
    do that.

(CONTINUED)

197 CONTINUED:

                         TRUDY
e-   What's the matter? Isn't the
      place good enough for you?

                         GIL
f-   No, you don't understand. I've
      got to get back home.

                         TRUDY
g-   Well, I like that. Do you think
      I only brought you home here to
      sleep on my couch? There's a
      little more to life than good
      deeds, you know.
              (she puts her hands
              on Gil's shoulders and
              stares seductively
              into his eyes)
      Now come on, honey. You don't
      want to run out on me. Think
      of all the fun we had the other
      night, out there on the beach.
      We do all right together, you
      and me.

But Gil is concerned with other things and immediately
yanks down Trudy's hands.

                         GIL
h-   Trudy, listen. Have you a car?

                         TRUDY
i-   A car? Why yes. But....

                         GIL
j-   A closed car? A sedan?

                         TRUDY
k-   It's a little coupe.

                         GIL
l-   Good. Will you do me a favor
      and drive me out to my place?

                         TRUDY
m-   You certainly have a lot of
      nerve. After the way you
      abandoned me on the beach the
      other night....

                                                (CONTINUED)

197   CONTINUED: (2)

                    GIL
n-   Trudy, please. I'll explain
        everything someday. But you've
        got to drive me out to my place.
        Please. You don't realize how
        important it is. I'll... I'll
        even pay you.

Trudy looks at him curiously, then crosses the room to a
little table next to the door. She picks up her purse,
which is lying there, and removes the car keys from it.
She dangles the keys in front of her.

                    GIL
o-   Trudy, this is really wonderful
        of you....

                    TRUDY
                (almost a sneer)
p-   Come and get them.

Gil pauses and stands there awkwardly.

                    TRUDY
q-   What's the matter? You're not
        afraid of me, are you?

Gil takes a breath and crosses the room to get the keys.
But just as he is ready to take them from Trudy's outstretched hand, she flings her hands behind her back and
projects her bosom and pursed lips towards Gil -- urging
him to take her in his arms.

                    GIL
r-   Trudy, please....

                    TRUDY
s-   Don't you want the keys?

He takes her gingerly by the shoulders and tries to grab
her hands. But she is too quick for him.

198   C.U. TRUDY'S HANDS AND DOOR

With a deft action, Trudy pulls open the door and flings
the keys onto the front stoop.

199   M.S. GIL AND TRUDY

Gil sees what she has done and pushes past her to grab
the keys from the stoop.

84.

200   MORNING EXT. - M.C.U. KEYS ON STOOP

Gil lunges for them, but just before he can reach them, Trudy kicks them off the edge of the stoop and into the maze of shrubbery nearby. Gil is furious now.

                        GIL
          Why you little....

201   M.C.U. TRUDY (FROM GIL'S ANGLE)

She is laughing maliciously.

                       TRUDY
         You can't get away from me so easily
         when I'm awake, can you.

Her laughter grows louder and more malicious.

202   M.S. GIL

He rushes down the steps and begins searching desperately through the shrubbery for the keys. Sound of Trudy's laughter continues.

203   L.S. SUN

It is blazing down.

204   M.S. GIL

He is pawing through the shrubbery. Suddenly he feels himself grow weak and pauses in his search. Trudy's laughter grows louder and harsher.

205   M.C.U. GIL

He covers his face with his hands and sinks agonizedly to the ground.

206   L.S. SUN

It grows larger and larger until it engulfs the entire screen. Trudy's laughter rises to an agonizing crescendo.

207   M.S. GIL AND TRUDY

Gil is in foreground with back to Camera. Trudy is in background facing Camera. She is still laughing. Gil begins to raise himself up from the grass. He has undergone another transformation. Suddenly Trudy sees what he has become and her laughter dies. She looks shocked and horrified.

                    GIL
     You fool. You stupid little
     fool....

He gets to his feet and starts towards her (his back still to the Camera). She tries to back away but the wall of her apartment building stops her.

208   M.C.U. TRUDY

She is terror-stricken.

                   TRUDY
     No, no. Go away....

She begins to scream. Suddenly a hideous looking hand reaches into frame and grabs her by the throat. Her screams mount.

209   M.S. WOMAN IN ANOTHER APARTMENT

She opens her window and looks out. She is horrified by what she sees.

210   M.S. MAN IN ANOTHER APARTMENT

He opens the door and looks out. He, too, is horrified.

211   M.S. GIL AND TRUDY

Gil (back still to Camera) is strangling Trudy. She screams once more, then her voice grows hoarse and dies out. She slumps limply to the ground. Gil starts to turn.

212   M.S. WOMAN IN APARTMENT   (SAME AS SCENE 209)

She screams as she sees Gil's face.

213   M.S. MAN IN APARTMENT (SAME AS SCENE 210)

   He looks horrified, then grim, and rushes out into the courtyard.

214   MORNING EXT. - M.L.S. COURTYARD

   Man from apartment rushes up to Gil to block his way. Gil knocks him down and rushes out of the courtyard towards the street.

215   L.S. STREET (CAMERA SHOOTING TOWARDS COURTYARD)

   Gil comes running out of the courtyard and starts blindly across the street in front of an oncoming car.

216   M.S. DRIVER (THROUGH WINDSHIELD)

   He quickly jams on his brakes and blows his horn.

217   M.S. GIL

   He turns towards the car. We still don't see his face.

218   M.S. DRIVER (THROUGH WINDSHIELD)

   He sees Gil's face and is horrified.

219   M.L.S. STREET

   Gil is panic-stricken and runs away from the car.

220   M.S. GIL (DOLLY)

   Camera dollies after Gil as he races down the street. Finally he turns into an alley where he disappears into the shadows.

221   MORNING INT. - M.S. ANN AND HOFFMANN IN LIVING ROOM OF GIL'S HOUSE

   They are both looking very worried.

(CONTINUED)

221   CONTINUED:

                    ANN
    a-   Dr. Hoffmann, don't you think
          we'd better call the police?
          He's been gone for....

                    HOFFMANN
    b-   No, my dear. We must wait.
          That is all we can do.

Suddenly there is a faint noise from the front door, as if
someone was trying to fit a key into the lock.

                    ANN
    c-   Oh, that must be him now. I'll
          go and let him in.

                    HOFFMANN
    d-   No, Ann.

But Ann has already started towards the front hall.

222   M.S. FRONT HALL

Ann rushes to the front door and grabs the knob.

223   M.C.U. ANN (FULL FACE)

She pulls open the door and smiles in anticipation of
seeing Gil.

                    ANN
          Gil....

Suddenly she sees something which causes her to pause
in horror.

224   M.C.U. GIL   (FULL FACE)

He is transformed into the monster and looks truly
horrible. Ann is heard screaming.

225   M.S. FRONT HALL

Gil pushes past Ann and rushes to the back of the house
past Hoffmann who has just entered the hall. Ann just
stands there, too shocked to move. Hoffmann goes over
to her. She flings herself into his arms and sobs
brokenheartedly.

                                        (CONTINUED)

"The most memorable shot in the picture," according to Clarke: The Sun Demon makes a sudden entrance.

225 CONTINUED:

> ANN
> Oh Doctor.... I... I never realized....

Hoffmann can do nothing but stand there with a troubled look on his face and try to comfort Ann.

FADE OUT.

FADE IN:

226 DUSK INT. - C.U. TELEPHONE RECEIVER ON DESK

It rings. A hand enters and lifts the receiver out of frame.

> SERGEANT PETERSON'S VOICE
> Peterson speaking.... Oh yes, Jim... You did, eh...? Okay.... Yeah, thanks.

Hand re-enters frame and plunks the receiver back on the cradle.

227 M.S. POLICE STATION OFFICE

SERGEANT PETERSON is seated behind his desk. He is a late thirty-ish cop who has come up the hard way and who believes in "the system". He turns to face SEVERAL OTHER COPS who are standing next to his desk.

> PETERSON
> a- Well boys. It looks like we're going to wrap this one up before the day's out.

> FIRST COP
> b- You know who did it, Sergeant?

> PETERSON
> c- We've got a very good suspect, if nothing else. Those men we questioned at that bar swear they helped the girl take this guy home with her. And the two people in her apartment building who actually saw the murder this morning gave descriptions that seem to fit the same guy. At least, as far as the clothes were concerned.

(CONTINUED)

227 CONTINUED:

                    SECOND COP
d-   Clothes, Sergeant?

                    PETERSON
e-   It's a funny thing. Both the man and the woman say he didn't look like a man at all. He looked more like some kind of hideous creature.

                    THIRD COP
f-   Must have been the excitement.

                    PETERSON
g-   I think so myself. Anyway, it doesn't make much difference. We're going to bring him in for questioning.

                    FIRST COP
h-   What's the man's name, Sergeant?

                    PETERSON
i-   McKenna. Gilbert McKenna.

                    SECOND COP
j-   Say. Isn't that old Dr. McKenna's son? Used to live out on the highway in that big old house.

                    PETERSON
k-   Could be. He does live out on the highway. We'll find out the rest soon enough.

                    THIRD COP
l-   We going out there right away?

                    PETERSON
m-   Yeah. Tonight. Soon as we get the cars started.

                                    DISSOLVE TO:

228   DUSK EXT. - M.L.S. EXTERIOR OF POLICE STATION

The cops come running out of the door and climb into several police cars that are parked at the curb. (STOCK SHOT)

                                    DISSOLVE TO:

90.

229 NIGHT INT. - M.C.U. GIL

He is seated on the edge of his bed in the cellar room. His head is in his hands. He has changed back to normal but he looks terribly drawn and haggard. He raises his head and continues speaking as if he has paused in the middle of a sentence.

       GIL
a- ...and... and then something horrible seemed to come over me. I felt as if... as if a bomb was exploding inside me. And then I saw my hands around her throat and... and she had gone all limp.

Gil covers his face with his hands and the Camera pulls back to M.S. to reveal Dr. Hoffmann listening to him, patiently and sympathetically. Hoffmann says nothing, for there is nothing to say. Gil looks up again.

       GIL
b- Doctor, do you realize what this means? I've... I've killed someone. I'm a murderer.

Hoffmann puts a sympathetic hand on Gil's shoulder.

       HOFFMANN
c- My boy, my boy....

       GIL
d- I've become a monster inside as well as out. Oh why, why? Where's the reason behind it all? Here I've devoted all my life to science and now I'm a victim of something that sounds like... like a medieval horror story.

       HOFFMANN
e- Gil, you must not lose hope. There is perhaps still a chance for you. Yes, I think there is still a chance. But you must not think of these things now. You must rest.

Hoffmann turns to leave.

       GIL
f- Where are you going?

(CONTINUED)

229 CONTINUED:

        HOFFMANN
g- Upstairs. I am going to prepare an injection so that you will sleep. I shall be back in a few minutes.

Hoffmann exits.

230 M.S. KITCHEN

Ann is washing the supper dishes in the sink. She looks very preoccupied. Hoffmann enters and she immediately goes over to him.

        ANN
a- Doctor?

        HOFFMANN
b- I have just talked with him.

        ANN
c- Is he... is he better?

        HOFFMAN
d- Yes, he is better. But a terrible thing has happened.

        ANN
e- A terrible thing...?

        HOFFMANN
f- During this last attack, he... he killed someone.

        ANN
g- Oh no.

        HOFFMANN
h- I am afraid that the illness has begun to affect his mind.

Ann looks away hopelessly.

        HOFFMANN
i- There may still be a chance. But we must get him away from here as soon as possible. I am going to give him an injection so he will sleep. Then, we must put him in the car and take him away.

(CONTINUED)

230   CONTINUED:

                    ANN
    j-   I can have everything ready in
         a few minutes.

                    HOFFMANN
    k-   Good. We must waste no time....

Suddenly they hear a knock at the front door. Both of them
freeze in their tracks and look at each other.

                    ANN
                 (a whisper)
    l-   The police...?

                    HOFFMANN
    m-   Perhaps. We must find out.

231   M.S. FRONT HALL OF HOUSE

Ann and Hoffmann approach the front door gingerly. The
knocking continues. Ann takes a breath and calls through
the door.

                    ANN
    a-   Who... who is it?

                    PETERSON'S VOICE
    b-   The police. Open up.

Ann looks fearfully at Hoffmann.

                    ANN
                 (a whisper)
    c-   The police.

                    HOFFMANN
    d-   Ask them what they want. Perhaps.....

Ann turns back to the door and calls again.

                    ANN
    e-   What do you want?

                    PETERSON'S VOICE
    f-   We want to see Gilbert McKenna.

Ann turns back to Hoffmann, and he, in turn, looks beaten.

                    HOFFMAN
    g-   I'm afraid....

92.

232   M.L.S. HALL

Gil has entered from the kitchen. Ann and Hoffmann turn to look at him.

      ANN
a- Gil....

Gil rushes up to them.

233   NIGHT INT. - M.S. THREE OF THEM

Gil has a desperate gleam in his eyes as he faces Ann and Hoffmann.

      GIL
a- Is that the police?

      HOFFMANN
b- My boy. I'm afraid we must
   let them in.

      GIL
c- So they can take me to jail?
   Not on your life.

      ANN
d- But Gil....

      HOFFMANN
e- You can't be blamed for what
   happened. The court will understand.

      GIL
f- Court? Are you out of your head?
   Do you think I'm going to let
   myself be crucified by a bunch
   of stupid, small town....

      HOFFMANN
g- My boy, you won't be crucified.
   No one will hold you responsible.

A fresh burst of knocking is heard.

      PETERSON'S VOICE
h- Open this door. Open up or we'll
   break it down.

         (CONTINUED)

233   CONTINUED:

>   GIL
> i-   Do you hear that? They'll...
>   they'll drag me through the
>   streets like a... a public
>   spectacle. I'm getting out of
>   here.
>
>   HOFFMANN
> j-   No, Gil. It's too dangerous.
>
>   GIL
> k-   Everything's dangerous now. But
>   at least I won't be caught like
>   a mad dog.
>
>   ANN
> l-   Gil, please....
>
>   HOFFMANN
> m-   I cannot let you go. You must
>   listen to me. I am your doctor.
>   You do not realize what you are
>   doing.

Gil pauses and looks squarely at Hoffmann.

>   GIL
> n-   Dr. Hoffmann, are you insinuating
>   that I'm... I'm crazy?
>
>   HOFFMANN
> o-   My boy, you are confused....
>
>   GIL
> p-   Because if you are, you can
>   forget it right now. I know
>   what's wrong with me. I know what
>   I've done. And....
>
>   HOFFMANN
> q-   Then why don't you let us take
>   care of you? Running away won't
>   help.

For a moment Gil stands there indecisively.

>   PETERSON'S VOICE
> r-   Okay boys. Break it down.

The cops begin battering away at the door and this decides Gil.

                                          (CONTINUED)

233 CONTINUED: (2)

        GIL
s- Dr. Hoffmann, I appreciate all
  you've done. But I'm not going
  to let you stand in my way now.

Hoffmann grabs him by the shoulders and attempts to hold him back.

        HOFFMAN
t- Gil, you cannot go. I forbid
  you to go.

Gil tries to shake off Hoffmann's grip but the Doctor keeps trying to hold him back. Finally, Gil raises his arms in desperation and pushes the old man back into a chair.

        ANN
u- Gil....

        GIL
v- I'm sorry, Dr. Hoffmann.

He turns and opens a closet, from which he takes a long coat and a felt hat. He dons the coat, pulling the collar well up around his neck, and pulls the hat far down over his eyes.

        GIL
w- Don't try to stop me, Ann. My
  mind's made up.

        ANN
x- Oh, Gil....

He pauses and catches her by the shoulders.

        GIL
y- I'm sorry for all that's happened.
  It's too bad you had to get mixed
  up in it.

She gazes at him with tears in her eyes. Then she leans forward and kisses him. He holds her in his arms for a long moment then releases her.

        GIL
z- Goodbye.

He turns and dashes towards the kitchen. Ann stands there, watching him depart. Then she turns to Hoffmann who is still sprawled in the chair and they exchange sad glances.

234 NIGHT EXT. - M.L.S. BACK OF HOUSE

Gil comes running out of the back door and races over to the barn. He pulls open the doors and disappears inside. The Camera holds on the doors and there is silence for a second. Then, there is the sound of the sports car starting. It backs out into the driveway, swings around, then heads out along the driveway that circles the house.

235 M.L.S. FRONT OF HOUSE

Two cop cars are parked there with cops standing next to them. The front door is wide open now. Suddenly, the sports car is heard and it comes tearing around the corner of the house. The two cops dive for their guns and begin firing. Gil dodges between the two cars and starts down the drive. One cop tries to block Gil's path but Gil runs him down and races off down the road leading to the highway.

236 EXT. NIGHT EXT. - M.S. FRONT DOOR

Peterson and several cops come running out with guns drawn.

                PETERSON
a-   What happened?

                COP'S VOICE
b-   He just got away in his car.

                PETERSON
c-   What?

                COP'S VOICE
d-   Yeah. And he ran down Willis on the way.

                PETERSON
e-   Oh great. Which way did he go?

                COP'S VOICE
f-   Towards the highway. It looks like he's headed North.

Peterson heads back into the house.

237 NIGHT INT. - M.S. FRONT HALL

Hoffmann is sitting in the chair and Ann is beside him. Several cops stand nearby. Peterson enters.

                (CONTINUED)

237   CONTINUED:

                       PETERSON
a-   Well, I hope you two are
      satisfied. He's made a nice
      clean escape.

Ann leaps up almost joyfully.

                       ANN
b-   He has?

                       PETERSON
c-   And ran down one of my men in
      the process.
          (he turns to
            one of the cops)
      Jacobs. Call the State Police.
      Give them a description of him
      and his car and tell them to
      stop him at any cost. He's
      dangerous.

                       HOFFMAN
d-   Sergeant, I beg you. Do not
      use force on him. He is a very
      sick man. He must be taken to
      a hospital.

                       PETERSON
e-   Yeah? Well, we've got to catch
      him first, before we can take
      him anyplace.
          (he turns to
            the cop again)
      And Jacobs. Get an ambulance
      up here, too. He ran down Willis
      on the way out.
          (he turns back to
            Ann and Hoffmann)
      All right, you two. We're going
      down to headquarters.

Ann and Hoffmann get slowly to their feet and follow
Peterson to the door.

                       FADE OUT.

238   NIGHT EXT. - M.S. GIL IN CAR

He is racing through the night with the instrument lights
casting a green glow over his tense and grim face.

                       DISSOLVE TO:

239   M.S. TWO STATE POLICE OFFICERS IN CAR

   One is speaking rapidly on the radio. (STOCK)

                                           DISSOLVE TO:

240   M.S. STATE POLICE OFFICER AND GAS STATION ATTENDANT

   Cop questions attendant who nods and points off down the road. (STOCK)

241   NIGHT INT. - M.S. RADIO ROOM IN STATE POLICE HEADQUARTERS

   Man at radio is copying down something he is receiving over the radio. When he finishes, he hands it to another cop who is waiting nearby. Other cop goes to phone and picks it up. (STOCK)

                                           DISSOLVE TO:

242   M.S. PETERSON BEHIND DESK IN HIS OFFICE

   He is talking into the phone.

                     PETERSON
   a-   Yeah.... Yeah.... Good. Let
         me know if you get anything
         more.

   He hangs up and turns to face Ann and Hoffmann who are seated across the room.

                     PETERSON
   b-   Well, that was another report
         on your friend.

   Peterson gets up and walks over to a map that is hanging on the wall.

243   NIGHT INT. - M.C.U. PETERSON'S HAND AND MAP

   It is tracing Gil's course on the map.

                     PETERSON'S VOICE
         Now let's see. He was reported
         buying gas here.... And somebody
         else saw him up... here. And
         that last report put him... here.
         Looks like he's headed for the
         City.

                                           DISSOLVE TO:

244   NIGHT EXT. - M.L.S. SPORTS CAR

It is proceeding along the streets in a city. The traffic is somewhat heavy and Gil cannot make as rapid progress as he might wish.

245   M.S. GIL IN FRONT SEAT (THROUGH WINDSHIELD)

He is obviously being made quite impatient by the delay. Suddenly he looks towards something.

246   M.S. TRAFFIC LIGHT

It changes from Green to Orange.

247   M.S. GIL IN FRONT SEAT (SAME AS SCENE 245)

He grips the wheel and decides to beat the light. There is the sudden sound of squealing brakes.

                                    DISSOLVE TO:

248   NIGHT INT. - M.S. PETERSON'S OFFICE

He is behind his desk. Ann and Hoffmann are seated along the wall. Cop enters.

                    COP
a-   Hey, Sarge. We just got a flash
       from the City. McKenna's car had
       an accident.

                    PETERSON
b-   What?

                    COP
c-   Yeah. He ran into a truck at
       an intersection.

                    PETERSON
d-   Well, did they get him?

                    COP
e-   No.

                    PETERSON
f-   No?

                                    (CONTINUED)

248   CONTINUED:

                    COP
    g- Well, you know how it is,
        Sarge. There were a lot of
        people milling around. And
        they didn't know it was his
        car until they checked the
        registration.

                    PETERSON
    h- But....

                    COP
    i- He wasn't around. Somebody
        said they saw him walking away
        from the accident. I guess he
        wasn't hurt.

Peterson looks as if he is about to make a crude remark
on the situation.

                    COP
    j- But don't worry, Sarge. They're
        putting on extra men and setting
        up check points all around the
        city. He won't get far.

Ann and Hoffmann react with dismay to this.

                                        DISSOLVE TO:

249   NIGHT EXT. - M.S. GIL WALKING ALONG DOWNTOWN STREET

He looks slightly disheveled and there is a cut on the
side of his face. He has lost his hat and his coat collar
is pulled up as far as it will go. Crowds of people mill
around him. As he nears a corner, the sound of a newsboy's
voice can be heard. Gil stops short and looks towards
the newsboy.

250   NIGHT EXT. - M.C.U. NEWSBOY

He is holding up papers and shouting.

                    NEWSBOY
        Hey, all the latest editions.
        Police tracking mad killer.
        Believed hiding out in city.

Let's hope that Robert Clarke wasn't quite *this* deflated when *The Hideous Sun Demon* turned into a losing proposition for him (financially).

251   M.S. GIL STANDING THERE

   He looks wildly around, then pulls up his collar further
   and ducks into the crowd.

                                           DISSOLVE TO:

252   M.S. GIL WALKING ALONG DESERTED STREET

   Every so often he glances over his shoulder to see if he is
   being followed. Suddenly there is the sound of a police
   siren. Gil freezes, then ducks into the shadows of a
   nearby alley.

253   M.S. COP CAR

   It races past with siren blaring. (STOCK)

254   M.S. GIL HIDING IN ALLEY

   He is crouched back in the shadows, watching the police car
   disappear down the street. Siren fades into the distance.
   Gil is just about to move out of the alley when he hears
   the sound of voices. He turns towards voices.

255   M.S. MAN AND WOMAN WALKING ALONG STREET

                         WOMAN
       a-   Well, I don't care, Harry. It
             isn't safe to be on the streets
             with that killer loose in the
             city. No telling where he might
             be hiding.

                         MAN
       b-   Oh now, Bess. You worry too much.

256   NIGHT EXT. - M.C.U. GIL

   He starts to back quickly into the alley again. Suddenly
   he trips over a garbage can which falls over and makes a
   loud sound.

257   M.C.U. GARBAGE CAN

   It is rolling back and forth.

258 M.C.U. GIL

He looks more and more desperate.

                    WOMAN'S VOICE
a-   What was that?

                    MAN'S VOICE
b-   Probably just a cat.

                    WOMAN'S VOICE
c-   It came from that alley over there.

                    MAN'S VOICE
d-   Want me to take a look?

                    WOMAN'S VOICE
e-   No. Let's get the policeman on the corner.

Gil panics at this and turns and starts running back through the alley.

                    DISSOLVE TO:

259 M.L.S. GIL WALKING ALONG STREET IN FACTORY DISTRICT

Suddenly he stops and looks up ahead.

260 M.C.U. GIL

He is staring fearfully at something up ahead.

261 M.C.U. COP STANDING ON CORNER

He turns towards the Camera and light falls across his face.

262 NIGHT EXT. - M.C.U. GIL

He looks distraught, then turns and flees in another direction.

                    DISSOLVE TO:

263 DAWN EXT. - L.S. GIL WALKING THROUGH SOLITARY FIELD
     (HIGH ANGLE)

In the background, the sky is getting light.

264   M.C.U. GIL

He looks up at the sky, glances at his watch, and resumes walking a little faster. Suddenly he stops and sees something.

265   L.S. BATTERED OLD SHACK (FROM GIL'S ANGLE)

It looks as if it might be able to offer Gil some kind of shelter from the sun and from those who are chasing him.

266   M.C.U. GIL

He reacts to seeing the shack, then starts towards it.

267   L.S. GIL IN FIELD

He runs over to the shack.

268   M.S. GIL AT FRONT OF SHACK

He approaches the door and tries to open it, after first looking around to make sure that no one is looking at him. At first the door refuses to budge, but finally it yields. Gil disappears inside.

269   DAWN INT. - M.S. INSIDE SHACK

Gil enters and looks around. Something on the floor in one corner catches his eye.

270   M.C.U. CORNER

On the floor is a battered toy stove and other items of toy furniture.

271   DAWN INT. - M.C.U. GIL

He is looking at the items. Then he shrugs and turns away.

272   M.S. GIL IN SHACK

He looks towards the shack's one window (which is now beginning to let in more and more sunlight) and decides that it must be covered. Fortunately, there are various

(CONTINUED)

104.

272 CONTINUED:

lengths of wood around and also some large scraps of tar paper so it is not long before Gil has succeeded in turning the shack into a fairly lightproof hideaway for himself. With all this done, he sits down in one corner of the room, and, in an expression of exhaustion, sinks his head into his hands.

              FADE OUT.

FADE IN:

273 MORNING INT. - M.S. PETERSON'S OFFICE

Peterson is sitting behind his desk drinking a container of coffee. He has been up all night and looks it. Hoffmann is seated in a chair next to Peterson's desk and Ann is asleep in a chair in the corner.

      PETERSON
a- I don't know what's holding
  those guys up. We should have
  had a report by this time.

      HOFFMANN
b- Perhaps he has managed to slip
  through your net.

      PETERSON
c- Not a chance. Besides. What
  can he do in daylight? From
  what you've told me, daylight's
  what causes those spells of his.

      HOFFMANN
d- True.

      PETERSON
e- Naw, we'll get him. It's only
  a matter of time. The whole
  city's been alerted.

              DISSOLVE TO:

274 MORNING EXT. - L.S. SQUAD OF MOTORCYCLE COPS

They are racing along a city street with sirens blaring. (STOCK)

275 M.S. NEWSBOY ON CORNER

He is cutting open a bundle of newspapers that has just been dropped on the sidewalk from a delivery truck.

276 M.C.U. NEWSPAPER BUNDLE

Newsboy cuts it open and we see the headline: MAD KILLER STILL AT LARGE. CITIZENS IN DANGER.

                                        DISSOLVE TO:

277 MORNING INT. - M.C.U. RADIO IN HOME

                    VOICE ON RADIO
                      (filter)
                 ...and the entire facilities of
                 the Police Department have been
                 mobilized to apprehend this
                 man, wherever he may be hiding.

278 M.S. RADIO IN DINER

Several people are listening to it.

                    VOICE ON RADIO
                      (filter)
                 Since late last night, special
                 squads have been on duty patroling
                 the streets, while extra men....

The sound of passing sirens drowns the radio voice out momentarily and all in the diner turn to look in their direction.

279 M.S. RADIO IN STORE

                    VOICE ON RADIO
                      (filter)
                 ... Our search is proceeding
                 carefully, systematically, and
                 with as much speed as possible.
                 It should produce results
                 very soon.

280 M.C.U. POLICE CHIEF SITTING BEFORE MICROPHONE

He is making a special broadcast from a radio studio and it is his voice that we have been hearing.

                                        (CONTINUED)

280 CONTINUED:

                        CHIEF
           Once again, as your Chief of
           Police, let me assure you that
           everything possible is being
           done to rid our city of the
           menace that presently threatens
           it. I ask your cooperation in
           obeying the simple rules which
           will speed our search -- to stay
           off the streets as much as
           possible, to report all suspicious
           individuals to your nearest
           precinct or police officer, and
           above all, to keep calm.

Camera pulls back and we see that the Chief has been sitting at a small table. He stands up now and starts towards the door leading out of the studio, carrying his speech under his arm.

281 MORNING INT. - M.S. CHIEF ENTERING HALLWAY FROM STUDIO

A cop is standing there and with him are Peterson, Ann, and Hoffman. Cop approaches the Chief.

                        COP
a-   Pardon me, Sir. Sergeant Peterson
     is here.

Chief turns towards Peterson.

                        CHIEF
b-   Oh yes. Peterson? How are
     you?

They shake hands.

                      PETERSON
c-   We just got here a little while
     ago. Your office said you were
     over here, so....

                        CHIEF
d-   Yes, I'm glad you came.

                      PETERSON
e-   Any news on him?

(CONTINUED)

281 CONTINUED:

>   CHIEF
>   f-   Well, you know how many places
>   there are to hide in a big city.
>   But we've got an organized
>   search going and I think we
>   should be able to turn him up
>   before nightfall.

                                        FADE OUT.

FADE IN:

282 AFTERNOON INT. - M.S. KITCHEN

MOTHER is at sink, peeling potatoes. The radio is on.
Mother works and is only idly listening to the radio.

>   RADIO VOICE
>   (filter)
>   ... and the killer is believed
>   hiding out somewhere in the
>   Western section of town. Police
>   headquarters reports that the
>   street-by-street search is
>   proceeding more rapidly than was
>   originally expected and indicates
>   that the killer, who is believed
>   to be mentally deranged, may be
>   brought to justice by nightfall.
>   Otherwise, it will mean another
>   night of fear and apprehension
>   for all of us unless the search
>   can resume tomorrow.

News broadcast ends and music begins. Mother goes on
working. Presently there is a sound at the door and the
Mother looks towards it.

283 M.C.U. DOOR LEADING TO BACKYARD

It opens and the LITTLE GIRL enters, evidently coming home
from school.

>   LITTLE GIRL
>   a-   Hello Mommy.
>
>   MOTHER
>   b-   Hello darling. How was school
>   today?

                                        (CONTINUED)

283 CONTINUED:

Little Girl goes immediately to the refrigerator, opens it, and takes out a bottle of milk.

       LITTLE GIRL
c- Oh... I liked Kindergarten
  better. They make us work too
  hard this year.

Little Girl carries bottle over to the sink and looks up at her Mother. Camera follows.

       MOTHER
d- Would you like a glass, dear?

       LITTLE GIRL
e- Yes. A big glass.

       MOTHER
f- All right.

Mother gets a tall glass from the cupboard and hands it to the Little Girl.

       MOTHER
g- Shall I pour it for you?

       LITTLE GIRL
h- No, I want to pour it myself.

She pours herself a glass of milk rather clumsily but without spilling any. Then she drinks the milk, hands the empty glass back to her mother, and carries the bottle back to the refrigerator. Camera follows. She puts the bottle on a shelf inside and closes the door. Then she turns to face her mother.

       LITTLE GIRL
i- I'm going out now.

284 M.C.U. MOTHER

She casts an unconscious glance at the radio, then looks towards her daughter.

       MOTHER
  Darling, why don't you play
  inside today?

285   M.S. TWO OF THEM

                    LITTLE GIRL
    a-   No. I want to play outside.
         It's nice and sunny.

                    MOTHER
    b-   Suzy, please. Be a good girl
         and do as I tell you.

At that moment the phone rings. Mother crosses to the
other side of the room and answers it.

                    MOTHER
    c-   Hello? Oh, hello Grace....
         No, just starting supper.

286   AFTERNOON INT. - M.C.U. LITTLE GIRL

She is standing there, watching her mother.

                    MOTHER'S VOICE
         Oh really...? Tell me all about
         it....

Little Girl glances once more at her mother, then goes over
to the back door and slips out.

287   M.C.U. MOTHER ON TELEPHONE

Suddenly she hears the door slam and looks quickly in
that direction.

                    MOTHER
         Suzy? Suzy.
              (she turns back
               to the phone)
         No, it was just Suzy. She
         managed to sneak out while
         my back was turned. Honestly,
         that child....

                                        DISSOLVE TO:

288   AFTERNOON EXT. - L.S. LITTLE GIRL OUTSIDE

She walks across her backyard and out through a gate in
the fence.

289   L.S. LITTLE GIRL WALKING THROUGH FIELD

In the distance we can see Gil's shack and it is towards this shack that the little girl is heading.

290   M.S. LITTLE GIRL AND SHACK

She approaches the front door and, without hesitating, pushes it open and disappears inside.

291   AFTERNOON INT. - M.C.U. LITTLE GIRL INSIDE SHACK

She closes the door behind her and heads towards the toy stove in the corner. Camera follows her. She reaches the stove and squats down on the floor next to it. Suddenly a man's feet and lower legs appear in back of her. At first she doesn't notice but goes on playing with the stove. But presently she stops, turns and sees the legs, and looks up at the man's face.

292   AFTERNOON INT. - M.C.U. GIL (LITTLE GIRL'S ANGLE)

He is looking down at her with an odd gleam in his eye and a curious expression on his face.

DISSOLVE TO:

293   M.S. OFFICE IN POLICE STATION

Chief is sitting behind his desk. Peterson is seated in a chair drawn up next to the Chief. Ann and Hoffmann are seated a little way off.

               CHIEF
a-   ...and as far as we can figure,
       he must be hiding somewhere in
       the Western section of town.

               PETERSON
b-   He couldn't have gotten out of
       town, could he?

               CHIEF
c-   No, I doubt it. We blocked all the
       roads last night. He must be
       hiding out somewhere.

Peterson turns to Hoffmann.

(CONTINUED)

293   CONTINUED:

                        PETERSON
d-   Well, that jibes with what you
      told me, doesn't it, Dr. Hoffmann?

                        HOFFMANN
e-   Yes. He would have to stay
      inside during the daylight hours.
      His transformation is always
      brought about by the rays of
      the sun.

                        ANN
f-   If we could only talk to him.
      Maybe we could persuade him to...
      to....

                        PETERSON
g-   Give himself up? You tried that
      once. It didn't seem to do very
      much good.

                        ANN
h-   But he was frightened then. He
      was afraid that....

                        CHIEF
i-   He's probably more frightened
      now. I know how these things
      work.
            (now he grows
             more reflective)
      It's funny. Everybody in this
      town is terrified of meeting up
      with him. They've locked them-
      selves in their houses, warned
      their children not to go out
      alone, and are gathered around
      their radio and TV sets, waiting
      for news that he's been captured.
      But he's more frightened than
      any of them. He's so frightened
      that he's apt to do anything.
      That's why we've got to catch
      him soon.

                                        DISSOLVE TO:

294   M.S. GIL AND LITTLE GIRL

They are sitting on the floor of the shack facing each
other. The Little Girl has evidently been talking to
Gil quite volubly while Gil, on the other hand, looks
frightened, unsure of himself, and confused.

                                            (CONTINUED)

Above: Gil's (Clarke) little helper Suzy was played by his niece Xandra Conkling. One of her delightful memories of doing *Sun Demon*: "I got to keep the tea set that I played with in the movie, and *that* was big-time!" *Below:* "Tanks a lot!": Suzy (Xandra Conkling) tries to help Gil (Clarke), and her reward is to be used as a human shield.

294   CONTINUED:

        LITTLE GIRL
a- But you shouldn't be out here
  if you're sick, mister. You
  should go to a doctor.

        GIL
b- No, I... I....

        LITTLE GIRL
c- A doctor would make you well.
  And he wouldn't hurt you very
  much. I went to a doctor last
  week, and it didn't hurt at all
  when he stuck me with a needle.

Gil's eyes dart back and forth but he seems unable to say anything.

        LITTLE GIRL
d- Sometimes the doctor will even
  come to your house. That's when
  you're real sick. Maybe he'd
  come to your house, mister.

Gil looks around wildly.

        GIL
e- I... I can't go to a doctor. I
  can't leave here.

        LITTLE GIRL
f- Why not?
    (there is no
     answer from Gil)
  Why not, mister?

        GIL
g- I... the sun's bad for me.

        LITTLE GIRL
h- Oh no. The sun is good for you.
  One time when I had a cold,
  Mommy had me sit in the sun all
  day long. And it made me get
  well.

Gil looks away as if he is too bewildered to reply.

          (CONTINUED)

294   CONTINUED: (2)

                            LITTLE GIRL
i-   And you should eat a lot, too. That's what Mommy says. Feed a cold and starve a fever. Don't you get hungry out here?

                            GIL
j-   Hungry...?

He looks away. He is very hungry.

                            LITTLE GIRL
k-   Would you like me to bring you some cookies?

She looks at Gil who stares back at her, as if trying to understand what she has just said.

                            LITTLE GIRL
l-   I love cookies. And Mommy always keeps boxes and boxes in the kitchen. Would you like me to get you some?

                            GIL
m-   You'd... you'd do that for me?

                            LITTLE GIRL
n-   Oh yes. We have lots of cookies. And Mommy can always get some more when she goes shopping.

                            GIL
o-   All right. But...but listen. You're my friend, aren't you?

                            LITTLE GIRL
p-   Your friend?

                            GIL
q-   You want to help me?

                            LITTLE GIRL
r-   Oh yes, mister. I like to help people.

                            GIL
s-   Then that makes you my friend. And that means you musn't tell anybody that I'm out here.

                                        (CONTINUED)

294 CONTINUED: (3)

                    LITTLE GIRL
     t-   Not even Mommy?

                    GIL
     u-   Not even Mommy. We have to
          keep it a secret from... from
          them.

                    LITTLE GIRL
     v-   Them?

                    GIL
     w-   Never mind. It's our secret.
          That's all you have to remember.

                    LITTLE GIRL
     x-   All right. I won't tell anybody.

The little girl goes to the door and exits, leaving Gil
pacing nervously up and down the room.

                              DISSOLVE TO:

295 M.S. KITCHEN

Mother is still telephoning.

                    MOTHER
     a-   Yes, Grace.... Yes, I know....
          Well, I'll see you tomorrow
          then.... All right, Grace.
          Goodbye.

She hangs up the phone and walks over to the stove. As
she is checking the pots, the door opens and the Little
Girl enters.

                    LITTLE GIRL
     b-   Hello, Mommy.

                    MOTHER
     c-   Hello, dear. You shouldn't
          have gone out when I told you
          not to.

The little girl says nothing and simply watches her mother
who continues messing around with the stove.

296 M.C.U. LITTLE GIRL

She is watching her mother. Then, she walks slowly to a
cupboard near the floor and opens the door. Inside are
several boxes of cookies.

                        MOTHER'S VOICE
a-   What are you after now?

The little girl turns around quickly.

                        LITTLE GIRL
b-   I just want some cookies.

297 M.S. MOTHER AT STOVE

She turns around exasperatedly.

                        MOTHER
a-   Now, Suzy. You know it's almost
       supper time.

                        LITTLE GIRL
b-   Oh, I'm not going to eat them
       now.

                        MOTHER
c-   Then leave them alone. You can
       have some for dessert.

298 M.C.U. LITTLE GIRL AT CUPBOARD

She looks frustrated. Then, after a moment, she starts into
cupboard again.

                        MOTHER'S VOICE
a-   Suzy.

The little girl withdraws from the cupboard again. Her
mother enters the frame, looking distinctly annoyed.

                        MOTHER
b-   What's gotten into you today?
       You're not usually this bad.

The little girl looks very upset.

                        LITTLE GIRL
c-   I want some cookies.

(CONTINUED)

298   CONTINUED:

                          MOTHER
        d-   You can have some for dessert.
              I told you that.

                          LITTLE GIRL
        e-   But I want some now.

                          MOTHER
        f-   Why? You can't eat them now.
              It's too close to supper.

                          LITTLE GIRL
        g-   I know....

                          MOTHER
        h-   Then why...?

299   M.S. LITTLE GIRL AND MOTHER (ANOTHER ANGLE)

Suddenly the little girl begins to cry. Her mother is
amazed and looks at her curiously.

                          MOTHER
        a-   Darling....

                          LITTLE GIRL
        b-   They're for my friend.

Her mother holds her at arm's length and looks at her again.

                          MOTHER
        c-   What friend?

                          LITTLE GIRL
        d-   My new friend.

                          MOTHER
        e-   New friend? Where is this new
              friend?

                          LITTLE GIRL
        f-   It's a secret.

                          MOTHER
        g-   A secret? Now really Suzy.
              You don't expect me to believe
              all this, do you?

                                              (CONTINUED)

299   CONTINUED:

         LITTLE GIRL
h- But it's true, it's true. He's
  out there all alone. And he's
  sick and hungry. I promised
  to bring him some cookies.

Her mother holds her at arm's length again. This time, however, she looks at her daughter a little differently, sensing that something peculiar is going on.

         MOTHER
i- Out where?

         LITTLE GIRL
j- I can't tell. It's a secret.

         MOTHER
k- Suzy. You must tell me.

         LITTLE GIRL
l- No, I can't....

         MOTHER
m- Suzy.
      (she shakes the little
      girl perhaps harder
      than she meant to)
  Now Suzy. Listen to me carefully.
  Who is this new friend of yours?

The little girl is silent.

         MOTHER
n- Is... is he a man? A grown-up
  man like Daddy?

The little girl says nothing for a long moment, then, very slowly, she nods yes.

         MOTHER
o- Suzy. Where is he? Where is he
  hiding?

The little girl is silent and her mother shakes her violently.

         MOTHER
p- You've got to tell me. Please
  Suzy. Where is he hiding?

The little girl wants to keep her secret, but now she is frightened and confused.

         (CONTINUED)

299   CONTINUED: (2)

                             LITTLE GIRL
        q-   He's... he's in the....

                             MOTHER
        r-   Where? Tell me.

                             LITTLE GIRL
        s-   The... the shack.

                             MOTHER
        t-   The shack?

     Mother leaps up and races over to the phone.

300   M.C.U. MOTHER AT PHONE

     She picks it up and quickly dials the Operator.

                             LITTLE GIRL'S VOICE
        a-   Mommy, mommy. It's a secret.
              You musn't tell.

                             MOTHER
        b-   Operator? Give me the police.
              Hurry.

                             LITTLE GIRL'S VOICE
        c-   No, Mommy. No.

301   AFTERNOON INT. - M.C.U. LITTLE GIRL

     She looks terribly upset.

                             MOTHER'S VOICE
              Hello? Is this the police.
              I think I know where that man
              is hiding.

     A look of agony crosses the little girl's face and she
     turns and rushes from the room.

302   M.C.U. MOTHER AT PHONE

                             MOTHER
        a-   Yes. Yes, that's right. The
              killer.... My name? Why....

     Suddenly there is the sound of a door slamming. Mother
     looks up fearfully and calls.

                             MOTHER
        b-   Suzy.

303   M.C.U. SPOT WHERE LITTLE GIRL WAS STANDING

The little girl is gone.

                        MOTHER'S VOICE
                  (she screams this)
        Suzy.

                                       DISSOLVE TO:

304   AFTERNOON INT. - M.S. CHIEF'S OFFICE

Chief, Peterson, Ann and Hoffmann are gathered there as before. A cop enters.

                        COP
a-   Excuse me, Chief. We just got
     a call from a woman out near
     the oil fields. I think this
     could be the break we've been
     waiting for.

                        CHIEF
b-   She knows where he is?

                        COP
c-   She thinks so. Hiding in a shack
     not far from her house. I've
     already alerted the squads out
     that way.

                        CHIEF
d-   Good.
        (he turns to
        the others)
     Let's get out there. If this
     is the man, I want to be there
     when they take him.

They all stand up and start for the door.

                                       DISSOLVE TO:

305   M.S. INTERIOR OF SHACK

Gil is still pacing back and forth. Suddenly there is a sound at the door and he turns quickly.

306   M.C.U. DOOR

It opens and the little girl enters, out of breath from running.

                    LITTLE GIRL
    a-   Mister, mister....

Gil rushes into frame and kneels down next to the little girl.

                    GIL
    b-   What's the matter? Why are
          you out of breath?

                    LITTLE GIRL
    c-   Mommy... called the police.

                    GIL
    d-   What?

                    LITTLE GIRL
    e-   I tried to stop her. I tried.

Gil looks at her wildly. Suddenly there is the sound of several sirens outside. Gil whirls around and rushes to the door. He opens it a crack and peers out.

307   AFTERNOON EXT. - L.S. OUTSIDE (THROUGH CRACK)

Two cop cars have drawn up on the road at the edge of the field. The COPS get out and look around and one of them points towards the shack (Camera). Then they start across the field towards the shack.

308   AFTERNOON INT. - M.S. INSIDE SHACK

Gil slams the door shut and looks wildly around. He realizes that he is trapped unless.... Suddenly his gaze fixes on the little girl.

                    GIL
          Come on. You're going to help
          me.

He grabs her, lifts her up in front of him, and yanks open the door -- standing so that the approaching cops can see him and the little girl.

309   AFTERNOON EXT. - L.S. WHOLE AREA

Cops are in foreground. Gil holding the little girl is in background standing in the doorway of the shack.

                    FIRST COP
a-   That must be him.

                    SECOND COP
b-   Yeah. But look. He's got a
     kid with him.

                    FIRST COP
                      (calling)
c-   Hey you.

                    GIL
                      (distant)
d-   Keep away. Don't come any
     closer.

Gil starts from the doorway, still holding the little girl, and starts to run across the field.

                    FIRST COP
e-   Stop in the name of the Law.

He raises his gun as if to shoot.

                    SECOND COP
f-   Be careful. You might hit the
     kid.

                    FIRST COP
g-   Yeah.
           (he lowers his gun)
     Listen. Go back to the car and
     call Headquarters. Tell them
     we need more men.

310   M.S. GIL RUNNING ACROSS FIELD

He is still carrying the little girl and this slows him down considerably.

311   M.C.U. GIL

He looks agonizedly up at the sun.

312   L.S. SUN

It is blazing down fiercely.

122.

313   AFTERNOON EXT. - M.S. GIL

   He reaches the road, crosses it, and plunges into the high
   grass beyond as he heads towards the stack of trolley cars.

314   M.S. COP IN CAR

   He is talking on the radio.

315   M.L.S. ANOTHER COP CAR RACING ALONG ROAD

   Siren blaring.

316   M.S. THROUGH WINDSHIELD OF COP CAR

   We can see the Chief, Peterson, Ann, and Hoffmann inside.

317   M.S. GIL

   He is running through the high grass still carrying the
   little girl. Suddenly he slows and wavers.

318   M.C.U. GIL

   He flings one arm over his face and sinks to the ground.
   Camera follows him and we see him writhing on the grass.
   The little girl escapes his grip and stands there, horrified.

319   L.S. THE SUN

   It grows bigger and bigger until it seems to engulf the
   entire screen.

320   M.S. COPS AROUND COP CAR

   One of them is still inside talking on the radio. Suddenly
   they hear the distant scream of a child. They all turn in
   the direction of the scream.

321   M.S. ROAD NEXT TO FIELD OF HIGH GRASS

   The little girl comes running out onto the road. The cops
   run over to her. The little girl is very upset. First cop
   kneels down next to her.

(CONTINUED)

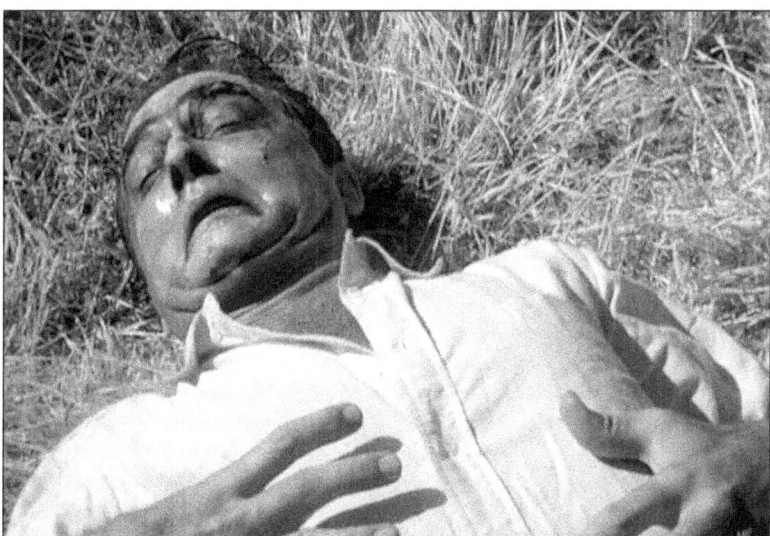

When it came time to shoot the scene of Gil transforming into the monster on the ground near the oil field (the movie's only on-camera transformation), *Sun Demon* costume maker Cassarino was not completely prepared to do the makeup application job, which annoyed Clarke. The best Cassarino could manage was to put black makeup around Clarke's eyes and a few pieces of rubber on his face. Clarke considered this scene a weak spot in the movie.

321   CONTINUED:

                        FIRST COP
     a-   It's okay, honey. You're safe
           now.

                        LITTLE GIRL
     b-   He's... he's sick. His face
           got all funny.

First cop stands up and turns to the other cops.

                        FIRST COP
     c-   All right. Let's go get him.

Several of the cops immediately plunge into the high grass with their guns drawn.

322   M.L.S. CLEARING AROUND STACK OF TROLLEY CARS

Gil (transformed into a monster) rushes past the Camera and heads for the trolley cars. He ducks inside one.

323   M.S. TWO COPS ENTER CLEARING

They stop and look around.

                        SECOND COP
           Be careful. He's probably hiding
           inside one of those cars.

They spread out and start towards the cars.

324   AFTERNOON INT. - M.S. GIL HIDING INSIDE TROLLEY CAR

He is crouched down behind a seat. A cop sticks his head in the door.

325   M.C.U. COP

He looks around but seems to see nothing.

326   M.C.U. GIL

He moves and inadvertently hits something.

124.

327 AFTERNOON INT. - M.C.U. COP

He hears sound and looks immediately in its direction. He raises his gun as if to shoot.

328 M.S. INSIDE TROLLEY CAR

Cop is about to shoot. Suddenly Gil grabs a broken seat and hurls it at the cop. It hits him and his gun goes off harmlessly, making a tremendous noise. Gil ducks out another door.

329 AFTERNOON EXT. - M.S. OUTSIDE

Gil starts in one direction, then sees cops approaching and ducks back. He turns and begins to climb up the stack of trolley cars.

330 M.L.S. OTHER COPS IN CLEARING

They point to stack of trolley cars. Gil can be seen climbing to the top.

331 M.S. COP

He starts climbing after Gil.

332 M.S. ANOTHER COP

He starts climbing from the other side.

333 M.S. GIL

He reaches top of the pile and starts making his way across the uneven roofs.

334 M.L.S. COP CAR ARRIVING ON SCENE

The Chief, Peterson, Ann, and Hoffmann get out.

335 M.S. ALL OF THEM

They look towards the stack of trolley cars and Peterson points.

(CONTINUED)

Three shots of the climactic sky-high fight... *Above:* The Sun Demon talks smack to Johnny Law (Cassarino). *Below:* The climactic sky-high fight to the finish between the Sun Demon (Clarke) and the pursuing patrolman (Richard Cassarino). Cassarino used three names in the movie's on-screen credits: Gianbattista Cassarino (as art director and assistant to the producers), Ben Sarino (as makeup) and Cass Richards (as an actor).

125.

335   CONTINUED:

                         PETERSON
              Look. He's on top. They've
              got him cornered.

        Ann and Hoffmann stare at the grotesque scene before
        them, utterly horrified.

336   M.S. GIL ON TOP OF PILE

        A cop sticks his head over the edge and starts to climb
        on top. Gil wrestles with him, succeeds in getting his
        gun, and throws him to the ground.

337   M.L.S. COP FALLING

        He screams agonizedly.

338   M.S. GIL ON TOP OF PILE

        He turns and sees another cop climbing onto the roofs.
        He fires and the cop fires.

339   M.S. ANN AND HOFFMANN

        They react to the shots which echo through the air. Tears
        well up in Ann's eyes and begin rolling down her cheeks.

340   M.S. GIL

        He is silhouetted against the sky on top of the pile,
        clutching his chest as he rocks back and forth unsteadily.

341   M.C.U. GIL

        Even though his face is utterly monstrous, we can see a
        look of pain and longing in his eyes. He turns his head
        slowly and stares at the sun.

342   L.S. SUN

        It is about to set, but still blazes forth fiercely almost
        as if it is smiling in grim and ugly triumph. At first, it
        is steady on the screen, then it begins to rock crazily
        and turn itself completely awry as if the viewer was
        losing his balance.

126.

343   AFTERNOON EXT. - M.L.S. STACK OF TROLLEY CARS (LOW ANGLE)

Gil falls forward over the edge of the roofs and drops down, crashing against the sides of the cars on the way.

344   M.S. GROUND

Gil hits the ground face down. He doesn't move. Cop enters frame and bends over Gil to see if he is still alive. Then he stands up and the Camera follows him, leaving Gil. The cop looks towards the group around the car and waves.

                              COP
                  It's okay. He's dead.

345   M.S. ANN AND HOFFMANN

Ann gasps and begins sobbing. Hoffmann sadly tries to comfort her. Camera pulls back to include Peterson and Chief in the shot.

346   L.S. WHOLE AREA

Ann and Hoffmann are standing together. Peterson and the Chief are standing a little way off and are looking towards the stack of trolley cars. Other cops are standing around except for two who have picked up Gil's body and are carrying it towards the group around the cop car.

Camera pans up to L.S. of sun as it is setting triumphantly beyond the hills.

                                             FADE OUT.

Promotional artwork for Clarke's never-made *Sun Demon* follow-up film *Sorceress*.

"SORCERESS"

Outline

by

Arthur C. Pierce

8/16/76

Property of:

Sun Demon Corporation
4841 Gentry Avenue
North Hollywood, California 91607

"S O R C E R E S S"

A palisade and beach area. A crowd of sun lovers on the beach, pleasure craft milling about beyond the surf, many curious persons beside parked cars along a seaside road, and a mobile TV crew covering the event everyone is watching. It is a peaceful demonstration being staged by a group of young environmentalists.

MAIN TITLES spaced throughout following action sequence:

The demonstrators, ten or twelve healthy young men and women, are soaring off the palisade, one at a time, on colorful hang gliders, each with a streamer with printed messages: "Ban Offshore Oil," "Stop the Smog Makers," "Save the Whale," "Zero Population," "Declare War on Pollution," "Most Endangered Species - Man," etc.

After last CREDIT TITLE, the final demonstrator comes off the bluff. CHRIS ERICKSON is a gorgeous young woman and the star attraction of the event. She appears to be totally nude as she glides over a cheering crowd, a banner trailing from each wing tip reading: "No on Nuclear Power" and "Yes on Solar Power." A lady TV commentator describes the excitement and success of the demonstration.

Chris makes her landing out beyond the surf, beside an awaiting power cruiser. Her boy friend, GLENN WILSON, a physical and handsome thirty, her younger brother, ERIC, and his friend, DONNA, all members of the organization, are aboard the boat. Relationships are briefly established as Chris is getting into a pair of water skies. The hang glider is attached to a tow line. Soon, the cruiser is skimming across the water with Chris airborne behind it.

With the banners flying, Chris and the glider are towed along the coastline, where thousands of people of an oceanside community get the message. Most important of all, the boat cruises as close as possible past a nuclear energy plant located along the coast. It is here that Chris gains as much altitude as possible, then releases the tow lines and her skis.

Aboard the cruiser important story points are established. The plan is for Chris to circle around the plant and return to sea for a landing. But something goes wrong. There is a radical shift in air currents. Chris is forced to soar inland, over a coastal range and out of view of her friends on the boat.

Chris finds herself over rugged terrain, rocky hills and crags, boulder canyons, and, beyond, rock strewn and cactus covered desert. Then she sees what appears to be a modern industrial complex, standing alone in the remote wasteland. And not far away, a small lake surrounded by desert palms. It is her only landing site.

An area in a boulder canyon. Three HIKERS have paused to have lunch. One of them sees the hang glider. They all watch as it soars overhead not far away and disappears from view beyond a hill. They aren't certain they saw what they thought they saw, then decide it's the hot sun and the beer they are drinking.

The glider sweeps down toward the lake, passing over a high chain-link security fence. And from an observation room in the complex a distance away, a SECURITY GUARD is watching the strange sight through binoculars. He reports it to the officials of the privately owned and operated research facility.

At the lake, Chris soars up over the palm trees, then down and out over the water. Near the middle she drops into the lake, letting the glider make a crash landing a distance beyond. After looking around at the shores, Chris makes her choice and begins swimming toward a bank about fifty yards away.

There is urgency outside the research facility as head bio-chemist, ARTHUR ROBERTS, and a party of security guards leave for the lake in a station wagon. It is disclosed that if the person on the hang glider has landed in the lake he could be in immediate danger.

Chris is nearing the bank of the lake. She reaches shallow water and begins wading. Suddenly, a strange sound behind her, a gasping sound.

She turns and is shocked to see ...

The head of a giant catfish coming up out of the water only a few yards away, its gaping, snapping mouth some five feet wide. Chris screams, splashes toward the bank. The mammoth fish pursues her, but the water has become too shallow. Chris reaches the bank, drops to her knees, looks around to see the monster settle back into the lake. Chris collapses.

* * * * * *

Solar Power and Research Corporation is located in a group of modern industrial buildings on the outskirts of a coastal city such as Long Beach. Its basic economy is based on the design, manufacture, and installation of solar cells in homes and industry. But its more important concern is in research and development of solar energy products for the near future. And the testing of one of these products is in progress at the moment.

In the large utility yard behind the plant, where numerous different vehicles are parked, ERIC ERICKSON, SR., Chris's father, founder and head of the firm, is in a medium-sized van with two of his engineers. They are about to test a solar torch, a device designed to be used in places where it may be hazardous to cut metal at close range. It is a complex optical device that concentrates a powerful beam of light from a five-foot parabolic mirror on the roof of the van, into a pinpoint of intense heat.

The test is successful. A pencil thin beam of light is projected out of the rear of the van to a two-inch thick metal plate fifty yards away, where it slowly melts through it, cutting a two-inch hole.

A call on the van's CB radio interrupts the operation. It is Glenn, informing Eric Sr. of Chris's disappearance into the rugged coastal range. Without hesitation, Eric asks Glenn to meet him at the airport.

A late model light plane flies low over rugged coastal foothills, an insignia on its side reading "Solar Power, Inc." Inside the plane Erickson is at the controls, Glenn seated beside him. It will be disclosed that the senior Erickson is Glenn's employer, that Glenn is one of his leading young engineers.

They discuss the rugged terrain below and Chris's skill at hang gliding. They are both concerned, but try to keep it from one another. Glenn spots the remote desert research complex and the small lake. They fly down to look the area over.

Both Glenn and Eric agree that the lake would have been a logical landing site if Chris had flown in this vicinity. They do not see the glider. But they do notice irrigated plots near the lake with various kinds of crops. Neither of them know the identity of the modern, isolated desert facility, and it does not appear on the map of the area. A call comes in over the plane's CB radio. It is Chris's brother.

Eric Jr. is in his early twenties, three years younger than Chris. He is sitting at the wheel of his jazzed-up van, his girl friend, Donna, beside him, studying a map. The colorful van is parked outside a sheriff's station in a small, modern, desert town. Via the CB radios (using much of the CB jargon), Eric and Glenn compare notes. The sheriff's department has come up with nothing, but they are still inquiring and searching the area. Glenn wants Eric to ask about the industrial facility located off the main highway and up in the boulder canyon, then meet them at the local airfield.

The infirmary of the desert research firm is as modern as any first class hospital. Chris is lying on a bed in a private, well-equipped room. She is in a deep sleep. The resident DOCTOR and a NURSE are nearby, looking over medical reports. Bio-chemist Arthur Roberts enters the room, concern on his face. It is disclosed that blood tests indicate Chris is definitely infected by mutagen, a chemical compound the researchers have put into the lake. Just what effect it will have on her, and how soon, is uncertain. Roberts leaves the room, obviously a troubled man.

In the sumptuous office of OTTO KRAMER, located in his penthouse apartment atop the administration building of the research complex, Roberts expresses his concern for the girl. He wants to begin treatments with his experimental antidote immediately. And he is in favor of notifying the local sheriff that they have found the girl.

Kramer, an eccentric, middle-aged genius and sole owner of Kramer Industries, is excited about the opportunity of studying the effects of the genetic chemical on a human being. He wants the girl's whereabouts kept secret until they have observed some results. He insists that Roberts wait until then before starting the treatment.

The solar power company plane lands on a small airfield where Eric and Donna are waiting. Eric informs Glenn and his father that they have learned the industrial facility in the desert is a branch of Kramer Industries, some kind of privately owned agricultural research firm, and that the sheriff's office had already checked with them. They knew nothing about Chris.

It is too late in the day to resume the search. It is decided that Eric Sr. will return to his company near Long Beach while Glenn and the others will remain in the small town in the event something develops.

The nurses' station in the infirmary. Roberts and the doctor are there, engaged in brief conversation about a genetic engineering project going on in the research labs. Suddenly, a chilling scream comes from a room nearby. They hurry to the room, a NURSE joining them, and are shocked to see ...

Chris, sitting up in the bed, staring at her hands in disbelief, hands that have undergone a physical change. The fingers and nails have grown longer and become clawlike. But it's what Chris can't see that is most frightening. Her beautiful face has distorted into a mask of evil, elongated eyes, flaring nostrils. Not so much a hideous face as it is sensual and she-devilish.

Frantic and bewildered, Chris wants to know where she is, who they are, what has happened to her. It takes both the doctor and Roberts to hold her while the nurse gives her a tranquilizer shot. Then, as Chris calms down, Roberts explains that she has had an accident and is suffering from shock; that they have given her drugs to help her rest; and that she is hallucinating. He tries to convince her that what she sees is not real; that it is only her imagination. Chris wants to know if what she saw in the lake was only a figment of her mind. Roberts skirts around the question.

As Chris begins going under, Roberts asks the nurse to bring his equipment. He is going to start the treatments. The doctor reminds him of Kramer's order to wait. Roberts no longer gives a damn about Kramer's egomania, and he's about had it with tampering with the natural laws of nature. He only hopes that it isn't too late to reverse the mutation process going on within Chris's body.

* * * * * *

Early evening inside a motel cocktail lounge. Glenn, Eric and Donna are in a booth, wine on the table, their attention, like others in the room, on a TV set up above the bar. A news bulletin has interrupted a sports event. It is a report about the missing demonstrator, showing pictures of Chris and a few film clips of the hang glider event at the beach location earlier in the day.

The previously established hikers are seated at the bar, feeling their beers and becoming excited about what they see on the news report. One of them wants everyone in the room to know what they saw earlier, up in the boulder canyon. Another backs him up, disclosing that they had thought they were seeing a UFO. Everyone laughs with them. Everyone except those at Glenn's table. They move quickly to the bar and ask some questions. The answers convince them that the hikers saw Chris and that she must have landed within the grounds of the research complex.

As they leave the cocktail lounge, Glenn is sure that something strange must be going on inside the desert facility, something its authorities want kept secret. He formulates a plan, and he and Eric get busy on the CB radio, calling on other members of their group in the city.

A few hours later Eric's van turns off a desert road and begins grinding and bouncing across rugged terrain. And following close behind is a utility truck equipped with a sky hook boom. An emblem on the truck denotes it to be equipment of the previously established Solar Power company. Both vehicles turn lights off as they leave the road.

The trucks drive up alongside a stretch of the high, electrically charged security fence in a remote area of the research firm's grounds. A platform is attached to the sky hook cable. Then Glenn and Eric are hoisted up and over the fence and lowered to the ground on the other side. They quickly make their way off into the darkness.

In Chris's room in the infirmary, Roberts is giving her another shot of the serum. She is awake and is almost completely her beautiful self again. Roberts explains that she must have a treatment every eight hours over a forty-eight hour period.

Chris wants to know if Roberts has called her father as she asked. Roberts, forcing himself to lie, tells her he has, and that her father has agreed that she should remain in his care until the following day. Chris accepts the situation. They then have a brief conversation, disclosing Roberts' growing interest in Chris and her interest in what kind of research he is engaged in. Roberts is evasive on this matter.

In the darkness outside, Glenn and Eric come up to what appears to be a large stable with fenced corrals and pens. They are forced to enter the building as a GUARD, making his rounds, approaches.

Inside, they find themselves in a dimly lit animal shelter, with rows of large cages on either side of a long corridor. They are unable to see what is in the cages as they walk along the corridor, until Eric stops to peer into the darkness of one of them.

Suddenly ... a gigantic desert boar charges them, a massive head with gaping mouth full of razor sharp teeth. The beast is some six feet in height, and only a heavy duty wire screen prevents it from taking Eric's head off.

Jolted, Eric and Glenn lunge back against a cage on the opposite side of the corridor, only to be shocked again. A huge, two-headed monstrosity of a dog leaps at them from the darkness of its cage, stopped only by bars and wire screen. Glenn and Eric run for the door at the end of the corridor.

Outside again, they make their way to the main building of the complex, where they find a GUARD on duty at a reception desk. They take him by surprise, disarm him, and force him to lead them to Chris.

In the corridor of the infirmary, Glenn and Eric take a NIGHT NURSE as second hostage and, after learning which room Chris is in, force her and the guard into a closet and lock them in.

They find Chris alone, asleep, and seemingly perfectly normal. They awaken and tell a bewildered Chris that they are taking her out of the place. Chris tries to explain that she is undergoing treatment, but Glenn won't buy it. Why did the authorities lie to the sheriff's office? Why didn't they inform her father that she was okay? Does Chris have any idea what kind of genetic experiments are being conducted in the research center? Chris can't answer the questions. Glenn is sure the scientists plan on using her as a human guinea pig.

Wearing only hospital pajamas, Chris hurries out with them and they reach the hoisting crane and safety before the security alarm sounds.

* * * * * *

In the van, enroute back to their home coastal town, Chris changes into a neat, form-fitting jump suit. Then she learns that the group is having a bash that night in celebration of their successful demonstration that made the prime time news that evening. Though Glenn thinks she should see her family doctor first, Chris insists that she is okay and wouldn't miss the party for anything. Glenn knows better than to pressure his very independent lady.

At the home of the highly successful rock music group known as ECOLOGY, a palatial old mansion located in the hills overlooking the ocean, the environmentalist group has gathered for the celebration, and they are all glad to see that Chris is okay.

After they have all had a little wine and beer and/or pot, and toasted to their success, Chris announces their next target. They are going after the polluters of the rivers, lakes and oceans; the oil refineries, chemical companies, steel and paper mills. The next demonstration will be against the oil company, near Long Beach, responsible for a recent spill into the bay.

As the party progresses, the music group really get it on, and this leads to some clothes coming off and some of the guys and girls getting things going in the pools, gardens, and bedrooms of the estate. But, as if something has come over her, Chris and Glenn have nothing going. She has drifted off someplace and no one has seen her for over an hour.

Chris is in a darkened upstairs bedroom, lying across the bed in a disturbed sleep. She is unaware that her face and hands have undergone a slight change. She is reverting back to the she demon.

LINC JEFFERSON, a tall and virile black man and member of the "Ecology," enters the room with his CHICK. They do not notice Chris in the semi-darkness. As soon as the door is closed, Linc's hands are all over the girl. She doesn't resist, and they lock in a hot embrace. As

They are kissing, the girl kicks off her shoes and one lands on a dressing table across the room, knocking a perfume bottle to the floor.

The sound awakens Chris. She sits upright on the bed, sees Linc and the girl across the room. Her eyes narrow as some primitive emotion possesses her. She springs off the bed and lunges at the lovers, grabbing the girl by the neck with her taloned hands, yanking her around and slapping her across the room, where she falls, bleeding and unconscious.

Chris, now the she devil, turns her attention to a bewildered Linc. Before he has time to react she is tearing at his clothes, ripping his shirt off. Linc tries to stop her, but he is no match for her newly developed strength. She knocks him to the floor and begins tearing at his jeans. Linc gets to his knees, shouting for help. Chris slaps him back against a wall, knocking over a table and lamp.

In another bedroom, two LOVERS part lips to listen to all the racket above them. They are amused, naturally assuming that some guy's girl is really doing a number on him.

The wild sounds are also heard by Glenn, who is coming up a stairway. He recognizes Chris's voice shouting profanities at Linc. He hurries down a corridor.

Inside the darkened bedroom, it is a pagan sex scene, with the she demon, now nude, astride a struggling Linc. She has his arms pinned against the floor, shouting obscenities at him. Linc manages to push her off him, and they tumble about the floor.

At this moment, Glenn bursts into the room and, in the shaft of light from the corridor, it appears to him that Linc is trying to rape Chris. He lunges across the room, grabs Linc by the arm, hauls him up and slugs him hard. Linc stumbles backwards, trying to explain what is going on as he goes. But Glenn is at him again. Then, in self-defense, Linc returns the blows.

While they are fighting it out, Chris grabs up her jump suit and leaves the room through French doors that open onto a terrace.

Glenn is no match for the more physical Linc, and soon finds himself pinned against the wall. Other members of the group now rush into the room, turning on the lights as they enter. They all stare in disbelief at Linc's girl friend, lying on the floor with her face lacerated, her throat slashed.

In the van outside the mansion, Chris zips up her jump suit, then looks at herself in the mirror on the inside of the closet door. She is shocked at her image. She looks at her hands. Her face becomes a mask of hate and evil. She smashes a fist against the mirror shattering it. Then she runs out of the van.

Chris runs up to a group of parked motor bikes, grabs up a helmet, puts it on, its dark visor concealing her face. Glenn, Eric, and some of the others come out of the mansion, begin calling for Chris. She mounts one of the bikes, starts it up, roars off into the night. Glenn and the others hear the cycle engine speeding away. They hurry for their cars and bikes and pursue Chris.

* * * * * *

Chris easily loses the group in the labyrinth of winding, connecting hillside roads, and is soon speeding down a freeway. And little does she know that one of the cars she passes, going in the opposite direction, is driven by Arthur Roberts, on his way to the Erickson home in hope of finding Chris and continuing the treatments. Also unknown to Chris, an APB has been put out on her.

On a side road outside the desert town, a sheriff's DEPUTY spots the motorcycle and gives chase. Chris finally pulls to the side of the road. As the officer gets out of his car and approaches her, one hand on his side arm, Chris gets off the bike. The officer asks to see her ID. The question triggers some primitive response in the changed Chris. She lashes out at the officer, her claw hand slashing his face with a force that knocks him to the ground.

The officer is seriously injured, but still has strength enough to draw his revolver. Chris reacts automatically and swiftly, kicking the officer's wrist, cracking it, sending the gun flying into the roadside ditch. The man collapses in agony. Chris stares down at him a moment, then at her hands, amazed at her newly developed strength. She mounts the cycle and roars away.

At the Kramer research facility, a night GUARD at the gate hears the sound of a motorbike in the distance, drawing nearer, but he sees no lights. Then the engine stops, and there is only silence. The guard returns to the guard house and his newspaper. Then he hears the sound of crunching gravel. He steps outside again, looks off into the darkness beyond the lighted area. The sound has stopped. Then suddenly...

The she demon springs out of the darkness, stands directly before the guard. He is petrified by the sight of her. She has removed the helmet, revealing that she is now fully mutated into a shocking she devil, with even the suggestion of horns on her forehead. Before the guard can react, the demon slashes his throat with her long talons, cutting his jugular veins. He crumbles to the ground in a bleeding heap. The she devil runs toward the administration building and enters.

The GUARD on duty at the reception desk looks up to see the demon running across the lobby toward him. Before he can get to his feet, she dives over the counter for him, knocking him to the floor. As he starts to get up, she cracks him hard on the back of the neck with one hand, flattening him unconscious onto the floor. The she devil then runs to the elevators.

In the massive, mirrored, darkened bedroom of Kramer's penthouse apartment, he is indulging in his favorite sexual pleasures: bondage and sadism. In a kneeling position on the bed, bound hand and foot and gagged, is a bountiful, nude ORIENTAL GIRL. And standing on the bed, wearing tight black leather shorts, boots and a mask, Otto Kramer is lashing her with a black leather horse whip. There are a dozen welts, some bleeding, on the girl's bare back. Loud, erotic music drowns out the sound of the apartment door being kicked open.

Unseen by Kramer, the she demon enters the bedroom, watches the debauchery a moment, her animal sexuality becoming inflamed. As Kramer is about to strike the girl again, the demon grabs the end of the whip, yanks him off the bed onto the floor and, without hesitation, begins flailing him viciously. Kramer tries to flee, but she stops him, hurling him back to the floor, and continues lashing him until he is unconscious. Then she lifts his bleeding body above her head and hurls it through a large view window.

The in-bondage Oriental girl has been watching the pagan spectacle, helpless to escape, actually excited by the savage exhibition. The she demon approaches the bedside, stares down at the girl. Their eyes meet. The she devil throws down the whip, reaches out and cuts the gag loose with a talon. Then, standing directly before the girl, she begins unzipping her jump suit.

* * * * * *

The following morning a police car and an unmarked car are parked outside the fashionable, ranch style Erickson home in an upper middle class section of town. Inside, a HOMICIDE DETECTIVE has been explaining what happened at the research facility and on the highway to Eric Sr., Glenn, Roberts and the others. He informs them that the murderer left the complex in one of its vehicles and has had enough time to be miles away. The officer further states that, until Chris is found and clears herself, she is the prime suspect.

After the officer has gone, they all agree that they must find Chris before the police. Then Roberts explains to them what actually happened to Chris, facts about mutagen and other genetic engineering experiments taking place at the Kramer research firm. Glenn lets Roberts know what he thinks of their scientific progress, tampering with the natural laws of nature, etc. Arthur Roberts agrees, confessing that he let himself be taken in by Otto Kramer. Interrupting this ...

A phone call from Erickson's solar power company. The truck with the experimental solar torch has been stolen. In its place is a vehicle from Kramer Industries. Also a note reading, "Death to the Polluters!" Glen and the others agree, Chris means to destroy some industrial complex. But which one?

Roberts remembers something Chris had said during their conversation in the infirmary. She talked about the target of their next demonstration... a tanker that caused a massive spill into the bay. Glenn and Eric Jr. know the super tanker must be it as it is due to arrive around noon this day. They conclude that one of the isolated roads on the Palos Verde peninsula, overlooking the shipping channel, would be the logical place for Chris to set up the equipment and it is a large area to cover before noon.

The Palos Verde peninsula is shrouded in a light fog, but it is still early in the day. The question is, will the fog burn off before noon. The medium-sized solar company van bounces and grinds along a remote dirt road high up on the palisade, overlooking the channel.

At the Long Beach airport, Eric Sr., alone, taxies his sleek plane out to the runway, gets okay from tower, and takes off. Meanwhile, Glenn's van is rolling through the colorful village of Palos Verde. He is at the wheel, Arthur Roberts beside him, Eric Jr. and Donna seated behind them. And not far out to sea, a huge oil tanker, riding low in the water, cuts through the fog and rolling swells.

In his plane, Eric Sr. makes CB contact with Glenn. The fog is beginning to lift. Shortly they make visual contact, the plane flying low along the coast line, Glenn's van traveling in the same direction on the palisades road. Elsewhere on the peninsula, the larger van is parked off the road in a ravine, a location that will be difficult to see even from the air. The large, disk-shaped mirror on the top of the truck is now uncovered, the first condensing mirror in position above it.

Inside the semi-darkened van, the she demon is making adjustments on the beam projector that is pointed out the opened rear of the truck toward the channel down beyond. Glenn's voice crackles over a CB unit, asking Chris to direct him to her. Then Arthur Roberts pleads with her to let him help her. The demon smashes a fist against the CB unit, silencing it.

The sound of an aircraft engine overhead causes the she demon to pause a moment. She listens until the plane has passed on, then continues with what she is doing. Erickson's plane is flying low over the area, but he doesn't spot the truck. And on the palisades road only a short distance away, Glenn's van cruises past. He and the others do not see the larger van in the ravine.

At eleven-thirty, the tanker is in the channel, headed for the Port of Los Angeles, a little ahead of schedule. It is nearing the she demon's position up on the palisade. The sky is clear, the sun blazing overhead. The huge mirror atop the truck is on automatic tracking, following the sun's movement.

And inside the van, the demon is tracking a section of the tanker's hull through a telescopic sight. She has only to press a button. She does, and instantly a pencil size beam of brilliant light streaks to its target, where it begins melting through the heavy metal hull plate.

A few hundred feet overhead, Erickson is making still another pass over the area. Suddenly, a bright flash lights up the interior of the cabin, almost blinding Eric. He looks down in time to see a bright, glittering object. Then it vanishes. He knows he has passed through the reflection of the parabolic mirror. He knows Chris is focused on the tanker. He radios the location to Glenn in the van, but he is sure there isn't enough time for them to reach Chris before the torch sends the tanker sky high. There is only one thing for him to do...

He shoves the throttle forward and maneuvers his plane down and out over the channel toward the tanker. Halfway between the ship and the palisade, he turns and heads back, just above the water, lining his plane up between the tanker and Chris's position.

Glenn and the others see what Eric is doing from where they are on the palisade road. They know he is going to try and interfere with Chris's line of sight, prevent her from keeping the cutting beam concentrated on one small spot on the ship's hull. They are right.

At high speed, Eric maneuvers the plane in and out of Chris's line of sight, pitching and yawing, and each time he crosses through the intense beam, it slashes through a section of the craft's thin metal skin, cutting control cables, fuel lines, anything in its path.

The maneuver is effective. The she demon is unable to track her target. But after a few moments, Eric's plane is trailing smoke, and as he fights to maintain control of the craft, flames flare up in the cabin behind him.

From where they are watching in the van, Glenn is shouting into the radio mike, telling Eric to ditch the plane in the channel.

But Eric knows what he must do. On and on the plane comes, like a kamikaze, toward the palisade and the truck where Chris, the she demon, is now watching. She realizes what is happening, that her father is ready to make the ultimate sacrifice to stop her.

She starts to flee, but it is too late. The plane is up over the cliffs and into the ravine, one wing clipping a rocky bluff, then ... the ship hits the ground just beyond the van, skids and slams into it, bursting into a blinding ball of fire.

Glenn, Roberts, Eric Jr., and Donna, now out of their parked van, look on in disbelief and horror. Finally, Roberts breaks the silence, suggesting it might be just as well it all ended the way it did; that he is sure Chris was past the point of return to normalcy, and how could any father want his once beautiful daughter to live the rest of her life an incarcerated mental and physical monster.

End

THE SUN DEMON: ITS DRIVE-IN WORLD PREMIERE

by **Gary D. Rhodes**

This chapter is an abbreviated version of Gary D. Rhodes's article "A Drive-In Horror by Default: The Premiere of The Hideous Sun Demon*," first published in* Monsters from the Vault #13.

By 1958, actor Robert Clarke had grown weary of starring in low-budget films and playing secondary roles at the major studios and on television programs. He had a wife and family to support, but he also had something else: "A really burning fever to make movies. Crazy, really, to want to make a film of my own independently, but that's what I wanted almost more than anything." That burning fever became *The Hideous Sun Demon* (1958). Over the years, it has turned into a cult classic, and has been released over and over again on VHS and DVD. But Clarke — who was exhausted after finishing the film — originally had difficulties finding a distributor.

In June 1958, he clipped a series of articles on the "how and why of horror movies" printed in the *Los Angeles Herald and Express*. The title of the first entry, "Horror Films Lure Teeners," stuck in his memory: the under-20 crowd had definitely become the major constituency of horror. According to the newspaper, "Chances are that when Junior borrows the family car, he and his date will hold hands at a drive-in while the monster with three heads and a million eyes pursues a teenage movie heroine through outer space."

But to Bob Clarke, the most important and inspiring proclamation of all was:

While most Hollywood producers are in deep mourning for the bonanza days when television was something out of

This ad ran in Texas newspapers in the days leading up to *The Sun Demon*'s world premiere.

science fiction and big stars meant big money, the makers of horror movies...laugh all the way to the bank. The horror cycle is at its peak. Independent producers, geared to cheap production and fast returns, have gotten rich.

Clarke wanted fast returns and the chance to produce more films. But to get rich, producers have to get their films projected. And *The Sun Demon*, as it was originally titled, had no pending screenings. Nothing had been booked.

So Bob Clarke's brother William came up with a brilliant plan. Since 1952, Bill had been sales manager at KGNC-TV, Channel 4 in Amarillo, Texas. During his years there, he had come to know many people in the Texas movie and entertainment business. For example, he regularly chatted with Blue Doyle, manager of the Crossroads Company, which owned three drive-in theaters in Amarillo. They often spoke about Bob Clarke and his film career.

When Doyle suggested, "Why not premiere *The Sun Demon* in Amarillo?", Bill Clarke quickly phoned his brother. Bob excitedly agreed to the idea. After all, drive-in theatres had reached their zenith of popularity in the late '50s, and no one else was knocking at his door.

Plans solidified, with Amarillo's Tascosa Drive-in chosen as the best venue. It was the largest and best attended of Doyle's theaters, featuring more parking spaces than the others. It was also was geographically adjacent to KGNC-TV, which soon acted as a kind of headquarters for the film's publicity. "You could walk from the back door of the station straight into the concession stand of the Tascosa; they were that close together," Bill Clarke later remembered.

Doyle scheduled the premiere for August 29, 1958, booking Allied Artists' *Attack of the Crab Monsters* (1957) for the bottom of what would be a double-bill. He also wanted to feature Bob Clarke in person, along with Nan Peterson, thinking the actress's attractive appearance would help generate interest among local movie fans.

The Crossroads Company arranged for Ray Johnson Advertising to design two different 3x7 newspaper ads and one more sized at 4x10. All proclaimed, "See the star of the picture in person. He will change from man

Nan Peterson and Robert Clarke arriving in Texas for the festivities.

to monster before your eyes. Never before attempted in any theatre. Don't miss it." Rather than keep the creature hidden from view, each ad showed Clarke wearing the Sun Demon mask.

The same ad agency also designed and printed 6000 heralds to be distributed in and around Amarillo. Nearly 11x14 in size, they could be posted in area businesses and given to would-be patrons. The design was similar to the newspaper ads: they pictured Bob undergoing the transformation into the Sun Demon, as well as a somewhat provocative image of actress Nan Peterson.

Ray Johnson Advertising also wrote and arranged airplay for several radio ads, which ran on various Amarillo stations. For example, KZIP ran a 30-second ad 40 times and a ten-second ad 20 times. The half-minute ad also ran 50 times on both KGNC and KLYN. The ten-second ad was also heard on two other stations: ten times on KLYN and 50 times on KAMQ. All were aired between August 28 and September 1, 1958. The script for the ten-second commercial read:

A beautiful girl…A handsome man…A sunny beach…Romance…Then…Before her very eyes…[Scream…Snarls]…From man…To Monster! See The Sun Demon*…Tonight at the Tascosa Drive-in Theatre…North on Fillmore Street!*

The 30-second commercial allowed time to build on the modern scientific aspects of the story:

SOUND: <u>BUBBLING SOUND</u>
ANNOUNCER: Born in the seething cauldron of an atomic furnace…and came to life with a roar like thunder!
SOUND: <u>EXPLOSION</u>
ANNOUNCER [*in echo chamber*]: *The Sun Demon!*
SOUND: <u>SCREAM AND SNARLS</u>
ANNOUNCER: Never in the wildest nightmare…was there a creature like this unbelievable product of a scientific mistake! A normal human being in the cool of night. But in the ultraviolet rays of the sun…
SOUND: <u>EXPLOSION</u>
ANNOUNCER [*in echo chamber*]: *The Sun Demon!*
ANNOUNCER: See the stark and startling story of *The Sun Demon*…Tonight at the Tascosa Drive-in Theatre, north on Fillmore Street. He changes from man to monster before your eyes! *The Sun Demon*! Tonight at the Tascosa Drive-in Theatre, north on Fillmore Street. Also showing…*Attack of the Crab Monsters*.

Sounds of explosions and buzzwords like "atomic" created a modern texture for the film; they placed it more firmly in the cross-genre of horror-science fiction, a combination that those *Los Angeles Herald and Express* articles had claimed were hits with teenagers.

Bill Clarke was also able to schedule some television commercials. The KGNC-TV continuity for the first commercial, dated August 29, 1958, is as follows:

Announcing — the world premiere of a motion picture that will long be remembered for its terror, its fright, and shocking suspense…The searing rays of the sun — that has been worshipped and feared by humans since the beginning of time — turns Man into Monster.

Before your eyes, you will see the terror that is unleashed by the Sun Demon. Experience the shock and suspense that the Sun Demon brings to a mighty Metropolis. Thrill to the brutal tower of strength that flows in its veins — the hypnotic spell cast by his evil face.

Oddly, the TV script did not build on the science fiction aspects of the story. Much like the shorter radio spots, the script reads like the horror film advertisements of the 1940s.

Publicity also came from free press, much of it focusing on Bob Clarke and Nan Peterson attending the premiere. "Two Actors Due for Premiere Here Friday," one article announced. "The actors will appear onstage… one time only on Friday. The stage appearance will take place between the two features and will last for approximately ten minutes…"

Interest in the premiere continued throughout the weekend of August 29, 1958, spurred in part by Bill Clarke's friends in the local media scene. KGNC broadcast a TV interview with Bob Clarke, and his radio interview on KLYN caused enough advance excitement for the station to sell ad time to support it.

Bill McReynolds, staff writer at the *Amarillo Daily News*, caught Clarke and Peterson shortly after their arrival in Texas, writing that they were "understandably tired, [having] left Hollywood Friday morning and land[ing] in Amarillo to the customary fanfare of television and interviews." Clarke also spoke to the newspaper about his choice of making a "monster picture" as his first film as producer:

"Well, it all goes back to why people go to see picture shows. Survey after survey indicates that our audiences of today are predominantly teenagers. At least, the teenagers are the ones that most frequently attend…

Naturally, then, I decided to tailor my film to those who would be most likely to see it."

Clarke was drawing once again on the ideas he had read about in the *Herald and Express*, still hoping for the same kind of box office success that the newspaper had described. All that remained was scoring a hit in Amarillo. Good press and large crowds: they would be key.

Clarke and Peterson look at a local newspaper ad for the *Sun Demon* show.

On the evening of the premiere, excitement grew. Bob's wife Alyce sent a telegram that arrived late that afternoon, which read, "The most of everything tonight darling, especially all my love." A few hours later, at twilight, the film began, flickering onto the Tascosa screen. Cars filled the parking area, meeting and soon exceeding attendance expectations.

The Sun Demon played well, eliciting a number of audible screams and laughs. The carloads of people sitting in the summer heat weren't disappointed. While the film lit up the screen, Bob Clarke was sitting a few blocks away, hoping and praying the evening would go well.

By the time **THE END** flashed on the outdoor screen, a motorcade had begun a few blocks away. Police cars led a Cadillac convertible into the Tascosa parking lot. Bob Clarke and Nan Peterson waved from their open-air vehicle while police sirens sounded in front of them. Searchlights beamed into the night air as the two stars made their way up a makeshift flight of stairs that led to the top of the Tascosa concession stand. Amidst cheers from the crowd, other lights illuminated Bob Clarke and Peterson.

The following is a transcript of the premiere, which was recorded on an audio transcription disk by Patterson Recording:

ANNOUNCER: Ladies and gentlemen, *The Sun Demon* now…Robert Clarke and Nan Peterson, escorted by the highway patrol and the sheriff's department. Here they come in the big white Cadillac [*laughs*]! Stars of the show *Sun Demon* [*applause*]…world premiering here in Amarillo [*applause*]!

ROBERT CLARKE: That was some chase, wasn't it? [*apparently referring to the police vehicles in the motorcade*]

ANNOUNCER: Can you hear us out there, ladies and gentlemen? Can you hear? Can we get a little more volume, please? Need just a little more volume. Can you hear us all right now? Not yet? Is that all the volume we can get? Hello, testing. Hello, testing. Hello, testing. [*Banging sound against the microphone.*] More volume, Mr. Projectionist…Ladies and gentlemen, we'd like to welcome our stars for *The Sun Demon*, Nan Peterson, the very lovely lady that you saw in our movie…I think we're getting a little more volume…and Mr. Robert Clarke, who flew in from Hollywood, California, early this afternoon. He left California early this morning, and we'd like to talk to him just a few minutes to find out just how he came about making this picture, *The Sun Demon*. First of all, ordinarily it's ladies first, but Bob, we'd like you to get another fellow for us in a little bit, so we'd like to talk to you for just a few minutes before we call Mr. Brooks [Hal Brooks, executive manager of the Crossroads Theater Company].

CLARKE: Okay, Larry, just so that I don't crowd Nan here. She is *sooo* pretty, this girl.

ANNOUNCER: Oh, isn't that the truth? Can ya'll see this pretty young lady? [*Cheers*] Can ya'll? Wooooo! [*Cheers and wolf whistles*] Bob Clarke has been in the motion picture industry for quite some time. Bob, I wonder if you can tell us where you came from originally.

CLARKE: Well, originally my home is right near Amarillo. Oklahoma City.

ANNOUNCER: And whatever prompted you to go out to Hollywood to become a movie actor?

CLARKE: Well, I guess, crazy ambition like anybody would have who wanted to get in this crazy business.

ANNOUNCER: I see. Did you have any background before you went to Hollywood?

CLARKE: Yeah, I was at the University of Wisconsin, in the theatrical school there.

ANNOUNCER: Can you give us a list of a few of the pictures you've played in, in Hollywood?

CLARKE: Well, perhaps some of you remember *The Man From Planet X* [1951], and the picture I did with Claire Trevor, called *Hard, Fast, and Beautiful* [1951], and more recently one that was here in Amarillo, *Girl with an Itch* [1958]. 'Course I've been on TV.

ANNOUNCER: *The Benny Goodman Story* [1955].

CLARKE: *Benny Goodman Story*. That was a while back. And been on *Sea Hunt* of course, and *Dragnet* and quite a number of TV things.

ANNOUNCER: Quite a lot of TV shows, and we've seen you over several of the channels here in Amarillo.

CLARKE: Thank you, Larry. Keep lookin'.

ANNOUNCER: Oh, we'll certainly do that. And Bob, how did you ever get the idea for *The Sun Demon*?

CLARKE: Well, it came about as a result of my having a very sincere interest in pictures that are full of action and science fiction type of story. I remember the picture, the original *Jekyll and Hyde*. You probably recall?

ANNOUNCER: Oh yes. Oldtimers remember that.

CLARKE: The old ones remember that. Well, I got a big kick out of that as a kid. Not too big a kid. And it's been kind of an ambition to do something along that line and bring it up to date, with science fiction and radiation poisoning and so on.

Peterson serves up hots-pitality to Clarke in beach and bedroom publicity shots. The trailer's narrator calls Clarke's character, "A man who loved with fierce, demanding passion!"

ANNOUNCER: Where was this picture shot? On location?

CLARKE: Well, this picture was made in the environs of Los Angeles, principally. We went on one location about a hundred miles away, but mostly around Los Angeles itself.

ANNOUNCER: How long did it take to shoot the picture *Sun Demon*?

Hot and "hotter": Clarke and Peterson in a classic publicity pose.

CLARKE: Actually, three weeks of shooting. In the entire preparation, planning and so on, about nine months. There's a lot of work in there.

ANNOUNCER: I imagine so.

CLARKE: And you have to pay a lot of money for a girl like this [Nan Peterson], you know. Her salary is at least 50 cents an hour [*laughs*].

ANNOUNCER: Well, that's about a quarter more than I make [*laughs*]. But Bob, we sure want to thank you for coming by, and I wonder if you would be kind enough now to get Mr. Brooks up here.

CLARKE: Mr. Brooks, who I think certainly should receive a wonderful hand, as well as Mr. Doyle, who made it possible for us to be here tonight. We want to thank them and thank all of you wonderful folks for coming. Let me get Mr. Brooks. I'll be back in just a second.

ANNOUNCER: Okay, fine. Thank you very much. While Bob is going to get Mr. Brooks, who is the executive… [*Cheers from the crowd for Nan Peterson*] Oh boy! This is one of the best jobs I ever had in my life, and they gave me two Cokes and a bag of popcorn for doing the job tonight — it was well worth it. I wonder, Nan Peterson, if you could tell us a little bit about your background. How did you ever get into moving pictures?

NAN PETERSON: Well, I come originally from Minneapolis, Larry. I've been out to Hollywood about a year, and I've always wanted to be an actress.

ANNOUNCER: You've always wanted to be an actress ever since you were a little girl. What did you do to prepare for it?

PETERSON: I went to the University of Minnesota and I took up radio-speech, and I spent my junior year at UCLA studying theater arts and then I spent a summer at the Sorbonne in Paris studying mime with [Marcel] Marceau.

ANNOUNCER: Is that right? And then you came to Hollywood. And how did you ever meet Bob and get into this movie *The Sun Demon*?

PETERSON: On a regular interview. He interviewed for the part…And I was tested for the part.

ANNOUNCER: And you made good by testing for the part. And I guess you all remember this young lady. You couldn't hardly forget her. Her first appearance in a movie was as the singer in the nightclub [*referring to a scene in* Sun Demon], is that right?

PETERSON: Yes.

ANNOUNCER: And from there you progressed admirably well.

PETERSON: To the beach! [*referring to the* Sun Demon *beach scene*]!

ANNOUNCER [*laughs*]: Is this your first picture, Nan?

PETERSON: This was my first picture, yes.

ANNOUNCER: I understand that there's some things in the works for future pictures for you.

PETERSON: Yes, I'm planning to do one called *Bourbon Street Blues* in New Orleans.

ANNOUNCER: Oh, in New Orleans. Wonderful.

PETERSON: I'll be playing a…[*Laughs*]

ANNOUNCER: Uh-huh, you'll be playing a…

PETERSON: A strip-dancer.

ANNOUNCER: A strip-dancer. Oh boy!

PETERSON: I'll have a double!

ANNOUNCER: She'll have a double! Well, Nan, we heard during the show tonight that they're never gonna go out in the sun again [*laughs*]. Did you have quite a thrill making this picture with Bob?

PETERSON: It was a lot of fun…The only bad part of it: We shot all the sequences at the beach early in the morning about 5 o'clock and —

ANNOUNCER: Oh my gosh!

PETERSON: And the one time when I had to go in the water, it was awfully cold.

ANNOUNCER: Ice cold! What was this thrilling incident while you were making the picture about the car, when you parked the car at the cliff with Bob after you left the nightclub?

PETERSON: Well, we almost went over the cliff!

ANNOUNCER: You almost went over the cliff!

PETERSON: In fact, one time I jumped out of the car. They thought I was silly.

ANNOUNCER: They thought you were silly for jumping out to save your life!

PETERSON: I don't believe in suffering that much for your art!

ANNOUNCER [*laughs*]: Wonderful! Nan, Mr. Brooks, the fellow who's made this world premiere possible, is standing back there. Wonder if we could get him up here. Mr. Hal Brooks, ladies and gentlemen, who is the executive manager of the Crossroads Theaters company. How did you ever happen to arrange for this world premiere here at Tascosa?

The Tascosa, site of *The Sun Demon's scream*iere.

HAL BROOKS: Well, we just been most fortunate that we were selected here in Amarillo to have the picture first, at the Tascosa Theater.

ANNOUNCER: Wonderful! And I'll bet it's been as big a pleasure for you meeting Nan Peterson and Bob Clarke as it has been for me —

BROOKS: It certainly has.

ANNOUNCER: — and lots of us here in the industry…I know the people of Amarillo have enjoyed this picture tremendously, and I think they owe you a big vote of thanks for bringin' it here.

BROOKS: Well, we've been very thrilled to have them, and I'd like to say now that we have been successful in talking both Bob and Nan into staying over for another night.

ANNOUNCER: They're going to be here again tomorrow night in person? Wonderful! Well, I hope some of the folks will come back and see 'em.

BROOKS: I hope so too.

ANNOUNCER: Fine. Thank you very much, and where did Bob go, Mr. Brooks?

BROOKS: I'll see if I can find him.

ANNOUNCER: Bye-bye, Mr. Brooks.

ANNOUNCER: Well, Nan, we certainly enjoyed your role in the movie tonight. Bob said it took about three —
PETERSON: [*screams twice, loudly*].

The archival recording of the premiere concludes with a number of screams, cheers and hollers from the crowds as the Sun Demon briefly ran into the parking lot. As a result, the film — incarnated in the personage of its title character — broke the boundary between movie screen and audience. In the best tradition of film ballyhoo, a live Sun Demon invaded the audience's space, moving from car to car as the recording comes to an end.

After Clarke ran behind the concession stand and took off the mask, he wiped the sweat from his forehead. It was time to remove the scaled claws and prepare for a night of glad-handing. A cocktail party honoring him and *The Sun Demon* began at ten that night at the Tascosa Country Club.

The Sun Demon attracted 1469 moviegoers on opening night; 1343 on Saturday, August 30; 1172 on Sunday, August 31; 482 on Monday, September 1; and 244 on Tuesday, September 2, the last day of the film's run. The drop-off on the last two days was not unexpected, as weekdays (especially Tuesday through Thursday) generally brought in much smaller crowds than weekends. Instead, the one surprise was probably

August 31, a day when Clarke and Peterson were not present in person but the turnout was almost as large as on the two days that they were.

When Clarke eventually received a Percentage Engagement Report from Blue Doyle, it included a check for $785.84, which amounted to half of the net proceeds. The gross had been $3,061.50, but authorized deductions amounted to $1,489.81; they broke down to $660.83 for newspaper ads, $214.72 for Clarke and Peterson's airline tickets, $499.26 for radio ads and ad designs-heralds, and $15 for *Attack of the Crab Monsters* rental fees. The percentage that Bob received did not include a cut of the concessions, which generated a large percentage of the profits drive-ins make. "We didn't even bother asking Doyle for a cut of those," brother Bill said. "We knew they wouldn't give a cent of that take, so we didn't even try to get them to budge."

Clarke had done well, not only in attendance, but also in the overall deal itself. Most drive-ins of the era preferred to pay flat fees to screen the films they rented, and when they did pay percentages in 1958, they weren't usually deals for 50 percent.

Happy with the outcome, Doyle offered to fly Clarke in his Piper Cub airplane to Dallas, where he could screen *The Sun Demon* for the city's Universal Studios Exchange. According to Clarke, "It was really hot weather and my God I was sweating as I carried film cans for a few blocks to get to the Universal people. When I finally got up to speak to them, they said they had been watching me trudging down the street. That must have been a sure signal to them that I was in deep and wasn't in much of a bargaining position."

The Sun Demon was screened and the response was relatively warm. On September 5, 1958, R.N. Wilkinson of the Dallas office penned a letter to Clarke:

> Pursuant to our conversation of yesterday, I wish to advise that there is a possibility of our using a picture such as your *Sun Demon* which might possibly be placed as a lower half of a double bill with a suitable companion picture for the top half. It may be possible for us to use this picture with a subject currently going into production based on *The Phantom of the Opera*.
>
> As I discussed with you yesterday, after you have been able to work on the print some[,] our people would be interested in screening this picture on the basis of a distribution deal only. We are currently not interested in buying any small pictures outright.

Clarke waited for a response, hoping for a distribution deal, even if it meant a delay in receiving much-needed funds. Days went by, turning into weeks. On October 8, 1958, Clarke tore open an envelope from F.J.A. McCarthy of Universal's New York City office. After reading several kind words, Clarke saw the news: "We had our Screening Committee look at *Sun Demon*, and they were of the opinion that this picture

"Made it, Ma! Top of the world!": When *The Sun Demon* had its successful Texas run, Clarke must have felt as though his new moviemaking career was off and running.

would not fit into our schedule of releases." His heart sank. Warner Brothers also passed on the film, giving an even quicker "no" than Universal had.

Possibilities with the major studios had crumbled, and Clarke was too leery of American International Pictures (AIP) to sign a distribution deal with them. A friend directed him to a third option: Miller Consolidated Pictures. Two business partners had started the company to compete with AIP. They happily offered to pair *The Sun Demon* with their own first film, *Date with Death*. Clarke agreed and even ended up acting in their movie.

On January 27, 1959, the film — now sporting the title *The Hideous Sun Demon* — opened at the bottom of the *Date with Death* double-bill at the indoor Plains Theater in Roswell, New Mexico. Clarke appeared live onstage in the Sun Demon costume. Two days later, the double feature played the indoor Lyric Theater in Odessa, Texas. The *Odessa American* reported that Clarke would once again "wear his monster suit at the personal appearance," which was scheduled for January 29.

Thanks to Miller Consolidated's distribution, *The Hideous Sun Demon* played in various cities and towns in the United States and England. Many of those bookings returned Clarke's film to where it premiered: the drive-in theater. But Miller Consolidated went bankrupt shortly after distributing *The Hideous Sun Demon*, meaning that Clarke never got a single dollar from them.

Despite its lasting cult status among horror and science fiction film fans, *The Hideous Sun Demon* does not really exemplify the typical drive-in horror film. Certainly, some films in that category made a profit; a smaller number generated very large grosses. Many drive-in horror films also provided the chance for their producer-directors to move on to bigger-budget projects. Bob Clarke received no such rewards.

But Bob always remembered having been the featured attraction at the premiere. That was the night under the stars in West Texas when it seemed that the possibilities for his film were endless. And in a way, despite the film's distribution troubles, some of his hopes and dreams came true. Over 50 years later, *The Hideous Sun Demon* is better known than so many of those movies that Universal and Warner Brothers did release in 1958. The film may not have made Bob Clarke money, but it did bring him lasting fame.

HIDEOUS SUN DEMON: THE SPECIAL EDITION

A Short History by **Tom Weaver**

Nineteen eighty-three, the silver anniversary of *The Sun Demon*'s 1958 drive-in world premiere, was marked by announcements that the newly formed Twenty Four Horses Company was producing *Hideous Sun Demon: The Special Edition*. Through a Hollywood talent agency, Twenty Four Horses (operating out of 358 North Doheny Avenue, Los Angeles) had contacted the original film's current owner Wade Williams about buying all rights. "They offered *beau coup* bucks—enough to get me to sell it," says Williams. "They said they were going to 'remake' it, but I later came to find out they meant 'remake' it like the Woody Allen *What's Up, Tiger Lily?* [1966]" (redub it comically and add new footage). According to the *Special Edition* presskit, the Twenty Four Horses moviemakers screened over 100 1950s horror flicks before choosing *Hideous Sun Demon*.

Williams suggested to producer Greg Brown that since new scenes would be shot for *Special Edition*, Robert Clarke should be in the cast. Clarke and the filmmakers did make contact; although he didn't wind up in the new footage, his actor son Cameron got a part. "That made it a little less…horrible for Bob," says Williams.

With new dialogue throughout, the *Special Edition* storyline has microbiologist Ishmael Pivnik (voiced by then-nobody Jay Leno) becoming a Sun Demon as a result of using plutonium and lizard semen in his newest innovation, a suntan lotion that you drink in order to tan from the inside out. Nan Peterson's Trudy is called Bunny (voiced by 1972 Oscar nominee Susan Tyrrell), Patrick Whyte's Dr. Buckell is called Major Clive McGonad (voiced by Bernard Behrens),

In new footage in *Hideous Sun Demon: The Special Edition*, Cameron Clarke *(right)* recreated the role of the Scientist originally played by his father (set visitor Robert Clarke, *left*).

Lt. Peterson is called Lt. Peckerwood (voiced by John Mayer), etc. Cameron Clarke plays the part of Pivnik in new footage. To avoid audience confusion, he is seen only in distant shots or with his back to the camera. And Leno goes mysteriously unbilled; in both the list of voice actors in *Special Edition*'s end credits crawl and in the presskit, the new voice of Pivnik is unaccountably credited to—Robert Clarke!

Once *Hideous Sun Demon: The Special Edition* was finished (circa spring 1986), the filmmakers couldn't find a distributor. Financial headaches ensued, and 21-year-old Hadi Salem, who had supplied the money, pulled out. (Williams: "The sheik went back to Araby!") Williams told producer Brown that he wanted to buy back the rights to the 1958 original, and Brown bit. When Williams got all his material back, he discovered that the *Special Edition* crew had cut up the original negative to morph it into the new movie.

About six months later, Brown called Williams to ask, "Would you buy *The Special Edition* from me?" Williams went to California and saw it in a Selznick Studios screening room, "and I'll be damned if I didn't laugh my butt off. So I made a deal with him, and I got it for like ten cents on the dollar."

Special Edition fixes a few of the technical mistakes of the 1958 flick, including the addition of needed punch, slap and gunshot sounds that the original moviemakers neglected to incorporate. Hilariously, Gil's many missed punches in his fight with George here have whiffing sounds; when Bunny begs Pivnik, "Let's get out of here!," Pivnik complains, "But I haven't *hit* him yet!" In new footage, there's even a happy ending for the Sun Demon: Still alive after his gas tank fall, he wanders the streets and encounters Bunny the nightclub singer, now a Sun Demon herself (she also drank the suntan lotion). They walk together into, yes, the sunset.

Williams sneak-previewed *Hideous Sun Demon: The Special Edition* at the Fine Arts Theatre in Mission, Kansas (a suburb of Kansas City, Missouri, Williams'

The *Special Edition* presskit says that the head used in their new monster footage was the original; it wasn't; Clarke sweated so much in the original in 1958 that it was starting to fall apart *then*. For *Special Edition,* a new mask was made from Bob Burns' mold.

```
                                              10.

   Nurse June exits.

                       GRANNY
                  Pardon me, young man.  Is there
                  perchance a magazine on the table
                  called "Bondage and Health?"

                       PIVNIK
                  Let's see.

   Pivnik hands her the magazine and looks for one
   himself.

                       GRANNY
                  I hope you won't think me rude
                  if I don't talk to you for a
                  while.  I'm anxious to get at
                  my article.

                       PIVNIK
                  Whatever you say, Granny.

   Pivnik and the old lady peruse their magazines.

   INSERT PIVNIK'S MAGAZINE -- "THINK AND DO."

   He loosens his robe in order to catch some rays.
   The sun beats down on him...

   Pivnik grimaces.  He begins to squirm in his chair.
   The sun gets larger and hotter.

   Pivnik now writhes in pain.

                       PIVNIK (V.O.)
                  Ugh!  Damn hospital food.

   LOUDS SOUNDS OF FLATULENCE.

                       PIVNIK (V.O.)
                  Ooooh!  Do I have gas.  Oh boy!

   MORE FLATULENCE.

   Granny looks up from "Bondage and Health."

                       GRANNY
                       (to Pivnik)
                  What's your opinion of nipple
                  clamps?
```

A page from *Hideous Sun Demon: The Special Edition*'s raunchy script.

home town). In his three-star review (May 17, 1989), *Kansas City Star* critic Robert W. Butler called the original *Sun Demon* "awful" and this new one "an instant cult classic…Granted, the project is in awful taste… But some savvy wit is also in evidence…[W]hen it's in high gear, this movie makes you laugh until the tears come. It isn't art, but it sure is funny." Robert Clarke ruefully disagreed; he told *Psychotronic* magazine's Anthony Petkovich, "It's not very good. Wade thinks it's funny. I don't think it's funny. I think it's dirty. Real low-grade humor."

Wade Williams: "I can understand why Bob did not like it. It made fun of his efforts and hard work and diminished the original. *Sun Demon* was made as a serious horror shocker but even in the late '50s it was a little antiquated in its concept. And some of the acting was 'hideous'! Today the original film does not scare as much as it entertains as a quaint B-movie of a simpler era. It actually is more of a '40s-type 'werewolf' film with the atomic radiation added to bring it up to date [1958]. But whatever its shortcomings, it's entertaining and a lot of fun.

"I like the original *and The Special Edition*. Both are fun. I believe the remake has a lot of entertainment value, and it's done good word-of-mouth business wherever it's played."

Unfortunately, Williams couldn't get *Special Edition* going theatrical distribution-wise the way he would have liked, and eventually released it on home video under the title *Revenge of the Sun Demon*. Several sources call it *What's Up, Hideous Sun Demon* but it appears that the movie has never had that as an on-screen title.

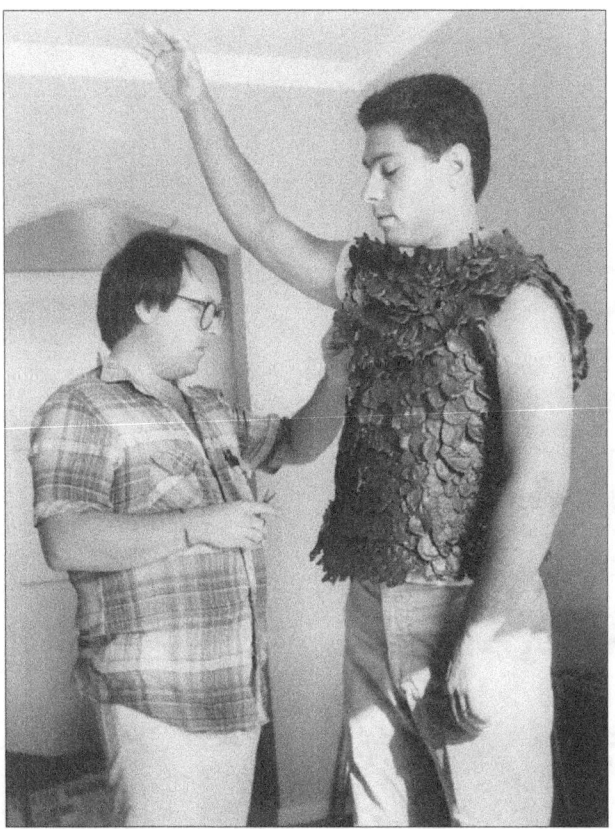

Special effects costume designer Robert Joyce (*left, with actor Stuart Blatt*) at work on the scaly tunic. His other credits include 1978's *The Wiz* (he created the Winkies) and 1983's *Spacehunter: Adventures in the Forbidden Zone*.

ABOUT ROBERT CLARKE...

Wade Williams, the sci-fi film distributor and entrepreneur, shares memories of his longtime friend Robert Clarke.

One Saturday in the winter of 1952, at one o'clock in the afternoon, my Aunt Virginia was getting married at City Hall. The man about to become her *seventh* husband was a very nice, recently divorced GI with three daughters. The immediate family was supposed to be there, including her father (my grandfather) and me.

A big problem: Across town at the very same time, at a Saturday matinee, a movie called *The Man from Planet X* was playing only one time. I *had* to see this movie. I had recently discovered the outer space TV shows *Space Patrol* and *Tom Corbett, Space Cadet*, and traded away my Hoppy outfit and six-shooters for spacesuits and ray guns. I was now a real Spade Cadet, hooked for life.

Under unrelenting pressure, and after a tantrum or two from me, my grandfather decided that his presence was not necessary at Auntie Virginia's wedding. He'd given her away six previous times; he wouldn't be missed. We were off to the Gladstone Theatre.

Sitting in the dark theater, I was introduced to Robert Clarke and the Man from Planet X. I was entranced by that 70-minute black-and-white invasion film, told in flashbacks by Clarke as a newspaper reporter. It had moody atmosphere and a feeling of isolation, and the appearance of the Man from Planet X was based on the recent descriptions of the little men of the purported Roswell flying saucer crash. What could be better?

Robert was every inch the dashing hero with an Errol Flynn look. He saved the world, he saved leading lady Margaret Field (a Jennifer Jones lookalike) and he thwarted the Man from Planet X.

Dashing Robert Clarke and his leading lady Margaret Field, mother of Sally Field, in a publicity shot from *The Man from Planet X.*

The movie occasionally played around town until 1956 and then the two prints in the Kansas City film depot were ordered junked. I was able to get one of them, plus a Holmes 35mm portable sound projector. I projected it hundreds of times on the living room wall.

Three decades later, Robert and I would become friends and I would even produce a film, *Midnight Movie Massacre* (1988), with Robert and Ann *War of*

Clarke got to enjoy himself in silly *Captive Women* publicity poses.

the Worlds Robinson.

Bob always gave believable performances and had the ability to make cheap films work. Another one of his pictures that did big business was *Captive Women* (1952) which re-teamed him with *Planet X* co-stars Margaret Field and William Schallert. In the early 1960s I saw Bob's *The Hideous Sun Demon* at a packed drive-in theater. It was a lot of fun and there were some chills. Bob also produced and directed *Hideous Sun Demon* and was proud of it. It was made on a shoestring budget with the help of college film students. The actors were a mix of amateurs and professionals. The Demon costume was well done.

Bob was stuck in low-budget movies like these, and others such as *The Incredible Petrified World* (1957), *The Astounding She-Monster* (1958) and *Beyond the Time Barrier* (1960). Back then, he was the leading man in more science fiction films than almost anyone. He could be counted on by such producers as Jerry Warren, Ronnie Ashcroft and Edgar Ulmer to look good and play the role well.

In the '70s, when I started buying the rights to science fiction and horror films, I was told that Bob

Robert Clarke in 1950, the year he began playing starring roles.

wanted to sell *Hideous Sun Demon*, among others. I had never met Bob but contacted him and went to L.A. for a meeting. We hit if off and became good friends. I bought the rights to *The Hideous Sun Demon*, *Date with Death* and *Beyond the Time Barrier*.

Bob and I also talked many times of making a movie together. We considered a sequel to *Sun Demon* and other ideas. He was always excited about the business and enthusiastic. Many young aspiring filmmakers came up with various concepts, scripts and ideas to remake *Demon* but Bob just couldn't raise the money or pique the interest of distributors.

In the early '80s I raised money to make a feature version of the TV series *Space Patrol* and I hired Harry Essex, the scripter of *It Came from Outer Space,* to do the writing. (1953). After the initial $20,000 for a treatment, I realized we had a turkey of a script and scrapped it. Writer-director Mark Stock and I rewrote it, and brought in a Hollywood crew who turned out to be more interested in the catering of food than in making the film. To star, I hired Bob and Ann Robinson, who gave credible performances. However, there was not enough plot for the film to stand on its own. Desperate to save what we had shot, a new "wraparound" story was written. A Kansas City director and crew shot the new footage, including a musical number. *Space Patrol* with Bob and Ann became "a movie within a movie" in a picture that was now called *Midnight Movie Massacre.* It got some good reviews.

It was great to work with Bob, a fine actor who had rubbed shoulders with greats like Boris Karloff, Clark Gable and Ida Lupino, and even a new-to-Hollywood Marilyn Monroe. Bob was slumming in most of his later films, working below his level, but always did the best he could with what he had. He had "matinee idol looks" and a commanding speaking voice. Why didn't he go farther? Perhaps he looked too much like Flynn or Robert Taylor, or did not have an agent who would work for him. Or maybe he did not want or need stardom all that much: He married into a famous singing group, the King Family, and helped manage them. He joined the Mormon Church and raised a family. There was not a lot of time to work at being a movie star. He lived in a luxurious home with a swimming pool and everything Hollywood stars are supposed to have. He toured the world with his wife's singing group, played for presidents and hobnobbed with the rich and famous.

Bob was a Midwestern boy who went to Hollywood and made movies. His handsome good looks are forever captured on celluloid and he will always be known as the Hideous Sun Demon and as the man who defeated the Man from Planet X.

He was a great friend and I miss him.

Wade Williams
November 25, 2010

Clarke, Wade Williams, Ann Robinson and associate producer Brian Mossman on a Los Angeles soundstage dubbing *Midnight Movie Massacre* in 1986. "Bob still looked like a handsome leading man in the Gable mold," says Williams.

FUN FACTS

by **Tom Weaver**

Yet more tidbits of information about everyone's favorite thermo-dynamic monster movie of the '50s and the people who made it…

✸ Cinemanor was a two-story, six-bedroom house, about three-quarters of a block north of the Shrine Auditorium (walking distance from the USC campus). *Sun Demon* co-director Tom Boutross and sound man Doug Menville were two of the earliest occupants. "It was perfect for us, and we all got along well," says Menville. "Over the years, some people moved out and others moved in. The landlord, Mr. Hill, allowed us to cut a hole in the living room wall for a projection setup and we installed a screen so that we could watch movies in comfort. One of our fellow occupants, Jack Stonnell, had a 16mm Bell & Howell projector and we would rent films from Films Inc. Often other film students would come and join us for the showings."

✸ It occurred to me to ask crew member Ron Honthaner, "If Cinemanor was such a big place, why wasn't any of *Sun Demon* shot there?" His simple answer: "Well…because Cinemanor was pretty much of a dump [*laughs*]! It was an old house that had been added-onto and patched-up and plastered-together, really kinda shabby, and we didn't do much to fix it up; we just lived in it the way it was. Upstairs, there was a pay phone in the hallway, and the upstairs bathroom must have been eight feet wide and 40 feet long — we called it 'The Bowling Alley' because it was such a weird set-up for a bathroom! That house has been torn down long since."

Sun Demon costume maker Richard Cassarino handles some last-minute adjustments.

✱ Robin C. Kirkman's house (4201 Woodman Avenue, Sherman Oaks) was used as *The Sun Demon*'s "casting office," where various actors and actresses were interviewed. Some of the shooting later took place there: the scenes set in Dr. Stern's office, the hospital room where Gil flirts with his nurse, Gil's bedroom where he dreams about Trudy, and the kitchen of Suzy and her mother.

✱ Scenes in Trudy's apartment were photographed in the one-story house of a lady-friend of actor Peter Similuk, who played the thuggish George. The police station scenes were shot in a little store on Ventura near Vineland; Richard Cassarino, who made the Sun Demon costume, decorated that set.

✱ Scenes set outside Gil's house were shot at the Canfield-Moreno Estate, perched high above L.A. on Micheltorena Street in the Silver Lake district. Built in the 1920s, it was once the luxurious mansion-home of silent screen star Antonio Moreno and his heiress wife Daisy; she died in a 1933 car crash, and to this day her ghost reportedly haunts the house. At the time of *Sun Demon* shooting, it was owned and run by a covey of nuns. It's now a recording studio and known as the Paramour Mansion. Other movies partly shot there include *Halloween H20: 20 Years Later* (1998) and *Scream 3* (2000).

✱ As cast and crew worked at the Canfield-Moreno Estate, Robert "Skip" Montgomery Jr. visited to watch the shooting. The actor-son of Hollywood heavyweight Robert Montgomery and the brother of Elizabeth (*Bewitched*) Montgomery, "Skip" had his own sci-fi spotlight moment when he played the teenage mathematician accompanying the first manned lunar flight in the indie *12 to the Moon* (1960).

✱ In our 1998 *Fangoria* interview, Tom Boutross said that Doug Menville brought in 24-karat kook E.S. Seeley Jr. as *Sun Demon* screenwriter. Menville, who I "met" online in 2010, sets the record straight: "I certainly wouldn't have recommended Ed, I would have recommended *myself*, for God's sake! I was a writer and would have loved to have had the job. I think Ed and Bob Clarke met independently, and Seeley talked him into it.

"Ed S. Seeley Jr. was a strange and amusing character. He was always so full of himself and so serious, we couldn't help but laugh at him. But the last laugh was his, as he was the only one who made any decent money from the film; I think Bob paid him $5000 for the script, but I'm not certain of the amount. Seeley had already produced several long, unpublished and unpublishable nihilistic novels with the theme 'God is evil.' I tried to read one of them and it was unreadable, little more than one long anti-religious diatribe. After he left school, he went on to write a number of soft-porn paperback novels. The porn novels were fairly well-written, in contrast, but boring." (According to Amazon.com, Seeley's novels are *Street Walker*, *Pillow Girl*, *Suburban Sexpot*, *Lens Girl*, *Sorority Sin* and *Double Date*.)

Menville continues, "Ed was always spouting his anti-God dogma to anyone who would listen, but he was quite intelligent. He drove a Packard and always used his driving gloves. Another Seeley trait was that he always carried an umbrella with him, rain or shine. Definitely an eccentric, he would have been right at home in England. We've all lost contact with him in the years since *Hideous Sun Demon*."

✱ Several crew members also played parts in the movie. Robin Kirkman, Ron Honthaner and Doug Menville are seen as policemen (see pages 16-17 of Clarke's introductory chapter for details); Cassarino plays the policeman who has a few Kelton the Cop-type exchanges with Lt. Peterson and chases the Sun Demon up the gasometer. He's also a beach frolicker in the scene where Gil (atop the cliff) contemplates suicide, *and* a customer in the bar where Gil meets Trudy. Script girl Margot "Deanie" Follis (wife of crew member Stan Follis) is another barfly; she'd already been seen in the movie as one of the hospital nurses. The service station attendant gassing up Gil's MG convertible is assistant director Tom Miller, grandson of Norman Thomas, umpteen-time presidential candidate on the Socialist ticket.

✱ Vivid in the memory of film loader and back-up cameraman Stan Follis is the day when his beautiful young wife "Deanie" (pictured on the facing page) told him that Fred La Porta, the elderly German glassware maker playing the role of Dr. Hoffman, had just propositioned her!

✱ Follis was an undergraduate and the other USC crew members were graduate students, so he laughingly calls himself "the lowest rung on the *Sun Demon* echelon." For him, working on the movie "was great, it was fun, and sort of exciting. It was as close as I ever got to real [theatrical] moviemaking." After graduation he went to work for the Navy, learning to scuba

Is that Ava Gardner? No, it's "Deanie" Follis, plum purdy on both sides of the *Sun Demon* camera. In the top photo she attends to her script girl job (with Richard Cassarino, right), in the bottom she's seen in her nurse's uniform in the opening hospital scene.

dive and photograph underwater; next he became part of an aerospace industry film production unit. Today he's president of Walkabout International *(www.walkabout-int.org/)*, a non-profit educational group that promotes neighborhood walking in urban, suburban, and rural environments.

✴ Marilyn King, Clarke's sister-in-law, told me that she was supposed to play "the bad girl" (Trudy) in the movie, but then *didn't* once she found out she was pregnant. Says Robin Kirkman: "I don't think that [Clarke and sister-in-law Marilyn as lovers] would have been a good idea. Almost incest there!"

✴ Clarke recalled going perhaps 14 takes on his hysterical scene, but for the rest of the movie, *one* take was more like the norm. Ron Honthaner says, "Bob was moving very rapidly. One day he said to me, 'For the hospital corridor scene, Ron, I need a shot of Deanie Follis' feet running. While I go get into my Sun Demon makeup, get that shot, Ron. You're the director.' I didn't know what the hell I was going to do [*laughs*]. Deanie ran in, and she was kind of mincing her steps, and so I asked her to do it again. By that time, Bob had come back in his Sun Demon costume, to do the scene where he breaks the mirror. He said to me, 'You haven't shot that thing *yet*, for cryin' out loud?!' and *he* shot it [*laughs*]! So, yeah, he was movin' like crazy. Well, hell, time is money, and he wanted to get it done."

✴ Clarke's six-year-old niece Xandra Conkling, who played little Suzy in the movie's closing reels, also remembers seeing a bit of "Uncle Bob"'s temper the day they shot on the Long Beach oil fields. "He wasn't able, of course, to block off the streets where he was shooting. It was a very deserted area, but occasionally a car would come through, and he'd run over and yell at the driver! And the cars would *continue* coming [*laughs*] — there was nothing he could do about it! I remember him yellin' at all the drivers that would come through, when he was trying to get a shot and they couldn't keep the traffic away."

✴ The daughter of Clarke's wife Alyce's sister Donna King and hit record producer James B. Conkling, Xandra was born Alexandra but soon became Xandra (and today calls herself Xan). When she was a kid, she says, she thought of "Uncle Bob" and Liberace (whose show she'd watch on TV) as her "first boyfriends" ("Quite a combination!"). "When Uncle

Bob asked me to be in his movie, it was like, 'I'm gonna be with my boyfriend!'" Her mother Donna taught her her lines and went over them with her — *and* played her mom in *Sun Demon*.

✹ Sound FX Defects: In the confrontation scene in Trudy's apartment, George slaps Trudy and Gil punches George, both without the needed sound effects. During the railroad yard chase, with the Sun Demon in the foreground and a cop in the distant background, the cop stops and points his gun, which bucks twice in his hand as he noiselessly "shoots."

✹ Other bloopers: Putting on an Irradiated Insect Life slide show for Ann and Dr. Buckell, Dr. Stern calls a hornet an ant and then calls a spider a grasshopper. In the beach scene, Gil's pants are wet up to the knees before he gets anywhere near the water. In Trudy's apartment, George thinks he's caught Gil with his hand in the nookie jar, pulls a gun and forces Gil to walk outside, where George now has a different gun. The barroom dust-up between Gil and George features more missed punches than Fight Night at the Helen Keller Institute; Gil eventually kayoes George with a series of weak uppercuts. The only "collateral damage" to the bar: a ring life preserver, hung on a wall, drops harmlessly to the floor. Nevertheless, the bartender frantically chases after the fleeing Gil and Trudy demanding, "Hey, what about the damage to the joint?!" At Suzy's house, watch how much milk she spills trying to fill the glass held by her mother.

✹ In the slide show projector scene, Tom Boutross wanted the images on Dr. Stern's slides (seen in insert shots) to be in color. The biology book seen in the movie was illustrated with color photos of various critters, so Boutross photographed some of the uglier ones on color movie film. But in those days, ev-er-y insert color shot would have had to be spliced into the proper spots in ev-er-y black-and-white print, a time-consuming, prohibitively expensive task, so the idea was dropped.

✹ The Sun Demon drives from the beach to his home, runs up a hillside and vaults over a wall toward the camera (see photo below). To make things easier for Clarke, a camera case was placed at the base of the far side of the wall; Clarke stepped up onto it before his jump. Unfortunately, when the crew moved to their next location (the beach), the base of that wall is

With *Sun Demon*, Robert Clarke leapt into the adventurous arena of producer-director.

right where the forgotten camera case *stayed*. Doubly unfortunate: It contained the filters needed to make the beach scene, being shot in daylight but set at night, look dark! It was Ron Honthaner who had forgotten the case; d.p. Vilis Lapenieks, in his thick Latvian accent, "chewed my ass good," says Honthaner. "Vilis was very dogmatic, very Germanic in his attitudes. And very vocal!" The camera's f-stop was adjusted and the "night scene" came out looking okay, but it coulda-shoulda been better.

✱ In the basement scene where the Sun Demon picks up a rat and crushes it in his hands, the dripping "blood" is actually ketchup. Clarke claims that the rat was not hurt. He admitted to me that the scene was not in good taste ("It made you want to throw up") and said he was happy that the footage was missing from some *Sun Demon* prints.

✱ The scene of Gil being beaten in the garbage-strewn alley behind the bar was shot in Santa Monica outside the Tumble-In Motel on Chautauqua Blvd., near the beach.

✱ I asked Ron Honthaner if working on *The Sun Demon* every weekend for months on end was fun, or did it "start to get old" after a while? "It was *always* fun and interesting, 'cause we [the USCers] were all new to moviemaking, and we felt we were making a... [*laughs*] ...classic! And I guess, in a way, we *have*! I have to admit, though...I saw it again recently, and it doesn't hold up as well as I had hoped. It was a lot more fun to make than it was to look at [*laughs*]!

"We all pretty much enjoyed making it. A couple of the guys dropped out; Tom Miller at one point dropped out, and then came back, and at least one other guy dropped out, someone who I guess just had better things to do. Or had to earn a living, perhaps! We weren't paid. I mean, we were paid the first weekend, and that was *it*. At least, that was *me*. But I stayed simply because I *wanted* to do it; to me, it was exciting."

✱ Running from the scene of George's murder, the Sun Demon stops, abruptly arches his back and throws his head back before climbing up the cliff side. Clarke did this because the mask had moved around on his head and he was trying to find the eye holes.

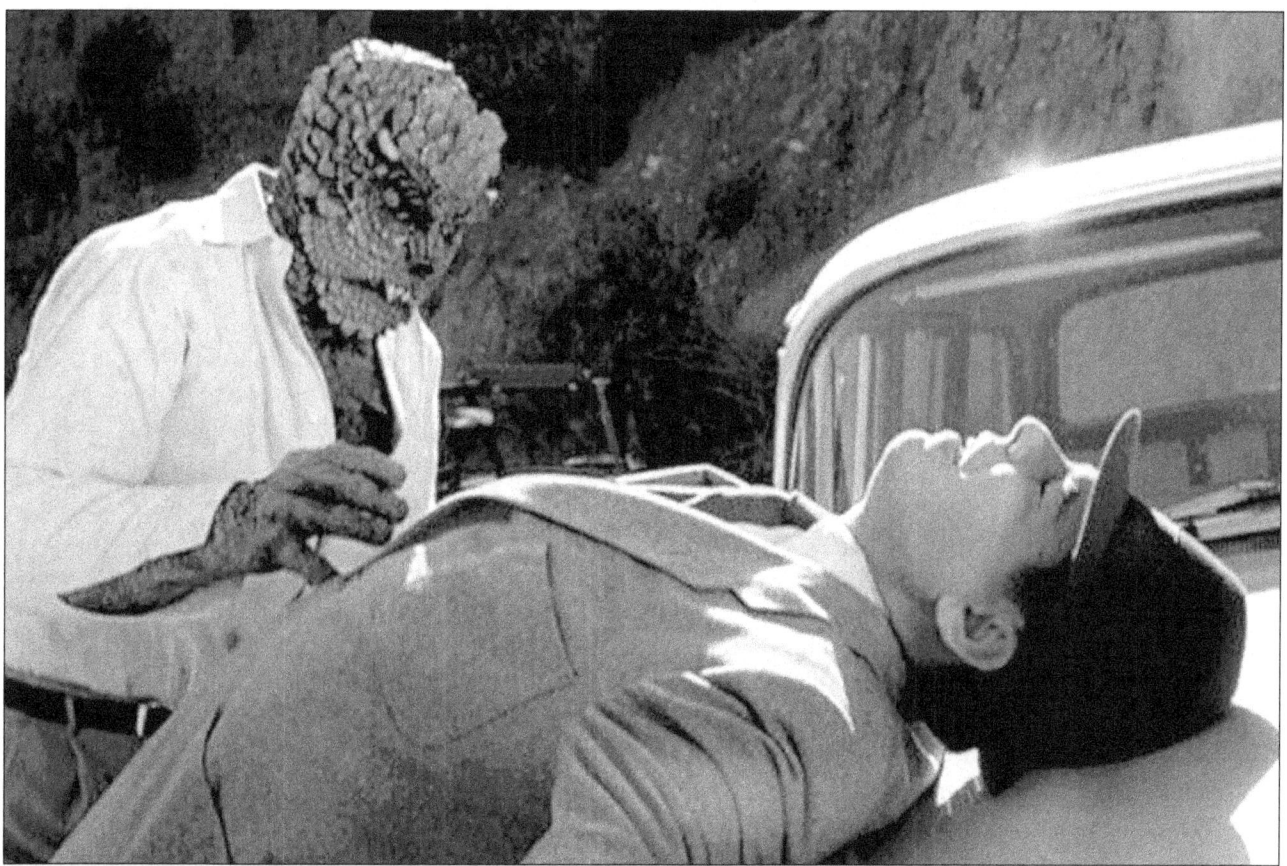

George (Peter Similuk) gets his hide tanned by the Sun Demon (Clarke). In the movie, watch perspiration (or *some*thing) dripping out of the Sun Demon mask as Clarke walks away.

✱ The newspaper-selling boy on the street ("Read all about it! Weird killer still at large!") is nine-year-old David Sloan, Clarke's nephew (the son of his sister Genevieve). In 1970, 21-year-old Sloan and his 19-year-old girlfriend Sheryl Lynn Benham were found dead in the trunk of Sloan's car in a lovers' lane northwest of Norman, Oklahoma. More than 20 bullets had been pumped into them. At the time, it was called one of the most savage crimes in the state's history.

For years the buzz was that Norman policeman Frank Gilley was the double-murderer, and in 1991 he was finally indicted and tried. There was something for everybody (mystery, sex, scandal, violence) in what became known as the Lovers' Lane Murder Trial, whose highlights included the testimony of Gilley (he pointed the finger of blame at a fellow officer, by then deceased) and the 12 jurors' trip through wintry winds and sleet to the crime scene. At trial's end, after four hours of jury deliberation, Gilley was found innocent. He died in a Texas rest home in 2002 but made no deathbed confession. Is the weird killer still at large?

✱ According to Kirkman, the cops' cars in *Sun Demon* were actually cars provided free of charge by the Chrysler Corporation, with police emblems added temporarily (and illegally!) by Cassarino. Much of the time, the shooting was done without permits.

✱ Although he co-financed the picture, Kirkman was seldom on the interior "sets": He had the job of sound recordist, and the recording equipment was kept in his station wagon. He would sit in the car outside the various location sites waiting to hear (through his earphones) Clarke, inside, yell "Roll sound!" Kirkman would then turn on the recorder and, when it was up to speed, blow the car horn as the signal that the actors could proceed!

✱ Kirkman was understandably apprehensive about some of the iffier things that he and the other *Sun Demon* moviemakers were doing (shooting without permits, wearing police uniforms in public, etc.) and occasionally voiced his concerns. One day when Kirkman was nowhere to be seen, Clarke referred to him as "a worried old lady" — unaware that sound man Kirkman, outside in his car wearing earphones, was hearing every word! Kirkman never brought the incident up to Clarke and laughingly told me that he forgave Clarke for making the comment.

✱ Arriving home from the beach in his MG convertible, Gil (as the Sun Demon) climbs out and walks across the top of a second car; it's co-director Tom Boutross' 1950 Dodge. The Sun Demon chokes George (Peter Similuk) on the hood of Similuk's Buick station wagon. When we see Dr. Buckell (Patrick Whyte) driving around, trying to find fugitive Gil before the police do, he's at the wheel of Clarke's 1951 Cadillac.

Robin C. Kirkman and Tom Boutross, *Sun Demon*'s associate producer and co-director, respectively; Clarke met them while taking Malvin Wald's screenwriting course at USC. (Ron Honthaner: "Malvin Wald was Jerry Wald's less successful brother. We always referred to him as 'And Malvin' because most of his screen credits were second-billed with someone else and always read '...and Malvin Wald.'")

✱ After broadcasting the bulletin about the police manhunt for Gil, the radio station announcer (Del Courtney) tells his listeners, "And now we return you once again to the King Sisters." Courtney was then the fiancé of King Sister Yvonne.

✱ No one was less "into" Clarke making *Sun Demon* than his wife Alyce, who thought he had lost his marbles and made sure he knew it. In fact, "she hated the whole thing," Clarke told me. "It was just that she was involved in getting over having [their son] Cam, and

I was off on weekends shooting this movie. So naturally she was not very happy about that." Alyce later apologized for her contrariness, writing a card which Clarke first read when he was in Texas for *The Sun Demon*'s premiere:

My dearest sweetheart,

I love you so very much and I want to be with you more than anything.

I've been a <u>stinker</u> [underlined twice] thru most of this and I beg your forgiveness, but I had to learn for myself — I have much faith in you and you have worked so very hard with so little support from me. I am ashamed! I will be thinking of you every minute and hope and pray you will have the success and happiness you deserve — for both of us!

I adore you.

With all my love,
Laloose

✳ One day when Clarke was a car passenger riding home from a location, still wearing his Sun Demon mask, tunic and gloves, he did a lot of waving at strangers in passing cars — and got zero reaction. For a guy who thought the Sun Demon costume was a good, scary one, this was worrisome: "I realized that if this was any indication of what I could expect [from movie audiences], I was up Shit Creek without the paddle!"

✳ An overheated Clarke arrived home (4841 Gentry Avenue, North Hollywood) that day, headed to his backyard swimming pool and jumped in, still wearing the full Sun Demon costume. Among the pool-frolicking crumb crunchers who saw it happen were various "King Family" nieces and nephews, including Xandra Conkling who was yet to play her role as Suzy in the movie. "I was in the deep end of the pool, and when I saw him walking across the lawn, I swam down to the bottom and said to myself, 'I am never coming up!'" she told me. "I didn't know who it was, I just saw this monster up there, and to a six-year-old that was pretty scary! That was my introduction to the Sun Demon."

Left: Sun Demon set visitor Alyce King Clarke gets a warm welcome.

✱ During the shooting at the warehouse, Honthaner and Doug Menville (standing outside, dressed as cops) were mistaken for *real* cops and waved at by LAPD officers passing in their cruiser.

✱ Clarke, exploring the abandoned warehouse prior to shooting a scene there, had just climbed a ladder to the loft when a sleeping tramp awakened, sat straight up right in front of him "and scared the shit out of me!" Then he realized that if it was scary in real life, it would be scary in the movie, and he got the tramp to agree to do the same thing on film. In the movie, Ron Honthaner is the cop who climbs the ladder, wakes the tramp and trains his gun on him.

✱ When Clarke (as the Sun Demon) jumps down from the warehouse loft at Honthaner (playing the cop), there was no mattress or pad on the floor to protect Clarke; "*I* protected him," Honthaner laughs. "He said, 'I'm going to grab your shoulder, Ron, just to help me when I come down.' I said okay." Weighing about a buck 45 at the time, Honthaner of course got flattened.

"I had been at USC for only a short time when Tom Boutross asked if I wanted to assist him on *Sun Demon*," says Honthaner. "I was excited, but I had no idea what it would entail. I don't think any of us did. It was a first for all of us. Bob Clarke was the only person who knew anything about making a movie and the rest of us just stumbled and bumbled around trying to learn and not trip over ourselves."

✱ Working in the heat-retaining Sun Demon suit was Hell in scales for Clarke, who nearly passed out a few times. His discomfort was probably never worse than when shooting on the fry-an-egg metal surfaces of the gas storage tank. Doug Menville's memory is that only Clarke, Cassarino and Lapenieks made the gas tank ascent for the shooting of the final scene; says Menville, "Most of the rest of us (wisely) opted to observe from below."

✱ To get an idea how gusty it was when the top-of-the-gasometer fight scene was shot, notice how fast and how far the wind carries the patrolman's (Cassarino) eight-point hat as it falls.

✱ At some point Ron Honthaner also climbed to the top of the gasometer, hauling along the Sun Demon dummy that would be taking the spectacular climactic plunge. Honthaner recalls, "They'd gotten a brand new dummy from whoever rents those things, and it wasn't light, so it was a struggle to get the thing up to the top of that tank. But I did, and when they all waved down below to let it go, I pushed it off. Well [*laughs*], this dummy was stiff, it wasn't limber, and it took off like a glider. Then the wind caught it, and smashed it against the side of the tank! It burst open, and everything came out! A few days later, we had to go back and I had to take up an *old* dummy that was more limber, and do it all over again." The dummies wore the Sun Demon costume; since this was near the end of shooting, it didn't matter if it was damaged.

This photo of assistant director Tom Miller indicates that he may also have been one of the movie's camera operators. A few years after *Sun Demon*, Miller (working under the close supervision of Saul Bass) cut the superb "prowling black cat" title sequence for *Walk on the Wild Side* (1962).

✱ Wanting to show the Sun Demon's plunge from the monster's point of view, Clarke had the idea of tying a camera to the end of a strong fishing line, turning it on and letting it fall. (The other end of the line was tied to the end of a 2x4 stuck out from the top of the tank.) First an Eyemo and then an Arri was dropped, both of them made "lens-heavy" so they wouldn't tumble as they fell. But for some reason, the falling cameras would spin on their axis, and so the footage was not used.

✱ Once *Sun Demon* was finished, little Xandra Conkling (who played Suzy) would regularly stand up on her school's "Show and Tell" days and talk about having acted in a movie — "but then it never came out, and never came out, and never came out, and I didn't know if anybody *believed* me," she told me. "Then when it finally did come to L.A., it went straight to the drive-in, and I had exactly *one* friend who saw it. And I felt like, 'Okay, they are *never* going to believe me, *ever!*'"

Vilis "Crazy Willie" Lapienieks "was a wild Latvian," says Doug Menville, "and drunk most of the time." Also the cameraman on *Night Tide, Eegah, Queen of Blood* and dozens more, Lapenieks died in 1987.

✱ Asked to rate her mom Donna King's performance as Suzy's mother in the movie, Xandra says, "It was exactly what my mom *was*: a little melodramatic [*laughs*]! With the *rest* of her sisters. My mom loved doing it " Asked to rate her *own* performance, Xandra offers instead: "I couldn't do now what I did then. I'm shyer now, I'm more introverted now, than I was then. Looking back, I'm pretty impressed that I could *do* that!" She saw the movie for the first time at a pre-release screening, then not again 'til TV showings with Elvira as its mocking mistress of ceremonies. In the interim, she "played" the Sun Demon herself: At one of Robert Clarke's birthday parties, he had her put on the mask and hide inside a box (representing a birthday cake), and pop out as the Sun Demon!

✱ Ron Honthaner got the job of assisting Tom Boutross with the *Sun Demon* editing simply because "Tom asked me if I *wanted* to do it. I said, 'Absolutely.' I didn't know what I was gonna *do*, because at the time I didn't know anything *about* editing [*laughs*] — I was just starting my first semester. I think we got the editing equipment from Birns & Sawyer [a movie equipment rental company]; we couldn't use anything from USC because all they had was 16mm. We cut it at Cinemanor."

✱ Adding greatly to the appeal of *Sun Demon* is the well-chosen and -integrated library music, including the pulse-pounding Jack Cookerly cue "The Monster Walks," later immortalized in the opening cemetery scene of 1968's *Night of the Living Dead* (the ghoul-chasing-Barbara music).

Xandra Conkling in 2011. She now has four children and eight grandchildren.

✱ On January 27, 1959, the movie world-premiered for the second time (following Amarillo) at the Plains Theater in Roswell, New Mexico, UFO capital of the world, double-billed with Pacific International's crime drama *Date with Death*. (By now the title was *The Hideous Sun Demon*; Ron Honthaner believes the extra word was added by Clarke.) According to Roswell newspaper ads, there would be in-person appearances by the "Stars and Producers of These Hits!": Clarke, Gerald Mohr (star of *Date with Death*), Penny Edwards (huh?) and Ed Erwin (who??). All seats that night were 70 cents.

✱ The Paul Frees-narrated *Hideous Sun Demon* trailer is well-made and exciting, piquing audiences' curiosity by not allowing a good look at the face of the monster. The screen-filling superimposition "Thermo-Dynamic Horror from Outer Space!" creates the wrong impression that the Sun Demon is an alien. The struggle between the Sun Demon and the patrolman at the top of the gasometer frame is recut so that it appears to be the patrolman who falls to his doom.

✱ Pacific International got Clarke to spring for the 100 *Hideous Sun Demon* prints that would play around the country on the nether half of the dual bill (under *Date with Death*). *Date* was advertised as being in the NEW PSYCHO-RAMA SUBLIMINAL PROCESS ("So different!…So shocking!…it has been banned on TV!"). Ads proclaimed the two movies "THE SCREEN'S BIGGEST **SCIENCE-FACT** SHOW!," an ad line that probably had people staying away in droves. Clarke, co-starring as a gangster in *Date*, climactically falls to his death in *that* movie as well!

✱ The British trade publication *Kinematograph Weekly* on *The Hideous Sun Demon*: "[It's] too crude to interest the intelligentsia, but its grisly highlights should give the undemanding a kick. …Incidentally, if the hero had signed the pledge and bought himself a decent suntan lotion, there'd be no film. A salutary thought this!"

✱ The *Kinematograph Weekly* reviewer also tossed in the zinger "[B]usty Nan Peterson can neither sing nor act as Trudy"— no doubt unaware that Trudy's singing voice was supplied by one of the King Sisters.

✱ Tom Selleck in *Entertainment Weekly*, 1997: "*Hideous Sun Demon* is my guilty pleasure. It's a great '50s horror movie about nuclear radiation and mutation. It's about this guy who turns into a lizard if he goes out in the sun. And that was really neat."

✱ The tricks that memory can play!: In the movie, the woman on the hospital roof who sees Gil's first transformation is elderly, wizened and in a wheelchair. But according to *Sun Demon* devotee Selleck in *Entertainment Weekly*, the rooftop eyewitness is a beautiful bikini-clad sunbather!

✱ Clarke's deal with Miller Consolidated Pictures (MCP) called for him to make three more movies. The actor next produced and starred in MCP's sci-fi *Beyond the Time Barrier* (1960), made back to back with another MCP flick, *The Amazing Transparent Man*. Much money was spent by MCP promoting the *Time Barrier-Transparent Man* twin bill in the Northwest, but a ferocious snowstorm hit and the movies played to near-empty theaters.

✱ The failure of MCP's expensive exploitation campaign triggered the collapse of the company, so Clarke received only his actor's salary ($2000) for *Time Barrier*, and *nothing* for *Sun Demon*. Years later he found out that MCP had been selling off the *Sun Demon* prints he had paid for, in order to recoup some of their own losses. ("Shame on them for what they'd done to me," he told interviewer Marty Baumann, "but shame on me for letting them.") Clarke estimated that *Sun Demon* burned a $50,000 hole in his wallet (over $373,000 in 2010 dollars).

From his autobiography:

> *Am I sorry that I turned producer and made* Hideous Sun Demon *and* Beyond the Time Barrier, *given the disastrous outcome? No, I wouldn't say that I'm sorry. If I had not done them, I would probably be sorry, and I'd be wishing today that I had put forth the effort. It was an interesting experience. I wish, of course, that it had turned out profitably and that it had led to other things that would have been more mainstream. With Roger Corman, pictures like those were stepping stones to bigger productions. But I took such a financial bath with the bankruptcy on* Sun Demon *and* Time Barrier *that I felt there was no way that I could continue as a producer at that point.*
>
> *But sorry? No, never.*

✱ From the ridiculous to the sublime: Around the same time as *Sun Demon*, several of the USCers who made it (Ron Honthaner, Stan Follis, John Morrill, Eric Darstaad, maybe more) were part of the crew of *The Exiles*, a semi-documentary depiction of one night in the lives of several young Native American Los Angelenos. Written, produced and directed by their college mate Kent Mackenzie (1930-80), it premiered at the Venice Film Festival. In 2009, the National Film Registry honored *The Exiles* by adding it to their list of "culturally, historically, or aesthetically significant films" to be preserved by the Library of Congress.

Clarke's second feature as producer was shot in Texas by director Edgar G. Ulmer. To save money, *Beyond the Time Barrier*'s scenes of a wrecked and abandoned Air Force base of 60-plus years in the future were simply shot at a wrecked and abandoned Texas Air Force base!

Left: For some Monster Kids, artist Basil Gogos' *Famous Monsters of Filmland* Sun Demon cover was their first exposure to the saurian beastie. Jon Fedele was one such fan; he hadn't yet seen the movie, but that cover made the Sun Demon his *favorite* monster of filmland. Fedele is now a special makeup FX wiz and monster maker, and circa 2005, just for fun, he used the *FM* cover as a guide to fabricate a Sun Demon mask (and also made the rest of the costume). *FM cover © 1974 Warren Publishing Co.* Famous Monsters of Filmland [words and distinctive lettering design] is a registered trademark of Philip Kim.

Top: In his Sun Demon costume, Fedele cameos in the wonderful *The United Monster Talent Agency,* a 2010 short by KNB EFX Group head honcho Greg Nicotero. In this behind-the-scenes *United Monsters* shot he poses with fandom legend Bob Burns.

✹ Despite his *Sun Demon-Time Barrier* trip to the cleaners, the indomitable Clarke retained his desire to produce movies and, in the mid-1970s, again worked toward making another picture — a follow-up to *Sun Demon*. He had schlock screenwriter Arthur C. Pierce write an outline that was called *Devil Sun Demon* until Pierce (or *some*body) XXXXX-ed out that title and typed *The She Demon* beneath — and then XXXXX-ed out *The She Demon* and put the title *Naked Sun Demon* beneath. Its cover page is dated August 10, 1976. A second version of this outline, titled *Sorceress* and dated August 16, 1976, is more neatly typed and (slightly) less ineptly written, so that's the one that appears in this book's Scripts Section.

✹ In the same way that Clarke got "beginners" (the USC students) involved on *Hideous Sun Demon*, he reached out to young Hollywood newcomer Eric Edson for screenplay help on *Sorceress*. In an e-mail to me, Edson says that, at the time, he was "a plucky youngster recently graduated with a Master of Fine Arts from the American Film Institute. One of the first things I did professionally was direct three episodes of a syndicated TV doctor series, *Westbrook Hospital*, and Robert Clarke was one of the stars. We got to know each other a bit. He showed me a screenplay he owned [*Sorceress*] and asked if I would be interested in the job of rewriting it. I was starting out and not in any position to turn down a paying gig. Rewrite it I did. I remember it as a fun romping sort of assignment. And I remember Robert Clarke fondly, as a warm and insightful man." After years of writing occasional movies and TV episodes, Edson became a university professor, and for some years now has headed up the Graduate Screenwriting Program at California State University, Northridge.

✹ In March 1977, Clarke prepared a 15-page "Picture Budget Detail" that called for *Sorceress* to cost a grand total of $222,996.68. In *Famous Monsters of Filmland* magazine, Robert Skotak wrote that the feature would mark the screen comeback of Kirk "Superman" Alyn in the role of a solar research scientist.

✹ According to Skotak in *Famous Monsters*, "[*Sorceress* will feature such monsters as] the 'Cobrat'— part scaly cobra, part rat; the 'Octa-Gator'; and Ammut — a half-lion, half-crocodile beast. This is Clarke's most ambitious project to date and will include an array of incredible special effects & action sequences and, he promises, 'a nerve-shattering ending!'"

✹ Clarke was apparently determined to revisit *both* his past (financial) failures: As *Sorceress* was being prepped for production, *Fantascene* magazine reported that Clarke also had in mind an "updated, large-scale" remake of *Beyond the Time Barrier*, in which "a pilot en route to orbit via the Space Shuttle breaks through time into the future." Neither movie was made.

✹ Bob Burns, king of the Monster Kids, was working weekends at Don Post Studios in the mid-1960s when Richard Cassarino brought in the original Sun Demon mold (probably for repairs). Getting permission from Post to make a pull from it, Burns created a mask for his now world-famous collection. Years later, Burns made a Sun Demon mask (complete with teeth and eyes) for Clarke, who was by then a member of the National Speakers Association and could use it as a prop in his popular presentation "The Magic of Sci-Fi Film Making."

✹ Cassarino created another scaly monster costume: the extraterrestrial amphibian in *Destination Inner Space* (1966). His work on the two fright flicks earned him a spot on TV's *To Tell the Truth*: That game show's celebrity panel tried to figure out who was "the *real* Richard Cassarino, designer of monster suits."

✹ In the latter part of his life, Clarke prided himself on his *Sun Demon* achievement, wearing *Sun Demon* T-shirts to monster movie conventions and writing letters to fans on "Sun Demon Corporation" stationery. A postage stamp-sized head shot of the Sun Demon appeared atop each sheet and the words "Robert Clarke — President" were on the top-left side.

✹ Inspired by the reception he got from fans at ComicCon in San Diego and at the Chiller Theatre convention in Hackensack, New Jersey, Clarke again began entertaining the notion of making another Sun Demon movie in 1992. He collaborated with a young writer on a script, this one titled *The Hideous She Demon*, but it was all for naught.

The Sun Demon and Planet X masks made by Bob Burns as gifts to Clarke, being displayed by Monster Kid Burns *(above)* and by Clarke *(below)*.

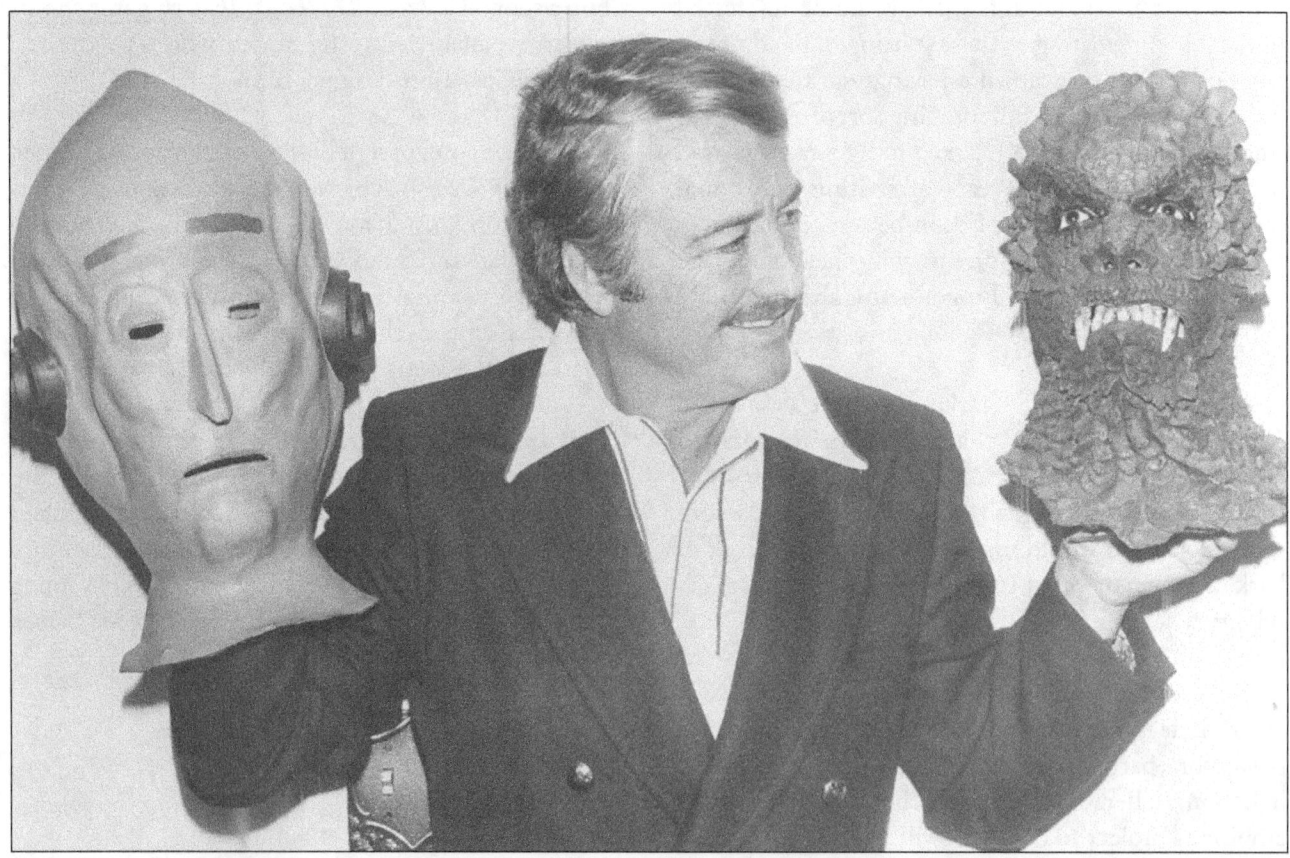

SHOWMANSHIP MANUAL

PACIFIC INTERNATIONAL

ADS...

Ad Mat 201

Ad Mat 301
(Also Available in 2-Col. Ad Mat 211)

SPECIAL SLUGS TO SELL THE NEW PSYCHORAMA PROCESS!

Ad Mat 202

Ad Mat 203

Ad Mat 307

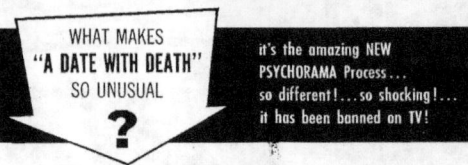

Ad Mat 204
(Also Available in 4-Col. Ad Mat 404)

ORDER THIS COMPLETE AD AND PUBLICITY CAMPAIGN AS ONE MAT FROM NATIONAL SCREEN SERVICE. MATS MAY ALSO BE ORDERED ON AN INDIVIDUAL BASIS.

Ad Mat 107

BEAUTIFUL redhead Liz Renay portrays a gun moll who offers the key to murder in the suspenseful "A Date with Death" currently screening at the................Theatre. Film stars Gerald Mohr, and makes use of hidden words and symbols to accent action. Mat No. 1B

Ad Mat 211

Ad Mat 102

Ad Mat 203

Ad Mat 105

Ad Mat 208

Ad Mat 103

Ad Mat 101

"THE HIDEOUS SUN DEMON" bursts onto a horrified group of his friends after a fateful laboratory accident. Robert Clarke stars in the thrilling science-fiction film screening at the........................ Theatre. Mat No. 2B

Ad Mat 209

AD-PUB MAT   **SPECIAL MAT No. 1**

PACIFIC INTERNATIONAL

CAST, CREDITS, SYNOPSES

"A Date With Death"

CREDITS
Produced by WILLIAM S. EDWARDS
Directed by.........HAROLD DANIELS
Executive Producer....JOHN MILLER
Associate Producer
          MICHAEL MILLER
Production Supervisor and Assistant
Director......LESTER C. GUTHRIE
Production Design by
          A. LESLIE THOMAS
Written by........ROBERT C. DENNIS
Director of Photography
          CARL GUTHRIE
Operator.....................BILL CLINE
2nd Assistant Director..DICK EVANS
Precon Psychologist
     DR. ROBERT E. CORRIGAN
Music Composed and Conducted
by...................DARRELL CALKER
Song, "Flim Flam":
     Lyrics: JULES FOX
     Music: DARRELL CALKER
Wardrobe.........ORA MAE CRUMMA
Edited..................JACK RUGGIERO
         and BEN MARMON
Running Time 81 Minutes

CAST
GERALD MOHR...........Mike Mason
LIZ RENAY................Paula Warren
HARRY LAUTER......George Caddell
STEPHANIE FARNAY.....Edith Dale
ED ERWIN.........................Art Joslin
ROBERT CLARK.........Joe Emanuel
RED MORGAN........................Urbano
LEW MARKMAN........................Potter
TONY REDMAN.......Mayor Langlie
FRANK BELLEW....................Weylin
WILLIAM PURDY.................Huber
RAY DEARHOLT.......................Sam
MELFORD LEHRMAN..........Bender
KEN DUNCAN...................Andrews

SYNOPSIS

Mike Mason (Gerald Mohr), ex-paratrooper, ex-used-car dealer, now down on his luck, broke and bitter, is hoboing his way across the desolate southwestern deserts from an unhappy past to an uncertain future. Hiking disconsolately along a bleak desert road he comes upon an abandoned car with a corpse in it. Confronted with the necessity of getting away fast, he hides the body, takes the car and the identification of the murdered man and speeds away.

He is stopped by two motorcycle police who escort him to Mindan City Hall where he is mistaken for a former New York policeman on loan to Mindan to clean up the town crime syndicate. He is sworn in as Police Chief.

His first official act is to release from jail a sexy erstwhile night club singer, Paula Warren (Liz Renay), a vagrant with whose plight he sympathizes. He arranges for her to secure airline tickets for them both to escape from Mindan. But before they can leave, evidence starts to accumulate pointing to his impersonation and he realizes he must stay on to find the real murderer.

Joe Emanuel (Robert Clarke), a suave gentleman of the underworld, heads the crime syndicate responsible for the killing. Mike realizes his only chance is to trap the crime czar into disclosing the real murderer. In Paula's apartment he discovers evidence that she was at the scene of the murder and he bursts angrily in on her while she is in the shower, nude. But he learns she is innocent and she gives him the identity of the murderer.

Mindan's cleanup committee meantime has discovered his impersonation but he is given a few days longer as Chief to find the murderer. In the vigorous cleanup, raids on roadhouses and arrests of bookies and thugs follow, and he flushes out the murderer as he had expected, but almost loses his life doing it.

The crime czar is besieged in his headquarters and in a burst of machinegun fire is blasted through a glass door. Mike has exonerated himself and destroyed the source of Mindan's crime, and so, his self-respect restored, he leaves with Paula.

"The Hideous Sun Demon"

CREDITS
Producer-Director ROBERT CLARKE
Associate Producer
          ROBIN KIRKMAN
Film Editor and Co-director
          THOMAS BOUTROSS
Production of Monster Sequences
          GIANBIATISTA CASSARINO
Screenplay by....E. S. SEELEY, JR.,
          and DOANE HOAG
Story by...............ROBERT CLARKE
          and PHIL HINER
Photographed by....JOHN MORRILL,
          VILIS LAPENIEKS, JR.,
          and STAN FOLLIS
Music..........................JOHN SEELY
Sound...................DOUG MENVILLE
Production Assistant....TOM MILLER
Editor's Assistant RON HONTHANER
Script Supervisor......DENIE FOLLIS
Running Time 74 Minutes
MUSICAL SCORE
Song "Strange Pursuit"
          MARILYN KING

CAST
Dr. Gilbert McKenna
          ROBERT CLARKE
Ann Russell......PATRICIA MANNING
Trudy Osborne........NAN PETERSON
Dr. Frederick Buckell
          PATRICK WHYTE
Dr. Jacob Hoffman FRED LA PORTA
Police Lieutenant......BILL HAMPTON
Mother.................DONNA CONKLING
Little Girl........XANDRA CONKLING
Radio Announcer........DEL COURTNEY

SYNOPSIS

Dr. Gilbert McKenna (Robert Clarke), atomic physicist, is rushed to a hospital as the result of an accident with fissionable material in which he was exposed to an undue amount of radioactivity. While under observation at the hospital he becomes a scaly, lizard-like creature. Dr. Stern (Robert Garry) explains to McKenna's close friends, Ann Russell (Patricia Manning) and Dr. Frederick Buckell (Patrick Whyte), that it has been brought on by a combination of the exposure to the radioactive material combined with the rays of the sun. McKenna's chromosome structure has been thrown out of balance causing him to revert backwards in the evolutionary cycle to the stage of the lizard. He must stay out of the sun for the remainder of his natural life.

Gil retreats to a big, empty, isolated mansion owned by his father. He goes to a nearby bar and has a flirtation with a singer (Nan Peterson) and he remains out until dawn. Terrified, he rushes to his car, drives home and in the house discovers that he has reverted to the horrible lizard creature.

Ann is waiting for him and tells him that she and Dr. Buckell have called in for consultation Dr. Jacob Hoffman (Fred La Porta), a world-renowned scientist, specialist on radioactivity. He warns the next sun-exposure may be fatal. But Gil keeps a date with Trudy, and her jealous suitor, George Messario (Peter Simuluk), and his henchmen give him a good going over. Next morning finds him on the street—in the sunlight—once more. Before their horrified eyes he is transformed to the loathsome lizard-creature. The scientist-turned-monster kills George and runs for a wooded area towards home.

The police await him but he escapes through the back door. They give chase through railroad yards, into an abandoned warehouse, and finally, he seeks escape atop a huge gas tank hundreds of feet high. In a terrifying climax there is a struggle-to-the-death with the monster plummeting to his death hundreds of feet below.

Ann turns away in horror while Dr. Buckell tries to comfort her with the words that perhaps Gil's sacrifice in the name of scientific progress will serve some useful purpose, after all.

PROMOTION

HOW'S YOUR SUBLIMINAL WORKING?

MAYBE you've always wondered how you would react to a lie detector test! Here's your chance: for in the lobby of the..............................Theatre where A DATE WITH DEATH is screening, the first six persons at the box office at the.....................o'clock show will get a free test... Have special posters announcing it, a special item in the newspapers, and have the detector set up by an attendant.

CONDUCT A CONTEST

HAVE patrons fill in a card and hand it in at show's end telling how many hidden words and symbols were flashed on the screen during A DATE WITH DEATH. Winner gets a couple of free tickets to the next film showing at the theatre.

GET COLLEGE COOPERATION

HAVE college psychology students turn in an essay explaining why they think Subliminal Perception Process should (or should not) be used in motion pictures. Give the winner or winners free passes to A DATE WITH DEATH & HIDEOUS SUN DEMON or the next attraction.

NEWSPAPER CONTEST

HAVE readers of any one (or more than one) newspaper in an area write into the drama editor stating why he or she would like to see A DATE WITH DEATH. Perhaps they could give instances of subliminal perception from their personal experiences. The drama editor (or editors) and the local exhibitor could act as judges. Give appropriate prizes.

HAVE SPECIAL SCREENING FOR PSYCHIATRISTS

INVITE a group of psychologists and psychiatrists to a special screening and ask their opinion of the films. If there is time, show a very small portion of the film two ways: with and without the subliminal process. Get their reactions and get quotes for feature stories for the press.

HAVE DRAMA EDITORS TAKE TEST

HOLD a special screening for the motion picture editors in various areas. Have the special equipment that measures their reactions while viewing the film. See how they react to the "hidden" words and symbols.

"HIDEOUS" CONTEST

HAVE Kiddies Matinee with prizes for most "hideous" costume inspired by "Hideous Sun Demon."

RADIO TRANSCRIPTIONS, TV SPOTS

BOTH radio and TV spots are available. The radio spots are devised as combinations selling both features as well as on each individual attraction. Order TV and radio spots from your local Exchange.

Action, Terror, Suspense Combine In Sensational Double Feature Bill

(Advance)

"A Date with Death" and "The Hideous Sun Demon" will open at the.................Theatre on.................and offer moviegoers one of the most thrilling double features ever seen.

Making use of The Psychorama by Precon Subliminal Process, "A Date with Death" stars Gerald Mohr as an ex-hobo sworn in as a small town police chief when he impersonates a murdered New York cop. Liz Renay, a vagrant released from jail by the new chief, and Robert Clarke as the crime syndicate's czar, turn in top-flight performances.

But what makes the film outstanding is the Subliminal Perception Process through which words and symbols are flashed on and off the screen with such rapidity that the eyes can not see them and only the subliminal —or subconscious—mind can receive them. Images to convey the strong emotions of love, hate, terror, suspicion, fear and the like, are used to heighten the viewer's participation in and enjoyment of the film.

"The Hideous Sun Demon," the other film on this thrilling bill, stars Robert Clarke as an atom physicist whose laboratory experiments cause him to revert in evolution to the giant lizard state. Advised by an eminent scientist (as played by Fred La Porta) that he must stay out of the sunlight for the remainder of his life, his friends, portrayed by Patricia Manning and Patrick Whyte, are helpless to save him when a honkytonk tavern singer, played by Nan Peterson, unknowingly triggers the first of a terrifying series of events which includes murder and a spectacular fight-to-the-death atop a huge gas tank.

KNOWN AS CHARACTER

Harry Lauter, who plays the role of George Caddell in "A Date with Death," is well known as a character actor in Hollywood motion pictures and television.

Lauter has had starring roles and co-starring roles in a number of westerns, including "Wyatt Earp," "Annie Oakley," "Maverick," "Cheyenne" and in "Texas Rangers" among others.

One of his most recent films was a character role in "The Last Hurrah" which stars Spencer Tracy. "A Date with Death" which is not a western but an exciting drama using a western town in Arizona as its locale, is the first picture Lauter has made on such a location where he does not appear as a cowboy.

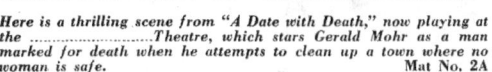

Here is a thrilling scene from "A Date with Death," now playing at the ....Theatre, which stars Gerald Mohr as a man marked for death when he attempts to clean up a town where no woman is safe. Mat No. 2A

Get Set For Giant Double Feature Thrill And Horror Show Today

(Opening Day)

Unprecedented terror and thrills mark the opening today at the..................Theatre of "A Date with Death" and "The Hideous Sun Demon."

"A Date with Death" allows audiences to provide their OWN response for it makes use of the Psychorama by Precon Subliminal Process, the screen's newest advance yet devised by scientists.

Gerald Mohr is seen as an ex-hobo who is sworn in as a small town police chief when he impersonates a murdered New York cop. Liz Renay is a gangster's moll released from jail by the new chief and Robert Clarke fills the role of the town's crime syndicate czar who almost succeeds in having the pseudo-policeman killed to escape detection himself.

By means of the Subliminal Process audiences will thrill to horrors not seen by their eyes but only felt by their subconscious minds. Symbols and words that evoke fear, hate, horror, love, suspicion and other emotions are used at intervals through the film and although audiences will not know *consciously* when or where they appear, the effect will be heightened excitement.

"The Hideous Sun Demon" stars Robert Clarke as an atom physicist whose experiments cause him to retrograde in evolution to the age of the giant lizard monsters. His close friends, portrayed by Patricia Manning and Patrick Whyte, call in for consultation an eminent scientist, played by Fred La Porta, who warns that the physicist must stay out of sunlight for the remainder of his life. But his infatuation for Nan Peterson, who enacts the role of a singer in a cheap bar, keeps him out until dawn and triggers a series of explosively terrifying events climaxing with a struggle-to-the-death atop a huge gas tank in one of the most frightening fight sequences ever filmed.

The pictures are released through Pacific International Pictures.

GERALD MOHR, a man marked for murder, fights back in "A Date with Death," suspense drama now screening at the.................Theatre. Film makes use of hidden words and symbols to heighten the excitement. Mat No. 1A

Mohr Top Actor in All Show Business

(Biography)

Gerald Mohr, who portrays the role of Mike Mason in "A Date with Death," was born in New York and began his career with CBS Radio, winning the 1951 Award for Radio's Best Actor. Since then, he has been in a long list of motion pictures and radio shows and has appeared frequently on live TV.

His motion picture credits include "Detective Story" with Kirk Douglas and Eleanor Parker, "Gilda" with Rita Hayworth, "Dragonfly Squadron" with John Hodiak, "Sniper," the Stanley Kramer production, "My World Dies Screaming."

In "A Date with Death" he enacts the role of Mike Mason, a man mistaken for a New York policeman who has been sent to a small desert town to take over as police chief and clean up the town.

Audiences Guaranteed Plenty of Excitement In Current Combination

(Current)

Currently screening at the..................Theatre is a double feature bill which provides one of the most harrowing and thrilling experiences ever evoked by motion pictures.

"A Date with Death" lets audiences provide their own emotional responses by use of the Psychorama by Precon Subliminal

SPECTACULAR LIFE LEADS TO FILM CAREER

(Biography)

Liz Renay enacts the role of Paula in "A Date with Death" and brings to the role a bright new motion picture talent. This is her first co-starring role.

The beautiful redhead was born into an indigent farm family, where there were many children and little food. Liz is an example of a classic Hollywood success story when, at the age of fifteen, she won a beauty contest and a bit part in a motion picture on location in Arizona.

Her life took on a spectacular turn when, through her nightclub work, she became acquainted with some of the top men in the underworld including Frank Costello, Anatasia, Mickey Cohen and "Coppy" Coppola.

BEAUTIFUL redhead Liz Renay portrays a gun moll who offers the key to murder in the suspenseful "A Date with Death" currently screening at the..................Theatre. Film stars Gerald Mohr and makes use of hidden words and symbols to accent action. Mat No. 1B

"THE HIDEOUS SUN DEMON" bursts onto a horrified group of his friends after a fateful laboratory accident. Robert Clarke stars in the thrilling science-fiction film screening at the..................Theatre. Mat No. 2B

BANNED ON TV

"A Date with Death," new film now screening at the..................Theatre, stars Gerald Mohr, and brings to the screen an entirely revolutionary technique of heightening suspense. That technique, which has been BANNED ON TELEVISION, makes use of the Subliminal Perception Process.

Also on the suspense-packed bill is "The Hideous Sun Demon" starring Robert Clarke as a young scientist whose experiments result in a horrifying series of events ending in death.

DOUBLE BILL THRILLS

One of the films now showing at the..................Theatre makes use of the newest motion picture technique since wide-screen. In "A Date with Death" which stars Gerald Mohr as a man marked for death, use is made of the new Subliminal Perception Process with hidden words and symbols flashed on and off the screen too rapidly for the eyes to see.

Another thrilling film on the same bill is "The Hideous Sun Demon" which stars Robert Clarke

Process, and it is safe to say that never previously has such participation-enjoyment been experienced through a motion picture. Starring is Gerald Mohr as an ex-hobo who assumes the identity of a murdered former New York cop and is sworn in as police chief to clean up a small town crime ring. Liz Renay is seen as a gangster's moll and Robert Clarke portrays the murderous czar of the crime syndicate which is the target for the cleanup campaign.

Throughout the film, audiences receive words and symbols which are flashed upon the screen too fast for the eyes to see but perceivable by the subconscious mind which reacts to them. Words and images providing strong stimuli to arouse love, hate, fear, terror and other emotions have been selected by the scientists who devised the process.

"The Hideous Sun Demon" is the other film on this excitement-packed double feature bill and stars Robert Clarke as an atom physicist whose experiments cause him to retrograde in evolution to the age of the slimy giant lizard. Appearing with him in the film are Patricia Manning and Patrick Whyte who are helpless to assist him when he ignores the warning to stay out of the sun or permanently revert to the monster. A bar room singer, played by Nan Peterson, unknowingly sets off a series of events which terrify the community. The film climaxes with a pursuit by police through railroad yards to the top of a huge tank and is one of the most frighteningly suspenseful scenes ever screened.

Both pictures are released through Pacific International Pictures.

IN a change-of-feature portrayal not equalled since the famed Jekyll-Hyde story, Robert Clarke stars in a tense science-fiction film where he turns from young physicist to "The Hideous Sun Demon" now screening at the.................. Theatre. Mat No. 1C

FOREIGN STAR MAKES DEBUT

(Biography)

Stephanie Farnay was born in Belgium and all her life has lived in various foreign countries. She began her dramatic career by studying at the Royal Dramatic Academy of Belgium.

She has acted on the legitimate stage in Paris, and for three years in the Montreal Shakespeare Theatre, and for three years in the French language at the Tricolor Theatre in Washington, D. C. Following that she appeared at the Georgetown Theatre in Washington, D. C.

Miss Farnay, who plays the role of Edith Dale in "A Date with Death," has had leads in three pictures made in Mexico.

"A Date with Death" is her first United States feature motion picture.

1 SHEET

11 x 14

22 x 28

INSERT

3 SHEET

SINGLE FEATURE CAMPAIGN

"A DATE WITH DEATH"

PUBLICITY

"A DATE WITH DEATH" BOOKED FOR EARLY RUN

(Advance)

"A Date with Death" opens at the ....Theatre on.................... and this picture will chill you in a way you have never experienced before!

Gerald Mohr is seen as a man down on his luck hoboing his way across a desolate part of the southwestern desert when he discovers a murdered man in an abandoned automobile. Taking the dead man's belongings, he is mistaken for a New York cop and is sworn in as Chief of Police of a small town to clean up the local crime syndicate.

Liz Renay plays the role of a gangster's moll befriended by the pseudo-policeman but before they are able to leave town, evidence forces the new law enforcement official to stay and clear his name by finding the real murderer. This does not fit into the plans of the crime czar, a role enacted by Robert Clarke.

"A Date with Death" takes on a new dimension in suspense by the use of what is known as Subliminal Perception. To perceive something subliminally means to perceive it below the threshold of the conscious mind. Words and symbols are flashed on the screen so rapidly the eye can not see them—but the subconscious perceives and reacts to them. The Subliminal Perception technique is considered so powerful that it has been banned on television!

The picture is released through Pacific International Pictures.

SUBLIMINAL PROCESS BANNED ON TELEVISION

"A Date with Death" which currently is screening at the.................... Theatre, makes use of the Subliminal Perception Process which caused a furore in television circles recently. The process, which makes use of hidden words and symbols throughout screenings, was considered of such a nature as to cause it to be BANNED ON TELEVISION.

The producers of "A Date with Death" believe that the process, which gets to the subliminal—or subconscious part of the mind—will greatly enhance the enjoyment of their motion picture and heighten the excitement by flashing such words as "death," "blood," "danger" and others at dramatic points in the story.

MANY STARTLING INNOVATIONS IN THRILL DRAMA

(Current)

"A Date with Death," the film currently playing at the............................ Theatre, brings you a completely new emotional experience.

The film presents Gerald Mohr as a down-on-his-luck ex-paratrooper hoboing his way cross-country when he discovers a murdered man in a stranded automobile and takes on the dead man's identity. Mistaken for a former New York cop, he is sworn in as Chief of Police of a small desert town to clean up the area's crime syndicate. Liz Renay is seen as a vagrant befriended and released from jail by the new Chief, but before their plans to leave town together can be carried out, the pseudo-policeman is forced to stay on to find the real murderer. Excitement flares when Robert Clarke, portraying the crime czar, moves in for the kill.

But the terror and lurking horror felt by seeing the film is heightened by use of the Psychorama by Precon Subliminal Process, which is the screen's newest innovation. By means of this new process, devised by scientists, words and symbols are flashed on-screen so briefly—and so rapidly—that the eyes can not see them, but only the subconscious part of the mind can perceive and respond to them. The result is breath-taking!

Thus, "A Date with Death" becomes more than just a motion picture to be seen and enjoyed: it becomes a NEW vehicle through which each individual in the audience provides his own response to the unseen images which make him for the first time a real participant in the film's excitement and drama.

"A Date with Death" is being released through the Pacific International Pictures.

Although the eye can not see the hidden symbols, you REACT in highly accelerated fashion. And that's what the process is supposed to do! Gerald Mohr stars in the film.

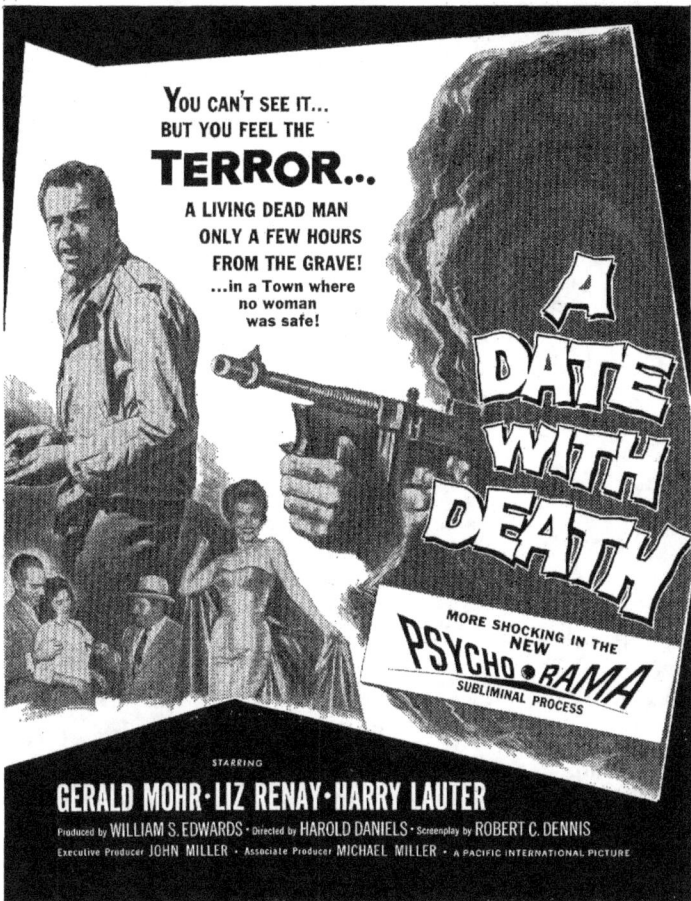

Ad Mat 304

Ad Mat 206

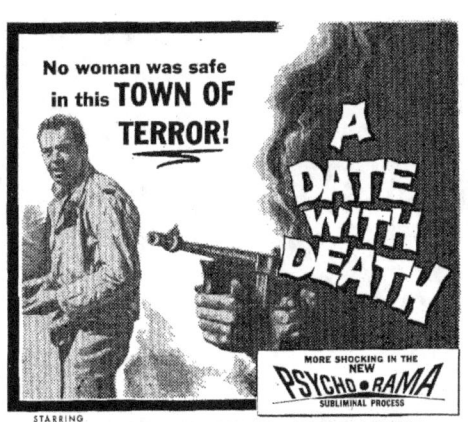

Ad Mat 207

Ad Mat 208

Ad Mat 103

Ad Mat 105

SINGLE FEATURE CAMPAIGN

"HIDEOUS SUN DEMON"

PUBLICITY

SENSATIONAL HORROR SHOW IS SCHEDULED
(Advance)

"The Hideous Sun Demon" commences its local showing at the ....Theatre on.........................

Robert Clarke is seen as the scientist whose experiments cause him to revert in the cycle of evolution to the age of giant, scaly lizards. With his only hope of regaining and retaining his human identity being to forever stay out of the sunlight, his infatuation for a honky-tonk singer keeps him out until daylight and proves his undoing.

Nan Peterson portrays the role of the blonde singer who unknowingly triggers a chain of terrifying events. Patricia Manning and Patrick Whyte portray the roles of the closest friends of the young physicist-turned-monster, but even their best efforts can not save him. Fred La Porta has the role of an eminent scientist famed for cures caused by radioactive burns. His warning about the sunlight is ignored and what follows when the man becomes the maddened monster makes an electrifying climax.

"The Hideous Sun Demon" is being released through Pacific International Pictures.

ACTOR ACHIEVES TRIPLE ROLE IN HORROR HIT
(Biography)

Robert Clarke produced and directed "The Hideous Sun Demon" in which he also stars. This is the first time the versatile actor has produced or directed a film.

Born in Oklahoma City, he attended the University of Oklahoma and received his B.A. degree in Economics from the University of Wisconsin. After serving in the United States Army Signal Corps, he moved to California where his appearance in several stage productions was spotted by a talent scout for RKO and he was put under contract to that studio.

Clarke played in a number of westerns at RKO and then went East to join the Newport Casino Theatre in Newport, Rhode Island, where for the season of 1947 he was leading man. Later, on Broadway he did the juvenile lead in "The Play's The Thing" which starred Louis Calhern and Faye Emerson. He was then brought to the attention of Ida Lupino and again landed in Hollywood where he appeared in two pictures which the actress-director made for RKO release.

'HIDEOUS SUN DEMON' STARTLES ALL FILM FANS!
(Current)

"The Hideous Sun Demon," the film currently screening at the............ Theatre, stars Robert Clarke as an atomic physicist whose experiments cause him to revert in the cycle of evolution to the age of scaly, giant lizards.

With his only hope of remaining human the necessity of staying out of the sunlight for the remainder of his life, the young scientist hides away in his remote hilltop home by day and roams the hills at night. On one excursion he visits a bar, meets a blonde singer and because of her stays out until dawn when the morning light causes him to revert to the lizard-monster.

His close friends, played by Patricia Manning and Patrick Whyte, bring in a world-renowned scientist, portrayed by Fred La Porta, and his verdict is that hope can be entertained but only if the physicist shuns the daylight forever. Another exposure could be fatal.

But desire to see the singer lures the young man to the bar once more and again it is morning when he finds himself on the street and threatened by the girl's jealous suitor. Reverting entirely to the animal he becomes a maddened monster who kills and terrifies. Through railroad yards, into an abandoned warehouse, he is pursued by the police and finally atop a huge gas tank hundreds of feet high where a struggle-to-the-death occurs and provides the screen with one of the most frightening climaxes ever filmed.

"The Hideous Sun Demon" is being released through Pacific International Pictures.

Ad Mat 302

Ad Mat 101

Ad Mat 205

Ad Mat 303

Ad Mat 209

Ad Mat 102

AFTERWORD

Blonde Bombshell **Nan Peterson** looks back on *Sun Demon* days

The Hideous Sun Demon was not a big, important movie, but it certainly was important to me because it was my *first* movie. There had always been a bug in me to act, and I'd *been* acting since I was a child in Mitchell, South Dakota — "declam" readings, humorous readings, little theater work, even my own 15-minute KELO-TV series in Sioux Falls, South Dakota. Shot in 16mm, the show was called *Pay's Art Store* and I also directed it and wrote my own scripts, talking about the store's different products. Very corny!

I arrived in Hollywood on Valentine's Day, 1956. In my little Chevrolet convertible packed to the brim, I came all the way out from South Dakota by myself. It took me about two weeks to get out here but I stayed only once at a motel because my worried parents had me staying with different relatives who lived along the way — Phoenix and Omaha and so on. And at my parents' request, they all tried to talk me out of going to California!

My first stop in Hollywood was going to be the home of my girlfriend Lois, who had once been a KELO-TV co-worker; Lois had moved to Hollywood and landed a job at Ziv Studios as secretary to Broderick Crawford, the star of their series *Highway Patrol*. Lois had told me that, if I ever came out to Hollywood to live, I could stay with her temporarily while I looked for a more permanent place. At one point on the freeway, I could see Hollywood quite a ways off in the distance to the left, so I drove into it. After getting a Coke at a drugstore, I stopped at a gas station to fill up and I asked the attendant how to get to the address where Lois lived. He said, "In what city?" and I said,

Twenty-six-year-old Nan Peterson made her film bow as sexquisite chanteuse Trudy in *The Hideous Sun Demon*.

"Here in Hollywood, of course." He laughed and said, "Well, this is Palm Springs. You've got a long ways to go yet!"

I eventually moved into the Studio Club, a rooming house for aspiring actresses on Hollywood and Vine. At first I did some modeling and also some stage work. As he prepared to make *Sun Demon*, Robert Clarke came to the Studio Club and interviewed different girls for the part of Trudy. I don't recall if I read for it — I probably did — but I sure remember him telling me I had the part. Probably a whole bunch of people had tried out for it, so I was surprised that I got it. I was thrilled. Of course, since it was a very low-budget movie, I had to do my own makeup and supply my own clothes. In those days, Jax in Beverly Hills was *the* place to go. It was on the corner of Wilshire, across from Saks, and I had one of their form-fitting, spaghetti-strap, low-cut black dresses that were all the rage. It was perfect for the bar scene in *Sun Demon* where I play the piano.

The *Sun Demon* crew guys were all very nice and seemed eager to do good work. And Bob Clarke as the director was very good. I didn't know it was his first time directing a picture. If I'm remembering right, we did a lot of "one-takes." Living at the Studio Club sometimes made things a little difficult, because they had hours there. To leave early in the morning as I sometimes needed to do for *Sun Demon*, you'd have to get permission; and then you had to be in by 12 midnight. But it was fun doing the movie. Then, several months later, it was also a thrill to fly down to Amarillo, Texas, for the world premiere. I was third-billed in the movie, but on the drive-in marquee it was just Bob's name and mine up in lights. *That* kinda threw me! At one point while we were in Texas, Bob and I were invited to some home and treated royally, like we were "really something," as though we were big movie stars. Well, Bob had been in a lot of movies opposite some top stars but *I* certainly hadn't. At that point, the only movie I'd ever been in *was Sun Demon*!

I guess *The Hideous Sun Demon* is a cult classic now, so it's fun to be able to say I was in it. Ten years ago, Tom Weaver interviewed me about *Sun Demon* for *Monsters from the Vault* magazine, and after the issue came out, Bob Clarke phoned and thanked me for saying nice things about him in the article. I was so surprised and delighted to hear from him. I told him, "If you're ever down this way, I would love to see you," but he said he was too ill. Some time later, I was really sad to see a writeup in *The Los Angeles Times* about his passing.

Nan Peterson in *The Hideous Sun Demon,* as captured by artist Frank Dietz *(www.sketchythings.com).*

My background is part-Norwegian and so I have light skin. Today I have a girlfriend who's younger than I am but looks 15 years older, and I think that's because she's *always* in the sun, sunning herself. For as long as I can remember I've tried to stay out of the sun, and… you know…maybe part of the reason is psychological, because of the memory of seeing *The Hideous Sun Demon* and the scenes where the scientist went out into the sun and how horrible his face became. I don't like to say this because it'll sound like I'm boasting, but a lot of people don't believe me when I say how old I am, because on my face I don't have any wrinkles at *all*. So maybe I can also be grateful to *The Hideous Sun Demon* for keeping my skin young!

Nan Peterson
February 2011

Wearing a Sun Demon mask he made from Richard Cassarino's original mold, Bob Burns cavorted as the helio-horror in the amateur short *Wrath of the Sun Demon* (circa 1965).

SUPPLEMENTAL PHOTO GALLERY

In closing, a few more photos of Robert Clarke, various incarnations of his Sun Demon and some miscellany

When RKO was preparing to make the swashbuckler *Sinbad the Sailor* (1947), contract player Clarke decided to try for the title role. Douglas Fairbanks, Jr., got the part, Clarke got this publicity photo.

Above: Clarke is visited by his parents on the set of the low-budget adventure yarn *Tales of Robin Hood* (1951). *Below:* Clarke and other members of the King Family. *Sun Demon*-related folks are highlighted.

Above: The actor-speaker spellbinding an audience.
Right: Clarke's flyer for his "Magic of Sci-Fi Film Making" presentation.

Above: One evening in the mid-1970s, Wade Williams ran his 35mm print of *The Man from Planet X* in his in-house theater for about 100 local friends. "Bob talked to the audience about the movie," says Wade, "and several women hit on him afterwards." *Below:* Three views of the Sun Demon mask that Bob Burns made for Clarke to use as part of his (Clarke's) "The Magic of Sci-Fi Film Making" lectures.

RKO Studios alumni Clarke and King Kong united! (Actually, the Kong puppet is the one built by stop-motion animator Dave Allen and seen in the classic 1972 Volkswagen TV commercial.)

Left: Sound man Doug Menville drew this sketch that he hoped would be used as the basis for the movie's poster, "but alas, 'twas not to be," he told me. Illustrator and lifelong *Sun Demon* fan Kerry Gammill *(KerryGammill.com)* tweaked and colorized it for this book's back cover. *Right:* At least one loyal Robert Clarke Fan received this gift from the actor: a Sun Demon bust with personalized plaque. That's the kind of guy Clarke was.

Bob poses with two old pals.

Robert Clarke was widowered in 1996. A constellation of health woes plagued him in the last decade of his life, and as he approached his mid-80s, there were enough day-to-day challenges that he needed to move into a Valley Village, California, hospice. Despite having to spend most of his time in bed there, he told me that he was managing to cope; "I'm kind of surprising myself that I *have* coped because, gosh, under circumstances like this, why didn't I flip out and kinda go ape shit and prove that I was a stereotype actor?" There were even days when his sense of humor re-emerged, for example when he told me, "If I eventually lose a leg [to diabetes], I lose a leg. Just so it isn't my *middle* one!"

Ten days after Clarke's 85th birthday, on Saturday, June 11, 2005, his caregiver Trish e-mailed me that he had died at 4:30 that morning. No autopsy was done to determine the cause for sure, "but if I were to guess, it would have been heart failure," she wrote. Services were held later in the week, at Forest Lawn.

From the family's press release: "While mixing in Hollywood with the best and brightest, Clarke retained his image as a Southern gentleman of grace, modesty, courtesy and kindness." Amen.

Bob's altered ego, immortalized in pen and ink by artist Frank Dietz *(www.sketchythings.com)*.

The Blaze of the Sun Makes Them Insatiable!

For even *more* dope on Robert Clarke, *The Hideous Sun Demon* and the other people who made that movie, feverish fans can check out my McFarland books *Science Fiction and Fantasy Film Flashbacks* (1998; a three-way interview with Robert Clarke, Tom Boutross and Robin C. Kirkman) and *A Sci-Fi Swarm and Horror Horde* (2010; an interview with Nan Peterson), as well as the autobiography *Robert Clarke: To "B" or Not to "B"* (Luminary Press, 1996).

Bear Manor Media

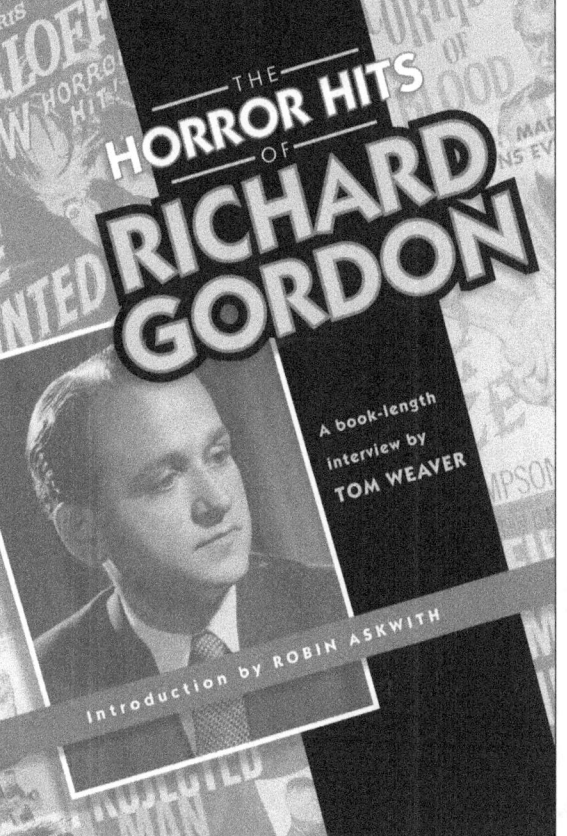

Classic Cinema.
Timeless TV.
Retro Radio.

WWW.BEARMANORMEDIA.COM

www.ingramcontent.com/pod-product-compliance
Lightning Source LLC
Chambersburg PA
CBHW081415230426
43668CB00016B/2246